STALKING THE RED BEAR

STALKING THE RED BEAR

THE TRUE STORY
OF A U.S. COLD WAR
SUBMARINE'S
COVERT OPERATIONS
AGAINST THE
SOVIET UNION

PETER SASGEN

ST. MARTIN'S PRESS ⚓ NEW YORK

Book design by Victoria Hartman

ISBN-13: 978-0-312-38023-6

To PJS

CONTENTS

Preface   ix

Introduction   1

PART ONE: GENESIS

Prologue   11

1. A Deadly Game   15

2. Running the Gauntlet   21

3. A View from the Inside Out   35

4. Subatomics: Making Power   53

5. High Stakes   59

6. On the Beach   77

7. To the Top of the World   89

8. Ice Cream and Blue Noses   99

9. Counterforce   111

PART TWO: STEALTH

10.	Fortress Polyarnyy	123
11.	Stalking Shadows	135
12.	First Blood	145
13.	Eyes and Ears	153
14.	The Coveted Prize	167
15.	Down Under	177
16.	Snoopers	189
17.	Cat and Mouse	199
18.	Fire in the Deep	207
19.	Sneak and Peek	219
20.	Into the Intel Abyss	225
Epilogue		229
Appendix One		237
Appendix Two		245
Appendix Three		257
Acknowledgments and Sources		269
Glossary		275
Bibliography		283
Index		287

PREFACE

Stalking the Red Bear is a true story about the U.S. Navy's covert submarine espionage operations against the Soviet Union. Code-named Holystone, this top-secret operation began in the late 1940s and continued through the cold war and beyond the collapse of the USSR. *Stalking the Red Bear* tells how in the 1970s, arguably the most dangerous decade of the cold war, the U.S. nuclear-powered submarines collected visual, electronic, and acoustic intelligence on Soviet military capabilities. It also tells how the U.S. Navy's nuclear-powered *Sturgeon*-class submarines, the workhorses of America's undersea spy program, were developed, designed, and built. Most important of all, it explains how they functioned and cloaked themselves in virtual invisibility to avoid detection by the Soviets.

Stalking the Red Bear also looks at the doctrine and tactics of what the Soviet navy called "the struggle against submarines" and the U.S. Navy called antisubmarine warfare or ASW. Indeed, it was a struggle, as the Soviets for decades lagged far behind the United States in submarine and sonar technologies. In their

mostly failed effort to thwart American cold war submarine operations in waters bordering Russia, the Soviets had to deploy submarines whose seaworthiness and reliability were questionable, to
say nothing of the safety of their nuclear reactors and weapons.
Stalking the Red Bear also examines other issues related to Holystone, such as the training U.S. and Soviet submariners underwent during the mid–cold war period, submarine weapons and
tactics, and the effects of long deployments on submariners and
their families. To place Holystone in its historical context, there is
a brief look at some of the clandestine U.S. and Axis submarine
missions that were carried out during World War II.

As for Holystone, during the cold war very few individuals
outside the intelligence and submarine communities knew anything at all about it. With good reason: The curtain of secrecy
surrounding submarine operations, beginning in World War II
and continuing today, was and is nearly impenetrable. The U.S.
Navy doesn't call it the "silent service" for nothing!

As information about Holystone began to leak out, first in the
1980s, then after the end of the cold war, the revelations proved
electrifying. Who knew that U.S. submarines had for years been
penetrating Soviet-controlled waters to spy on the Soviet navy—
its ships, bases, and missile tests—or to tap into the USSR's undersea communications cables? Yet as hair-raising as these missions
must have been, it struck me that most of the Holystone operations described in print seemed rather tame. Thinking about it, I
realized the reason was that most of the reporting on Holystone
concentrated almost exclusively on its historical and anecdotal
sides. What had been left out was all the details, the texture, of
the submarine espionage operations themselves, which would
have brought the Holystone story to life in an exciting way.

Interesting as these accounts were, I wanted to know more.

For instance, what was it really like to carry out a top-secret covert submarine intelligence-gathering mission against the Soviet Union? How risky was it? How difficult? What was life like aboard one of those Holystone subs operating north of the arctic circle or in the Sea of Okhotsk? What special skills did these submariners possess and what motivated them? What about the physical and mental toll Holystone exacted from the crews and the strain it put on marriages and families? Where did the idea for Holystone come from in the first place?

I sought to answer these questions and bring Holystone to life by writing a book that described the action principally from the perspective of a commanding officer (CO) of a Holystone submarine. Not that I wanted to ignore the officers and enlisted men— after all, it's not a one-man show—but the CO is the one guy aboard a submarine who makes it happen, while the crew plays an important but supporting role.

I also wanted to show readers what it was like to stand watch shoulder to shoulder with shipmates aboard a submerged submarine. I wanted them to experience, as much as words can convey, the sights, sounds, and smells unique to submarining. When it's sub versus sub in Soviet-controlled waters, anything can happen, and I wanted them to feel that tension. Finally, I wanted to take them closer to the Soviet target than any work on submarine espionage had ever done before.

To do this, I knew, I'd have to tell the Holystone story from the inside out, that is, from *inside* a U.S. submarine's hull, in the driver's seat, so to speak. Part of telling that story had to include a look at a Soviet submarine, her commanding officer and crew, and their operations against U.S. subs. Therefore, I've reported on a typical Soviet submarine operation into the Barents Sea. In addition, in the three appendices, I've included capsule descriptions of historically significant and trailblazing operations that were carried out by submarines during World War II and, later, the cold war. These operations showcased some of the innovative tactics submariners employed against the British, Japanese, and Soviets; perhaps someday they'll receive the full treatment they deserve.

I knew that to write *Stalking the Red Bear* I'd need help from a veteran submariner who'd commanded one of the nuclear subs that had penetrated Soviet-controlled waters, a man who knew his way around in the Barents Sea. He also had to know his way around America's defense establishment and the labyrinthine intelligence community that serves it.

Fortunately I found such a man, and after I convinced him that I had an exciting story to tell, he agreed to coach me through the intricacies of Holystone and share his experiences and recollections. Thus were born "Roy Hunter" and his submarine the USS *"Blackfin,"* both of whom appear in *Stalking the Red Bear* as pseudonyms.

Hunter and I have not divulged or compromised any current secret submarine operations or tactics, nor have we identified any individuals or submarines currently involved in such operations. Everything outside of Hunter's recollections was gleaned from open sources.

Given that this is Hunter's story, I put him aboard the *Blackfin* and turned him loose. Because *Stalking the Red Bear* is not a work of documented history, I felt free to reconstruct many of the scenes and operations and much of the dialogue Hunter described.

My thanks, then, to Roy Hunter, who, like all submarine commanders past and present, possesses a keen intellect and an amazing ability to bring order out of technical and literary chaos. Any mistakes—errors regarding technical and tactical matters, misreadings of history and geography, faulty interpretations—are mine and mine alone.

To my literary agent, Ethan Ellenberg, thanks for your mastery of the medium and reading of the market. I knew you were right all along. To my editor Marc Resnick and the staff at St. Martin's Press, thank you for making this the best book possible.

The U-boat [attack] was our worst evil. It would have been wise for the Germans to stake all upon it.

— Winston Churchill

It's the importance of finding out what they're planning ahead of time that is the task of intelligence, and you have to have a very special kind of intelligence to do that; and you have to understand that this is going to involve spying.

— Caspar Weinberger

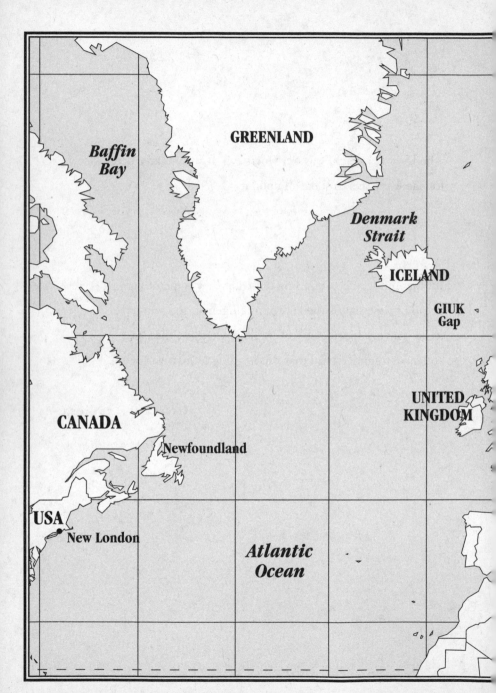

Cold War Submarine Operating Area

AUTHOR'S NOTE

The names "Roy Hunter" and *"Blackfin"* are pseudonymous. To create and maintain narrative flow, dialogue has been reconstructed and some of the time frame has been condensed.

STALKING THE RED BEAR

INTRODUCTION

THE COLD WAR had its origins in the titanic ideological and geopolitical struggle between the United States and the Soviet Union following World War II. Starting in 1946, and until the breakup and collapse of the Soviet Union in 1991, the USSR committed almost every available resource (by some estimates in the mid-1970s, at least 40 percent of its gross income) to the destruction of the United States, which the Soviet leadership regarded as a dangerous and predatory imperialist state. Newspaper headlines announcing the first Soviet atomic bomb test, on August 29, 1949, at Semipalatinsk on the Russian steppe, stunned America and the rest of the world. Overnight the United States had lost its postwar nuclear monopoly and faced a Soviet Union bent, so it seemed, on world domination. Six years later the Soviets detonated their first hydrogen bomb. Americans took seriously Nikita Khrushchev's threat, "We will bury you!" Thus for over forty years the United States spent trillions of dollars to defend itself and its allies against the Soviet Union, which Americans regarded as the most dangerous regime in recorded history, worse even than Nazi Germany.

Both countries began building long-range bombers to deliver nuclear weapons to targets within the other's borders. With help from former German rocket scientists captured by the Russians at the Peenemünde rocket works, the Soviets began building nuclear-armed intercontinental ballistic missiles (ICBMs), the early design of which was based on the V-2 used by the Nazis against Great Britain in World War II. Along with a buildup of their army and air forces, the U.S. and USSR increased the size of their naval forces, which included submarine-building programs that led to the development of nuclear-powered submarines.

Though the U.S. submarine fleet under construction in the 1950s was numerically smaller than the one the Soviets were building, it was technically more advanced. By the 1960s, lagging far behind the United States in nuclear propulsion, quieting, sonar, and, most important of all, safety, the Soviet sub fleet, in its early stages, relied principally on vast numbers of diesel-electric subs. Meanwhile, the U.S. Navy, driven by Admiral Hyman G. Rickover, the implacable force behind the nuclear sub program, made steady progress with the nuclear submarine technology that would keep the Soviets scrambling to catch up. Even so, given the speed with which the Soviets had developed an atomic bomb, albeit with help from spies within the U.S. nuclear program, experts like Rickover knew it wouldn't be long before the Russians built their first nuclear-powered submarine to compete with the United States.

The threat of nuclear war took an ominous turn with the deployment in the 1960s of American and Soviet submarine-launched long-range nuclear-tipped ballistic missiles. Large missile-firing submarines lurking in waters off the coasts of both nations and seemingly invulnerable to attack were capable of launching hugely destructive weapons able to reach their targets in just minutes. Under such conditions, civil defense was a concept in theory only; tens of millions of Americans and Russians would die in a nuclear attack.

Once the Iron Curtain fell across Eastern Europe after World War II, the United States had no way to know if war with the Soviet Union was imminent. Reconnaissance satellites had not yet been developed, and there were few camera-equipped aircraft capable of overflying Soviet territory to assess their capabilities. Many Western spies inside Russia had been captured or killed. The United States desperately needed information that would provide not just threat assessment but also early warning of a Soviet attack.

At that time the U.S. Navy assumed that if war were to break out, the Soviet Northern Fleet and Pacific Fleet would sortie from their bases. The only way to have adequate advance warning would be via submarines patrolling the Barents Sea and the Sea of Okhotsk. To effectively counter the looming threat of nuclear war launched from the sea, the United States also needed to infiltrate the Soviet military apparatus to collect vital information on the Kremlin's intentions and capabilities. It was essential that the intelligence contain hard facts, not just speculation, which too often led to gross overestimates or underestimates of Soviet capabilities.

As we now know, intelligence and its uses and interpretation are controlled to a great degree by political considerations. Officials who use it to shape foreign policy or to develop military plans often disagree with each other and may have wildly divergent points of view. Their disagreement may not be over what the intelligence shows but rather over what it means. This is especially true when trying to fit thousands of pieces of intelligence into a mosaic that will provide an accurate picture that can help determine whether perceived threats are real or imagined. Troop and ship movements or activity at missile sites might presage an attack. Then again, they might not.

Intel collection systems vary in their ability to perform. Relying on human intelligence, or HUMINT, has severe limitations. Spies may not be able to obtain certain types of technical data or to understand complex weapons and delivery systems. Reconnaissance aircraft and satellites, as well as ships outfitted for spying, are capable of photographing or watching ICBM tests with infrared sensors to measure heat from rocket engines or with radar to track flight paths. Such information is essential, as targeters have to know if an ICBM can be intercepted or attacked at its ground-based site or on board a ship before it's launched. But spy planes are easy to track on radar, and spy satellites can't always be where they are needed. And surface spy ships can't enter Russian territorial waters to collect intelligence; it takes a submarine to do that.

For the United States, collecting intelligence on the Soviet navy became a top priority, a major part of which consisted of U.S. attack submarines finding and then trailing Russian missile-firing subs in their operating areas to learn in advance what the Soviets planned to do and what they could do with what they had. Collecting this intelligence was a mission for which U.S. nuclear-powered submarines, with their inherent stealth and almost unlimited underwater endurance, proved the perfect tool. Moreover, by the time nuclear submarines joined the fleet, the navy had already been operating in Soviet-controlled waters for several years; U.S. submariners knew the environment in which they were operating, and they knew how the Soviet navy itself operated. Now, with the advantages offered by nuclear submarines, the United States had an intelligence-gathering capability that could function unseen and undetected to assess the Soviet navy's strengths and weaknesses. Such information would allow the United States to structure its forces to take advantage of that knowledge.

Submarines make ideal platforms for intelligence gathering. After all, a sub's principal characteristic is stealth, which it uses to infiltrate a denied area—a harbor, say, or naval base—where it can watch, listen, and collect information without being seen or heard. Within months of the end of the Berlin Blockade in 1949, and spurred on by the test of Joe One, the Soviet A-bomb, the U.S. Navy, utilizing modified World War II–era diesel-electric submarines, began its pioneering intelligence-gathering patrols against the Soviet Union. Despite their limited endurance and mobility compared to the nuclear-powered submarines that were soon to follow and, by today's standards, their lack of sophisticated snooping gear and their poor habitability, these older boats collected vital information about the inferior quality of the Soviet navy's radar, sonar, and communications systems. These early missions also proved that submarine espionage was possible and that the Soviets, while not to be underestimated, weren't very good when it came to ASW.

By the late 1950s, as these older boats retired, nuclear subs equipped with the latest electronic eavesdropping gear, their crews working in relative comfort, roamed far and wide in the hunt for intelligence while the subs' embarked communications specialists, or "spooks," as they were called, scrubbed the ether for nuggets of information about Soviet objectives.

The intelligence collected—visual, audio, acoustic, and electronic—underwent analysis by National Security Agency (NSA) and Office of Naval Intelligence (ONI) analysts, who were expert at putting it into a form that could be understood by decision makers. If relevant, the material was passed to higher authority. If, for example, the onboard intel team had collected telemetry data on the latest Soviet missile test or had reported on the deployment of a new type of strategic missile sub or attack sub, the information might prove relevant to ongoing U.S. weapons programs or treaty negotiations. A sudden surge of naval forces might indicate that war was imminent. If nothing else, the data might help to clarify the overall intel picture of the USSR to which the United States had been adding pieces ever since the end of World War II. This information, along with data that had been collected from other sources, would possibly warn of a surprise nuclear attack as well as keep track of new developments in Soviet offensive and defensive capabilities.

The Holystone missions carried out during the cold war encompassed everything from recording the acoustic signatures of individual Soviet submarines to collecting electronic communications to videotaping weapons tests. Holystone subs also snooped on Russian anticarrier operations, surveyed the underwater hulls of transiting surfaced Russian subs, and trailed Russian missile subs and attack subs. To get this precious intelligence, U.S. subs, operating with virtual impunity against stout Soviet opposition and shrugging off air and sea surveillance, crept as close as they dared to the main enemy's naval forces at sea.

The *Blackfin*'s mission detailed in *Stalking the Red Bear* (its sixty-day time frame has been compressed for the sake of narrative flow) took place in the Barents Sea, a part of the Arctic Ocean bordering Norway and Russia's Kola Peninsula. Other Holystone subs conducted missions in the Sea of Okhotsk, which lies to the north of Japan, inside the Kuril island chain. (See Appendix One.)

During the cold war the Barents was home to the Soviet Red

Banner Northern Fleet. It was also a test range for Russian ICBMs and nuclear weapons. Gathering intelligence in the Barents under the nose of a determined enemy on the hunt for snooping U.S. subs was dangerous and hair-raising work. It required extraordinary reserves of courage and resourcefulness. Moreover, the captains of these submarines, always operating in a wartime posture, had to be expert ship handlers and superb tacticians. They also had to have seasoned judgment because while both sides understood the rules of the espionage game they were playing, one misstep—say, the accidental sinking of one submarine by another—could have triggered the very war the United States was trying to prevent.

A submariner's biggest fear, then, was suddenly finding himself under the loaded torpedo tubes of a Soviet submarine. After all, one torpedo was all it would take to send a sub and her crew to the bottom in the blink of an eye. Nevertheless, because the stakes were so high, every mission successfully carried out proved a vital contribution to the overall espionage war submarines like the *Blackfin* waged against the Soviets. Commander Roy Hunter, the *Blackfin*'s CO, knew only too well the dangers he and his crew faced. He also knew that sooner or later the Soviets might declare war in the game of espionage that American submariners proved so adept at playing and that the Soviets were losing.

It wasn't just about weapons and tactics or winning or losing, though. Long deployments at sea took a toll not only on the submarine crews but also on wives and families. It was not at all uncommon for officers and enlisted men alike to have spent between four and six months at sea a year for every year they'd served in submarines. Because they believed that what the men were doing was vitally important, most families willingly made sacrifices that not only imposed hardships both financial and emotional but often wrecked marriages. In addition, because submariners could not discuss their work, the wall of secrecy that developed between them and their friends and loved ones sometimes had a ruinous effect on these relationships.

Clearly it took more than love to keep a marriage together under these conditions. It required courage for a woman with children and all the increased responsibilities that go with raising them to take on a dual-parent role for months at a time. Then, too, there was the ever present but unspoken possibility that a submarine might not return from a patrol and that the crew's fate would never be known. Such was the case with the USS *Scorpion*. The day the *Scorpion* was due to arrive in Norfolk, Virginia, from a long patrol, excited families and friends of the crew had been waiting on a pier for hours for the submarine's return. Unbeknown to them and the navy, she had sunk with all hands days earlier off the Azores. Her loss, the exact cause of which is still debated, was a terrible blow for the Navy; for the families and loved ones of her crew, it remains a mystery to this day.

More often, thankfully, for those left behind, the sight of a submarine returning from a long deployment meant that the separation had come to an end. While everyone knew the cycle would start again soon enough, all that mattered was that the ship and her crew were home at last.

Holystone submarine crews took extraordinary risks and accomplished extraordinary feats. The goal wasn't just the collection of intelligence for the sake of collection alone, in other words, sheer quantity. Nor was the goal of collection winning a race that was undertaken because war was imminent. Just the opposite was true: The goal of Holystone was to ensure a stable and lasting peace. That turned out to be its greatest accomplishment of all.

PART ONE

GENESIS

PROLOGUE

Washington, D.C., 1971

CHIEF OF NAVAL OPERATIONS Admiral Elmo R. Zumwalt Jr. took a seat in the CNO's briefing theater at the Pentagon. An aide standing at the podium ordered the room darkened for a slide presentation. The briefing was conducted by an officer from the Joint Chiefs of Staff.

Zumwalt, a thirty-plus-year navy veteran, was the youngest man ever to serve as CNO. Something of a maverick, Zumwalt, though not without difficulty, had shaken up the navy and set it properly on a course of modernization and efficiency. Old ships had gone to the breaker's yard; new ships were on the building ways. He also brought needed reforms to issues affecting the personal lives of enlisted personnel and their retention in a navy reeling from a shortage of critical ratings.

As a reformer, Zumwalt wasn't particularly enamored of the submarine force because it was gobbling up money the navy had earmarked for a new fleet of guided missile cruisers and destroyers. His main objective as CNO was to neutralize the growing Soviet threat by employing American sea power to its maximum effect without busting his budget. The submarine mafia, as it was dubbed by Zumwalt and his surface warfare brethren, with its insatiable quest for bigger and better multimission submarines, threatened to scuttle Zumwalt's plan to modernize the surface fleet.

Now he viewed a slide of the Barents Sea area and Russia's Kola Peninsula. A solitary blue dot marked the position of a U.S. submarine deployed on an intelligence-gathering patrol west of Novaya Zemlya. A fresh slide appeared. Zumwalt frowned as soon as he saw a cluster of red dots spreading out from around the Kola Inlet north of Severomorsk, the Red Banner Fleet's biggest and most important naval base. He didn't have to be told what the dots represented: Soviet warships. A big-picture man, Zumwalt knew that what he saw could only mean one of two things: a routine naval exercise had gotten under way—Zumwalt kneaded his brow—or a Russian ASW task force had begun searching for the U.S. spy submarine.

Zumwalt knew that the submarine had an experienced commanding officer and a seasoned crew, many of them veterans of earlier spy missions into Soviet-controlled waters. Still, he knew that anything could go wrong and sometimes did. After all, a U.S. sub snooping around the Kola Inlet was the equivalent of a Russian sub snooping around inside the U.S. Navy's Norfolk operations area. Risky business. More than once, Soviet and U.S. subs had collided; after one of those collisions, a Soviet sub was thought to have been sunk. Wars had been started over less provocative events than collisions at sea.

Ever since the end of World War II, in which Zumwalt had

served as a young naval officer, the USSR and the United States had been fighting the cold war. Armed with nuclear weapons and given the growing hostility that existed between the two countries, both sides faced the possibility of all-out nuclear war. Like all Americans, Zumwalt still took seriously Nikita Khrushchev's threat to bury them.

It was 1971, though, and U.S.-Soviet relations had come a long way since Khrushchev had banged his shoe on the lectern at the UN and issued threats to annihilate the United States. To improve relations between the two countries, President Richard Nixon would visit Moscow next spring for a meeting with Khrushchev's successor, Leonid Brezhnev. To win favor with the dour general secretary, an avid car collector, Nixon had elected to present him with a brand-new Cadillac that would be flown to Russia along with Nixon's armored limousine, in the hold of the C-130 accompanying Air Force One. In addition to engaging in private talks, both men had high hopes that their meeting would lead to the implementation of the Strategic Arms Limitation Treaty (SALT), which officials on both sides believed would reduce the threat of nuclear war. A Top Secret/Sensitive document originating at Defense and circulated to State set out the goals of SALT and rated its chances of acceptance by the Soviets as excellent. Nixon also had good reason to believe that negotiations under way in Paris to end the Vietnam War, in tandem with SALT, would go a long way toward easing cold war tensions. Everyone in Washington used the phrase "guarded optimism" to describe how they felt about the upcoming summit.

Everyone but Zumwalt. He recalled how the Francis Gary Powers U-2 spy plane shoot-down by the Russians in 1960 had scuttled President Eisenhower's summit meeting with Khrushchev. Now, a U.S. spy sub nosing around in the Barents Sea, a virtual

Soviet private lake, might have drawn the attention of a Soviet ASW task force.

Zumwalt decided that he'd seen enough and departed the briefing thinking, *Lots of things could go wrong. . . .*

1

A DEADLY GAME

U.S. NAVY COMMANDER Roy Hunter, captain of the USS *Blackfin*, heard the sibilant beat of ships' screws and, through the raised periscope, saw the masts of hull-down Soviet warships. Electronic Signals Measures (ESM) intercepts of radar and radio transmissions had confirmed the presence of several ships and ASW helicopters as well as the high-frequency polarized radar the Soviet helos employed for detecting exposed submarine periscopes and masts.

As he lowered the periscope, Hunter ordered, "Lower all masts. All ahead two-thirds. Make your depth two-five-zero feet. The officer of the deck has the conn."

Hunter announced his intention to track the contacts via passive sonar, then ordered the officer of the deck (OOD), a young lieutenant, to station the section fire-control tracking party, the team tasked with keeping tabs on a target's position. Rigged for red, the control room, with its lit up fire-control consoles and other vital instruments, had a spectral look.

"Conn, sonar; active sonar bearing one-three-zero," advised the sonar supervisor. "Frequency five kilohertz; ten-thousand-yard scale. Designate Sierra Ten."

The OOD toggled his microphone switch. "Conn, aye."

The report from sonar meant that the Soviet warships had shifted to high-powered active sonar, a sure sign they were searching for a submerged intruder.

"Officer of the deck, make your depth four-five-zero feet," ordered Hunter.

Greater depth would provide an extra layer of invisibility, like pulling a blanket over their heads. Since making sonar contact with the ships, Hunter had been thinking, *Avoid counterdetection.* In other words, don't let the Soviets know you're there. If they do, you lose. Hunter was confident he could give them the slip— unless they got lucky, and so far it didn't seem likely.

The Soviets relied on a rigid and highly codified ASW doctrine, what they called the "struggle against submarines." It was more a theory than a proven tactic. The Sovs, with their inferior passive sonar, often gave up searching for submerged U.S. subs simply because they were too quiet to detect. Yet when using active sonar they often regarded submerged contacts as anomalies caused by scatter or thermal gradients, or reverberations caused by shallow water. Moving west, the Sov ASW team's active sonar slowly started fading. So far so good. It seemed as if they'd lost the scent . . .

"Conn, sonar; picked up a three-hundred-hertz tone. Bearing two-nine-zero, drawing right, designated Sierra Eleven. Classified as a submerged Type II." Sonar had a submerged Russian submarine contact, perhaps a Charlie or Victor nuclear attack sub.

Hunter's submarine, moving silently, was nothing more than a hole in the ocean. Not so the Soviet sub.

"Come left to two-nine-zero," the OOD ordered.

The helmsman confirmed the order; the American sub turned northwest.

A moment later the OOD ordered, "Attention in the attack center. We'll maneuver to solve the target's course, speed, and range." Turning to Hunter, he asked, "Captain, should I try to get lined up for an ASPL?"

"Not yet."

Making absolute sound pressure level recordings of a Soviet submarine's noise levels was high on Holystone's intelligence-gathering list. First, though, Hunter had to determine what this one was up to and whether the contact intended to maintain the steady course and speed essential to making accurate ASPL recordings.

"Conn, sonar. Based on the tonal upshift, the range rate is a hundred yards per minute and closing."

"Conn, aye."

Hunter settled down to wait. After several minutes the OOD ordered, "Come right to course zero-two-zero."

"I have Sierra Eleven on course zero-one-zero," reported the fire-control coordinator. "Speed ten, range forty-one hundred yards." A touch over two miles. "Got a good solution on him for an ASPL—"

"*Conn, sonar!*" The sonar supervisor broke in on fire control; the urgency in his voice was unmistakable. "Heard a transient, a *thump*, from Sierra Eleven."

Hunter, his mind working like a computer, reviewed a picture of the setup in his head. He "saw" the approaching enemy sub in relation to his own sub, which he'd maneuvered to gain an advantage on the intruder. He was certain that the Soviet sub hadn't heard the maneuver, so how . . . ? It didn't matter how—that thump could only mean one thing, that he'd opened the outer doors on his torpedo tubes—

"Conn, sonar—a single ping from Sierra Eleven!"

Hunter heard it, too, on the UQC underwater phone at the periscope stand, a shrill pulse of pure sound energy fired by the Soviet sub at Hunter's sub. The ping meant that the Russian had painted the Americans with active sonar, a sign he was about to fire a torpedo at them!

Before Hunter could issue orders, sonar broke in: *"Torpedo in the water! Bearing three-one-two!"*

Hunter didn't hesitate; instinct and training took over. "I have the conn! All ahead flank! Right full rudder! Come to course one-three-five!"

Caught by surprise, Hunter at first refused to believe what he'd heard. No Soviet sub would ever fire a torpedo at an American sub in peacetime. There were rules in the espionage game both sides were playing, and if they were violated it could start a goddamn war—*a nuclear war*! His gut tightened. Everything suddenly ground to a halt. There was nothing more he could do, no way to avoid disaster. Like the watchstanders frozen at their stations, he heard the incoming whine of the torpedo's up-Doppler props, counted down the seconds to impact, and—

Lights snapped on in the control room.

A moment later a voice boomed from a speaker: "You're sunk, Hunter."

Chagrined, Hunter and his fire-control team blinked, looked around the attack center simulator's mocked-up control room, and then exchanged glances with each other. Hunter, at the periscope stand, blew through clenched teeth. It had only been an exercise, but goddamn it! The team running the simulation had slipped one in on him.

A week of circling, weaving, chasing down multiple targets, avoiding detection, and now getting sunk had left him exhausted. Still, better to make big mistakes in the attack teacher than up in the Barents Sea where a real mistake could kill you, not just bruise your ego. In the simulator at the U.S. Navy's submarine school in New London, Connecticut, with its perfect scenario reconstruction, a guy could learn from his mistakes and live to tell about it. After all, here it was Americans against Americans. In the Barents it would be Americans against Soviets. Hunter lit a cigarette and thought of all the things that could go wrong up in the Barents Sea—and how it would be his job to make sure they didn't.

2

RUNNING THE GAUNTLET

LOOKING NORTH UP the Thames River from New London, at the submarine base on the Groton side of the river, a visitor saw first the landmark water-filled escape training tower where submariners practiced getting out alive from a disabled or sunken submarine. Next came a jumble of old brick buildings, then, jutting into the river, a row of wooden piers, to which were moored perhaps a dozen black submarines.

One of those moored submarines was the USS *Blackfin*. Like all *Sturgeon*-class SSN submarines she was a bit of a hybrid. First and foremost she was a warship designed to attack and sink enemy ships and submarines, yet she was also a spy ship. It was the incomparable intel-collection capability of the *Sturgeons* that usually made CNO Zumwalt knead his brow whenever Holystone subs were routinely deployed against their Soviet adversaries. Some of the COs of these boats were hotshots who, like their forebears in World War II, weren't afraid to take risks, but this was the modern navy, not your father's navy, and Zumwalt didn't like risk takers. He was a surface sailor, though, not a submariner, a bureaucrat, not a sub driver. He wasn't the type to go looking for action in the Barents Sea. On the other hand, for Roy Hunter, who was neither a risk taker nor a hotshot, just a damn good sub driver, a Holystone deployment to the Barents Sea was exactly what he had been hoping for.

The U.S. Navy, like any navy, thrived on paperwork. Hunter was an old hand at dealing with it, separating wheat from chaff. One of his colleagues, the sub force's most notorious wheat-and-chaff separator, was said to have tossed overboard the mail his ship had received after a long deployment, deep-sixed it except for the registered stuff. Funny thing was, nobody ever seemed to notice that the regular mail they'd sent went unanswered.

Hunter had been in the *Blackfin*'s wardroom drinking coffee and smoking, sifting through the morning's arrival of official mail—the yeoman had organized it into two piles, wheat and chaff— searching for something special that still hadn't come. Then the shore-connected phone cradled on the wardroom bulkhead chirped. Hunter swept the mail aside and picked up the phone. He wasn't a mind reader, yet when he heard the voice of the deputy squadron commander, he sensed what was coming—orders.

"Hunter, you lucky SOB. SubLant says you're scheduled for spec ops," the deputy squadron commander told him. "Get a schedule worked up, then give me a holler. Tell me what you need and I'll see that you get it."

Holystone. An opportunity to stalk the red bear. There was no peacetime mission the navy assigned its submarines that was more important than Holystone.

· · ·

Roy Hunter was an experienced submarine officer, a veteran of tours aboard both nuclear-powered strategic ballistic missile submarines (SSBNs) and attack submarines (SSNs). Along the way he'd learned how to work the system. That was exactly what he did when he lobbied and arm-twisted the detailers at the Bureau of Naval Personnel (BuPers) in Washington, D.C., who, among other things, recommended officers for command of submarines. Hunter had wanted new construction, one of the *Sturgeon*-class boats then being built at the Electric Boat Division of General Dynamics in Groton. "How about the *Blackfin*?" Hunter had urged whenever he was in Washington on submarine business. "She'll need a CO." A nudge here, a hint there, a little more arm-twisting, and sure enough Hunter had his submarine. After a year or so of exercises and ASW ops, though, he craved more action. Now, the phone call from the deputy squadron commander proved that his lobbying, along with his reputation and his standing in the pack, had worked again. The shipyard was no place for an aggressive skipper to end up in, yet by taking command of a brand-new submarine, Hunter could start out with a new ship and crew, not inherit someone else's problems. In other words, he'd get to do it his own way.

Like many submarine COs, Roy Hunter was a graduate of the U.S. Naval Academy. His path to submarine command had run, as every submarine officer in the navy's nuclear power program had, through Admiral Hyman G. Rickover's office. Rickover was the visionary driving force behind the navy's development of nuclear power. An engineer, known for his abrasive personality and uncompromising standards, Rickover, among his other contributions, mustered the congressional support necessary for the success of the navy's nuclear power program. No less important was his unwavering demand for only the highest quality in nuclear construction and safety.

Summoned to Rickover's office, a young candidate, often a senior-class midshipman from the Naval Academy or NROTC (Naval

Reserve Officer Training Corps), underwent a rigorous interview by three of the admiral's staff associates, civilians he'd handpicked and molded to their jobs of serving just one man, Rickover. They forwarded to Rickover their recommendations as to whether the candidate should be accepted into the program. The candidate was then interviewed (many officers likened the experience to running a gauntlet) by Rickover himself. If he passed muster with Rickover, no small achievement itself, the candidate was off to a year of nuclear power training—six months of academics at the Navy's nuclear power school and six months at a shore-based nuclear reactor where a budding nuclear engineer learned how the back end of a submarine works, the part that produces the power.

After graduation from nuclear power school, an officer attended six months of basic officer's submarine school, where he learned about the front end of the submarine, the part that controls the back end. After graduation from the basic course, he was assigned to his first sub. Now came the hard part.

The officer had to qualify not only in submarines but also on the two key watch stations: officer of the deck and engineering officer of the watch. Upon arrival aboard ship the new officer received three stacks of qualification cards, one stack for sub quals, another for OOD quals, and one for engineering officer of the watch quals. To qualify for OOD, he had to know everything there was to know about the control room and attack center and, just as important, how to handle a ship on the surface and apply the rules of the road.

To qualify for engineering officer of the watch, he had to qualify on each enlisted and officer watch station related to the ship's power plant and then some. There was a lot of material to study for qualification, both practical and theoretical, as well as oral and written exams to pass and engineering-officer-under-instruction watches to stand.

Qualification generally took about a year, sometimes less, depending on how much of a go-getter the officer was. After working his way through the quals, the officer had to demonstrate his knowledge to an examining board made up of other officers. If he passed this exam, he was recommended to be "qualified in submarines," whereupon the ship's CO, if he concurred, awarded him the coveted Twin Dolphins.

The next hurdle the officer faced was qualifying as engineer officer. For the candidate, it meant long hours of study and practical experience to receive the necessary recommendation by the CO. Then it was back to Rickover for more grilling and exams. If the officer survived this phase, he was designated a "qualified engineer," responsible for the ship's power plant and half the crew.

The goal of any seagoing naval officer is command at sea. Yet an officer aspiring to command a nuclear submarine faced a formidable challenge since, with few commands available given the relatively small size of the sub force compared to the surface force, only the very best officers were selected. It goes without saying, then, that ideally a candidate for command possessed a keen intelligence and analytical acumen. If he was also resourceful, calm, and unlikely to buckle under pressure, all the better to succeed in a tough environment.

PCO (prospective commanding officer) candidates were—as they are today—essentially under a microscope, their personalities and records subjected to a careful screening process designed to weed out individuals who lack the qualities essential for command. Nevertheless, to achieve the designation "Qualified for Command," the already qualified engineer had to survive yet more hurdles, chief among them a recommendation by his commanding officer and approval by his squadron commander, who would have seen the candidate in action and could judge his abilities. The PCO candidate also had to have served a successful tour as executive officer aboard a sub and been selected for command by the chief of naval personnel, a process that included Admiral Rickover's informal approval.

Upon the receipt of orders to command, the candidate reported to Rickover's office for three months of study and exams. This period also provided an opportunity for the PCOs to meet with the admiral's senior staff members and discuss the complex technical issues related to nuclear propulsion.

The PCOs also participated in the interviews Rickover conducted, of non-PCO candidates entering the nuclear propulsion program. During this process, each interviewee was accompanied by a PCO whose job it was to take notes for the official record. Nominally an impartial observer, the note taker was sometimes unavoidably drawn into the interview (which could last anywhere from a few seconds to more than an hour), an uncomfortable situation for both interviewee and PCO but one that Rickover fostered. On the upside, the observer could later tell thigh-slapping stories, such as what would happen when Rickover would have before him an NROTC candidate who had majored in psychology or liberal arts.

Rickover relished these encounters. Indeed, it was the psych majors who bore the brunt of the wily admiral's barbs and sarcasm as he pressed for their opinions on the perceived shortcomings of his organization. Under prolonged interrogation and intense deconstruction and examination of the Rickover organization, the dazed, sweating young man would, in the end, be forced to conclude that any shortcomings in the organization were the fault of Rickover's mother!

Notwithstanding the problems Mrs. Rickover had possibly caused and the navy had to endure, with an okay from her son, never a sure thing, the candidate was off to the PCO course at Pearl Harbor, Hawaii, or the submarine school at New London, Connecticut.

In Hunter's case, as he departed Rickover's office for PCO school, he encountered the admiral, his hooded gaze riveted on a report. Without looking up, Rickover said, "Hunter, did you learn anything while you were here?"

The PCO stopped in his tracks. "Well, Admiral, I . . ."

"Get the hell out of here."

. . .

At PCO school, candidates like Hunter undertook a demanding six-week course of training with a heavy emphasis on tactics, with many hours spent in attack simulators and, at sea, firing exercise torpedoes at submarines and surface ships. As in earlier discussions with Rickover's staff, classes were devoted to a wide range of issues that included the current state of the submarine force, both its challenges and strengths. Other issues included the problems of officer retention and the declining rates of reenlistment for enlisted personnel. The seriousness was leavened at times with insider gossip about which commanding officers had screwed up and how bad, and who'd been canned—lessons to be learned by the PCOs: A CO is, after all, head of a complex organization of men *and* machinery. The PCOs, with their working knowledge of the sub force, knew that once in command of a nuclear sub, they would have to apply all of their skills to the job. A ship's commanding officer faces enormous responsibilities; at sea there is no room for error or seat-of-the-pants submarining.

At last the big day arrived. Following graduation from PCO

school, the officers reveled in being on their way to command of a nuclear submarine.

. . .

Having survived the rigors of nuclear submarine instruction, to say nothing of Admiral Rickover's gauntlet, and having served in several submarines as engineering officer and executive officer (XO), Hunter had been fully prepared for command when he stepped aboard the *Blackfin* as her commissioning CO.

For enlisted men the pipeline to nuclear subs was similar to an officer's. After boot camp and special schools, it was on to a year of nuclear power training for engineering personnel, followed by sub school, then assignment to a sub. In addition to "nukes," sailors trained in nuclear power, submarine complements included machinists' mates, electricians' mates, electronics technicians, radiomen, sonarmen, torpedomen, navy corpsmen in lieu of a ship's doctor, and more. As with the officers, for the enlisted sailors aboard submarines there were qualification cards, study, and tests. They learned how submarine systems work, how to operate equipment and, most important, how to deal with fires, flooding, and radiation dangers that can occur aboard ship. Also like officers, enlisted men who mastered these complicated subjects were qualified in submarines.

Meanwhile, Hunter's lobbying for a special operations assignment had worked. ComSubLant (Commander Submarines Atlantic) in Norfolk, Virginia, the U.S. Navy's Atlantic submarine headquarters, had inserted Hunter and the *Blackfin* into the rotation of submarines assigned to Operation Holystone. The commanders knew who the best were and what to expect from them. Ongoing since the end of the Berlin Blockade in 1949, Holystone (the exact date when the name was applied to the navy's submarine spy program has been lost to history) had delivered impressive results. Intelligence on both Soviet surface combatants and submarines had helped fill the gaps in what little was known about their capabilities, which in turn developed a picture that exposed both the Soviet navy's strengths and weaknesses. Now, armed with advanced attack submarines like the *Sturgeons*, the U.S. sub force was operating virtually unseen and unheard against the Soviets in their own backyard. It stripped the Soviets of their feelings of invulnerability in their home waters and kept them off balance.

From prior experience Hunter knew that Holystone missions required lengthy predeployment preparation before sailing and that the most important preparations involved upkeep, training, and briefings. Nothing could be left to chance; there was too much at stake. He savored the challenge spec ops offered and had the confidence—some would say ego—needed to pull it off. Orders in hand, he had wasted no time making things happen.

. . .

For starters Hunter put his crew through a workout in the New London sub school's trainers and simulators, starting with the one that resulted in the *Blackfin* being "sunk" by a Soviet torpedo. That failure had prompted a renewed effort to rectify the mistakes made by Hunter and the fire-control tracking parties. Given the simulator's ability to reconstruct scenarios, and since no time was lost repositioning as would be necessary at sea with real ships, he reran the torpedoing scenario again and again. Among the other scenarios he ran was one that not only required masterful shiphandling skills but was dangerous in its execution: trailing a Russian submarine to record its noise levels.

Because of the time compression that was possible with the

simulator, these and other scenarios could be halted in midstride, so to speak, and started over if something went wrong. Hunter typically did a demo run or two, then turned it over to each of the *Blackfin*'s three watchstanding sections. As chief critic, he stressed over and over again the basics: detect, localize, classify, approach, surveil. The cardinal rule was *don't be counterdetected*. In other words, don't let the Russians find you. Still, it happened, and you had to be prepared for the unexpected. Sometimes in the scenarios Hunter had to defend himself by shooting torpedoes. What made the simulations realistic was that the fake Soviet ships sometimes shot back and, as Hunter discovered, sometimes scored hits.

Other training devices at sub school included the diving trainer, on which the crew practiced handling shipboard casualties such as flooding or a stern plane jam at high speed, either of which could cause loss of ship control and a disaster. There was also a very realistic damage control trainer with valves and pipe fittings that, upon activation from a glassed-in control booth, unleashed powerful jets of water capable of flooding the entire test compartment. Sailors undergoing training struggled to stop the leaks and get control of the flooding before the instructors had to shut off the water so that no one drowned. In the smokehouse trainer, sailors wearing oxygen breathing apparatus (OBA) had to cope with a simulated fire on board a submarine. In another facility they practiced the radiation control techniques they would use in the unlikely event of a reactor casualty on board the *Blackfin*.

Hunter also had to deal with the human aspect of a Holystone deployment. The welfare of the men's families was another of the myriad things that went into predeployment preparations. Wives and children had to prepare ahead of time for a long separation from husbands and dads. It was especially hard for the women, who would have to rely on the support of friends and family to help them cope with the problems that a one-parent navy house-hold presented. Thus Hunter's responsibilities encompassed more than a ship and crew at sea.

Fortunately the predeployment process was relatively unstruc-tured and informal and left in the hands of the CO. A good thing it was, too, since few officers at the various staff levels had the spec-ops experience they would need to meaningfully critique his effort. He would be free to do it his way, aware, of course, that a CO's experience and judgment determined how well prepared a submarine was for a Holystone deployment. Because some ships were better prepared than others, Hunter, a perfectionist supremely confident of his abilities, had no doubt that the *Blackfin* would be as well prepared as humanly possible. This meant not just the *Blackfin* herself but every man aboard, from Hunter and his XO to the ship's department heads, division officers, leading chiefs (who do much of the heavy lifting aboard a sub), right down to the leading petty officers and lowest nonqualified sailors who kept the ship humming like the precision instrument she was.

During this critical period the chief of the boat (COB), a mas-ter chief petty officer with vast experience in submarines, played an important role. Addressed as "Cob," he, like all sub force COBs, had authority over the ship's enlisted men and was respon-sible for maintaining discipline and good order.

• • •

After receiving his orders, Hunter moved the *Blackfin* into the nest of submarines alongside the submarine tender USS *Fulton* to begin an upkeep period.

Moored at State Pier downstream of the sub base, the *Fulton*, built during World War II to service diesel submarines in the Pacific, had been modernized to service nuclear attack subs. As big as a cargo ship, she was a semipermanent fixture in the Thames and the object of such fascination for motorists on Interstate 95 that Connecticut had long ago banned cars from stopping on the bridge connecting New London and Groton north of the *Fulton*'s berth to get a look at her and her submarines.

The *Fulton* provided submarines with almost any service a navy base ashore could provide except dry docking, from welding to electronics to periscope optics—food and laundry services, too. The *Blackfin*'s upkeep period was a time for the crew to undertake any needed corrective maintenance and to install new equipment, especially anything that would aid intelligence gathering. They would also make any possible modifications to existing equipment and machinery that would further reduce the ship's self-noise levels. Finally, they would carry out routine maintenance and top off spare parts and consumables as needed. Food stores would be added later as the date of departure drew nearer, enough for ninety days at sea. Everything that needed to be done had to be accomplished during the predeployment period. For sure there'd be no USS *Fulton* in the Barents Sea to turn to for help.

Though Hunter pushed his gang relentlessly, no one complained. The simulator training, readiness inspections, and constant drills had markedly improved the performance of all hands and had fine-tuned the crew's ability to handle any emergency they might encounter.

Hunter, meanwhile, kept an eye on the calendar as he reviewed reports on the *Blackfin*'s operational readiness. The executive officer, who had overall responsibility for running the ship, and his fellow officers—the ship's department heads, ranging from the engineering officer and weapons officer down to the supply officer (the *Blackfin*'s chief pork chop counter)—conferred with Hunter on an almost daily basis.

Hunter kept the squadron commander apprised of the *Black-fin*'s status as he, too, watched the clock run down to the scheduled departure date. The list of things to do grew shorter until one day everything that had needed attention—a packing gland here, a thrust washer there—had received it. Satisfied that his submarine was fully prepared for action, Hunter took up the next order of business: at-sea training and postupkeep shakedown.

3

A VIEW FROM THE INSIDE OUT

ROUGH WATER HAD TURNED Block Island Sound into a potato patch; the North Atlantic, too. But the *Blackfin*, moving swiftly under the sea, felt rock steady.

There were many things to accomplish during this first of several at-sea periods. One was to wring out newly installed electronic gear for any hidden mousetraps or bugs—flaws in its circuitry. Another was to allow the special intelligence operators assigned to the *Blackfin* time to check out their collection equipment and get comfortable with its installation and operating procedures. Yet another was to check the performance of the ship's towed sonar array, known as submarine towed array sonar system, or STASS.

Submarines like the *Blackfin* employed long towed sonar arrays principally because their hydrophones, mounted as they were on a cable streamed behind the towing sub, away from the noise generated by the submarine itself, had proven more sensitive than the ships' own bow-mounted array. The eight-hundred-foot-long

STASS cable was connected to the ship via a stub incorporating an electrical connection mounted on the starboard vertical stabilizer outboard of the stern diving plane. STASS utilized dozens of hydrophone modules to feed signals to the ship's primary sonar system for processing. Navy technicians aboard a small vessel attached the cable to the sub before departure and disconnected it upon return.

For the *Blackfin*'s at-sea trial periods the squadron commander had provided a couple of targets, a submarine and, in lieu of a destroyer or frigate, the submarine rescue vessel USS *Skylark*. With the two targets deployed as needed, the *Blackfin*'s crew began by practicing their techniques for submarine trailing, the same evolution they had worked on in the simulator.

To safely carry out such complex evolutions, the OOD had to master the hairy maneuvers they required, while the fire-control tracking parties had to be adept at target motion analysis (TMA), the technique submariners use for tracking a target to determine its course, speed, and range.

For input, TMA relied almost exclusively on passive (listening only) sonar to accurately provide a target's bearing—its position relative to the tracking submarine. Range was an important quantitative factor a tracker and plotter had to know before launching a weapon or conducting the trailing operation. Of all the necessary factors, however, it could be the most difficult one to nail down due to the loss of accurate sonar bearings caused by some combination of long range, high sea state, high own-ship speed, and a quiet or maneuvering target. It was, Hunter preached, a lot easier to practice this at sea on a target that was behaving itself, that is, one that wasn't diving, speeding up, or zigzagging the way a Russian target might do in the Barents Sea.

After practicing these maneuvers over and over again, chief

critic Hunter usually let the tracking and fire-control parties blow off steam by sneaking up on the submarine providing target services and putting a "torpedo" into her midsection. If it had been a Soviet sub and the torpedo a real one, the target would have been doomed.

While all of this was taking place, Hunter reflected on how truly extraordinary his ship was.

Deathly quiet, the *Blackfin* sped effortlessly beneath the surface like a black mirage. Divorced from the world above, she seemed not to exist except in a silent world of her own. Self-contained, independent of shore-based controllers, little affected by sea and weather, she was the perfect antiship weapon. She could strike at will and with devastating effect. During World War II, had the United States possessed even a handful of submarines like the *Blackfin* armed with reliable torpedoes, the Japanese would have been defeated within a year of Pearl Harbor and without the United States suffering any submarine losses. (That World War II U.S. submarine torpedoes had failed to run properly and to explode when they hit targets was a scandal the U.S. submarine force still hadn't forgotten.) For now at least, U.S. subs still had an edge on Soviet subs, and to stay ahead would require constant refinement and improvement of both existing and future submarines.

Hunter, aware of this, didn't dwell on it. He assumed that his crew, especially the enlisted men, hardly gave it a thought. Still, even if most of the submariners (that's sub-muh-REEN-ers, not sub-MARE-iners) aboard the *Blackfin* were too young to remember the first Soviet atomic bomb test, they at least sensed how important their mission was. Focused on doing their jobs, they may not have fully understood or even cared about the strategic aspects of Holystone and its operational details, but they surely knew how vital submarines were, regardless of whether the war was hot or cold.

. . .

An attack submarine's primary mission is to sink ships. During World War II, German Grand Admiral Karl Dönitz's U-boats almost defeated Great Britain and her allies by sinking millions of tons of Allied merchant shipping bound from the United States for British and Russian ports, sending to the bottom the food, fuel, and raw materials needed to survive and fight Hitler. In the Pacific theater, U.S. subs, operating primarily from bases in Australia and Pearl Harbor, torpedoed and sank 5.6 million tons of Japanese merchant shipping, the loss of which strangled Japan's far-flung military garrisons and ultimately helped defeat that country. For a submarine, stealth and mobility are essential, since its ability to operate with impunity against enemy opposition might mean the difference between victory and defeat. The Germans learned this only too well, especially during the latter stages of World War II, when hundreds of U-boats, lacking improved stealth, quieting, and undersea endurance, were sunk by Allied ASW units, whereas U.S. fleet-type submarines, having sunk a good portion of the Japanese navy, which lacked effective ASW, ruled the Pacific.

Even so, German advances in submarine design pointed the way to the future.

On April 30, 1945, the day Adolf Hitler committed suicide in his Berlin bunker, a submarine unlike any other in Admiral Dönitz's fleet, or any other fleet for that matter, put to sea from Bergen, Norway. She was a highly advanced Type XXI U-boat, the first submarine in history designed to operate entirely submerged for extended periods. She had a storage battery capacity three times that of a Type VIIC, the standard U-boat employed in combat during the war. This capacity gave the streamlined Type XXI high underwater speed and long range by the standard of the time. Then, most submarines could either run submerged at two or three knots and stay down for perhaps a day to a day and a half, or run at high speed at eight to ten knots for about an hour before needing to surface to charge batteries. Their underwater range was severely limited: sixty to eighty miles at best. By comparison the Type XXIs, with their increased battery capacity and a snorkel for drawing air into the boat to recharge the batteries by diesel when submerged, could make sixteen knots submerged for a short time and remain underwater almost indefinitely. The ability to hide from her enemies for long periods of time and to move stealthily across great distances, when coupled to an enlarged torpedo load, advanced sonar, and excellent seakeeping qualities, made the XXI the most deadly submarine of its day.

Though 119 Type XXIs were delivered and commissioned between 1944 and 1945, Allied bombing raids, lack of raw materials, and the difficulty encountered in training crews to handle a new type of submarine scuttled the plans Dönitz had to employ these boats against the Allies. Many incomplete Type XXIs were left rusting on the building ways. The only Type XXI to undertake a war patrol, the *U-2511*, was at sea when the war ended.

After the war, U.S. submarine officers, most of them combat veterans, were surprised, if not shocked, at how advanced Germany's new U-boat was. Because these officers had experienced firsthand the important role U.S. submarines had played in the projection of American sea power against the Japanese, they understood that had those U-boats been deployed earlier in the war, when Great Britain was staggering under the U-boat onslaught, the outcome for the Allies might have been vastly different.

With such issues in mind and after studying the advanced design principles found in the two Type XXI boats allocated to the United States after the war, the *U-2513* and the *U-3008*, the navy incorporated into its first postwar (or prenuke) submarine-building program much of the Type XXI's technology, including its streamlined hull forms and superstructures.

After studying alternate means of propulsion, such as the unproven Walter hydrogen peroxide closed-cycle system, as a replacement for conventional diesel engines, the navy authorized the construction of the *Tang* class of submarines. They were to be powered by a new compact radial diesel engine designed by General Motors, who had built diesel engines for the navy in World War II, after the Walter system proved too problematic to be of any practical use.

The six *Tang*-class subs, which the navy rushed into service starting in the early 1950s to blunt the threat of the rapidly growing Soviet sub fleet, bore a close resemblance to the Type XXIs. So, too, did the obsolescent World War II fleet boats after undergoing modernization to help fill the submarine gap.

In the rush, however, the *Tang*s entered service with a myriad of problems. Experienced officers called the *Tang*s' new pancakestyle GM diesels a disaster. These engines, with their sixteen radially stacked cylinders, had failed miserably, at times leaving submarines stranded at sea. They also found fault with the *Tang*s' torpedo control systems, their freshwater distilling apparatus, and their cramped living spaces. In time the six *Tang*s underwent modifications, including the replacement of their radial engines with conventional in-line engines. Though they would serve the navy for many years, conventional diesel-powered submarines had by then passed into history.

. . .

It wasn't too long after the Hungarian theoretical physicist Leo Szilard had his celebrated revelatory vision in 1933 of the shape of things to come—that it might be possible to release the power of the atom to induce a nuclear chain reaction and use the resulting release of energy to power machines and build atomic bombs—that other physicists and naval engineers had visions of their own about using atomic power to propel submarines.

After World War II, U.S. Navy scientists and engineers began work to determine the feasibility of a nuclear-powered submarine and what technical characteristics would shape her final form. By late 1946, plans were under way to begin the development and construction of such a submarine. With approval from the navy, a team was assembled to design and build a prototype nuclear reactor and, if it proved successful, an actual working combat submarine, not a test model. Thus was born the USS *Nautilus*, the world's first nuclear-powered submarine.

The *Nautilus* was the brainchild of many officers and scientists in and out of government and the navy. Even so, she was inextricably linked to the indomitable Admiral Rickover.

Launched at Electric Boat in 1954, the nuclear-powered *Nautilus*, with her subtle hints of the Type XXI's external design yet with many unique and innovative design touches of her own, had, the moment she touched water, made every submarine in the world obsolete. Overnight the *Tang*s and their sisters, the surplus World War II *Gato*-, *Balao*-, and *Tench*-class boats, had become relics of another age.

The navy, committed to nuclear propulsion in its development of submarines, built on lessons learned from the *Nautilus*. Submarine development in the United States accelerated as more and more nukes started coming online. Series production began in earnest with the *Skate*-class, boats which were similar in design and capabilites to the *Nautilus*.

The *Skate*s soon evolved into the *Skipjack* class, the first U.S. nuclear submarines designed with an improved pressurized water reactor capable of producing fifteen thousand shaft horsepower. Ironically, the *Skipjack*s echoed the design of submarine inventor John P. Holland's football-shaped SS-1 commissioned by the navy in 1900. Though separated by more than fifty years, both submarines had teardrop-shaped cylindrical hulls and a single centerline propeller, proving that good design never goes out of style.

Later still, the *Skipjack*s' basic design evolved into the first generation Polaris-missile-firing SSBNs, with lengthened hulls to house sixteen missile launch tubes. The first Polaris A-1 submarine-launched ballistic missile (SLBM) carried by these new strategic submarines had a range of 1,200 nautical miles. Improved versions such as the A-3 had a range of 2,500 nautical miles. The submarines themselves were reconfigurable to handle improved versions of Polaris missiles as they were introduced into the fleet.

The deployment of the A-3 in 1964 allowed SSBNs to patrol in areas more distant from Soviet coastlines than ever before, opening up ever vaster areas of ocean to utilize for concealment. In turn, Soviet ASW forces were stretched ever thinner by the need to search bigger and bigger ocean regions for the virtually invisible Polaris-firing subs. Unable to directly counter the Polaris threat, the Soviets, who had been the first to develop SLBMs, rushed to develop even more potent versions of their own SSBNs, though they were no match for U.S. strategic submarines, especially in areas of quieting and reactor technology.

As the first Polaris subs began deploying in the 1960s, the new, quieter, deeper-diving *Thresher*-class attack submarines started coming off the building ways. The *Threshers'* teardrop shape and single-screw design, with certain modifications and refinements, were utilized again in the new *Sturgeon*-class attack submarines known colloquially as the 637 class. Later still, this same design, with yet more modifications and improvements, would appear in the *Los Angeles–*, *Seawolf-*, and *Virginia*-class submarines of the future.

The *Thresher* embodied all of the characteristics the navy had hoped to achieve in its quest for the ideal nuclear submarine. She was in a sense the first true attack submarine for the age. Everything about her had been planned with utmost care and designed to work as an integrated whole—her sensor suite, combat systems, weapons, the whole package. Accordingly, the navy suffered a terrible blow to its prestige and confidence when the *Thresher* went down with all hands on April 10, 1963.

The wreckage, when it was found in the North Atlantic, at first held few clues to the disaster. Moreover, her design had been used in many other submarines, and there was no way to know whether the design itself was basically flawed or a piece of machinery or equipment had failed. Much later an investigation pinned the blame on a combination of cascading events: A leak in a seawater connection likely had led to electrical system short-circuits and the loss of reactor power. A contributing factor was the impossibility of blowing the main ballast tanks when ice, which had formed under high pressure inside narrow-gauge air piping, blocked the flow of compressed air to the *Thresher's* ballast tanks.

While it was impossible to know how accurate this likely

scenario was, the navy instituted the necessary changes in submarine design to prevent such disasters from happening in the future. As a result a host of refinements and safety features, along with the growing requirement for more intelligence-collection capability, were incorporated in the design of the new *Sturgeon*-class submarines that had been authorized for construction beginning in the early 1960s.

• • •

Though the *Sturgeon*s as built sacrificed speed for greater combat capability, there was no question that they embodied important improvements over their predecessors. As such, the thirty-seven *Sturgeon*s commissioned between 1967 and 1975 became the backbone of the navy's fast-attack sub force during the middle period of the cold war. Most of these submarines remained in service until the 1990s, replaced by the *Los Angeles*–, *Seawolf*-, and *Virginia*-class SSNs. The last *Sturgeon*, the USS *Parche*, fitted out for ultrasecret and highly specialized intelligence work, didn't retire until 2004, when the USS *Jimmy Carter*, a *Seawolf*-class boat, assumed her role.

Launched at Electric Boat in Groton, Connecticut, in the late 1960s, the *Blackfin*, like her sisters, was designed and built for both antisubmarine warfare and espionage operations. During construction she'd received the latest modifications and improvements developed in response to the various design deficiencies, both large and small, that are typically discovered only after a new class of warship in series production puts to sea. As her commissioning CO, Hunter worked hard to make sure his new ship met if not exceeded his and the navy's expectations.

Some of the modifications she received while under construction were advanced quieting features meant to ensure submerged stealth. Others included a strengthened sail—the tall, flat, vertical structure on a submarine—to house periscopes and retractable masts used for electronic eavesdropping and communication, sail-mounted diving planes that could rotate ninety degrees from vertical to horizontal for breaking through thick arctic ice, improved air-conditioning, more efficient internal arrangement of equipment, and the addition of vertical fins to the tips of the stern diving planes to improve handling when submerged.

Other enhancements included a Type 15D periscope, which augmented the standard Type 2F attack periscope. The 15D had a broadband ESM receiver housed in a cylinder at the base of the scope's eyepiece box. The 15D also came equipped with a periviz system designed to pipe video images to slaved video monitors in other parts of the submarine. This system represented a departure from previous doctrine in which only the CO saw what was happening topside through the periscope. Though periviz allowed for second-guessing by officers and enlisted men alike, Hunter, like most COs, didn't give it a thought.

Submarines like the *Blackfin* used passive sonar to locate and attack their enemies. A submarine must have the capability to hear everything and anything in the water around her, not just up close but also many miles away. The ability to do so depends on both highly skilled sonarmen and supersensitive sonar suites. Detectable noise can come from both the rotating machinery inside a submarine's hull and its propellers. It can also come from steam flow through the sub's nuclear propulsion system and transients such as the slamming of a watertight door or a dropped tool.

As well, the ocean environment is noisy. Wind-driven waves hiss and chuckle. Dolphins whistle and squeal. Whales croon. Fish clack and click. Merchant ships rumble and rattle. A submarine's sonar system relies first on a sonarman's hearing, then on signal processing by the system's computers, to sift through the background noise that radiates in all directions (as does the listening submarine's own noise) to identify the sounds made by another submarine. A submarine's sonar array therefore must have adequate size to detect low-frequency sounds; hence the huge spherical bow arrays in the *Sturgeon*s.

The noise a submarine makes—her sound signature—consists of three separate components. One component is continuous broadband noise caused by rotating internal machinery. The second component is narrowband noise caused by *specific* sound frequencies coming from the sub's machinery and propulsion system, and also from the low-frequency sound caused by the vibrating blades of its turning propeller, a phenomenon known as blade rate. While broadband noise varies in intensity, the tonals in narrowband noise are steady and continuous. The third component is self-noise caused by the flow of seawater over a submarine's hull. Self-noise varies in strength depending on the submarine's underwater speed and, to complicate matters, can degrade the sub's own sonar reception.

The sonar system aboard a submarine routes the broadband noise through a computerized narrowband spectrum analyzer set to specific frequencies that can be identified and isolated from the general broadband noise in the ocean to identify noise made by an enemy submarine. The strength of a sub's broadband signature is influenced by distance, background noise, and absorption by seawater, whereas a particular narrowband frequency with high energy—say, from a circulating pump—can often be heard at long ranges despite background noise and absorption.

Temperature layers in the ocean, because they're so variable, not only absorb broadband and narrowband sound but can also alter the direction of sound propagation and its intensity. Such conditions can further complicate the detection of an enemy sub-marine, which even under the best conditions is a somewhat iffy proposition. A submarine sonarman has to consider a host of vari-ables to find the enemy. He has to be able to differentiate between a trilling school of fish and a humming submarine generator. No matter, it all comes down to one objective: You have to hear the other guy before he hears you. For U.S. submarine sonarmen, it wasn't all that hard to do because, compared to their U.S. counter-parts, Russian submarines were pretty noisy.

The *Blackfin*'s primary sonar suite consisted of a BQQ-5 low-frequency passive and active system. It had a fifteen-foot-diameter bow-mounted spherical array fitted with more than 1,200 hy-drophones providing a "wide view" and great sensitivity. The system's computers had the ability to integrate the *Blackfin*'s bow-mounted array with its hull-mounted BQR-7 conformal array and towed STASS. Another sonar system, the BQS-14, was a dual-purpose, short-range, under-ice unit that would come in handy if the *Blackfin* was ever ordered under the arctic ice pack.

Though the *Sturgeon*s were bigger than their predecessors, they were not so big as to make them ungainly in littoral waters, where they might have to operate. The *Blackfin* displaced 4,780 tons sub-merged, had an overall length of 292 feet, a beam of 31 feet 6 inches, and a draft of 28 feet 10 inches. (*Los Angeles*–class sub-marines then on the drawing boards were sixty-two feet longer and about two thousand tons heavier.) Later *Sturgeon* units, starting with the USS *Archerfish*, had ten-foot-long sections added to their hulls to provide more space for intel collection. Nevertheless, creature comforts were minimal: The *Blackfin*'s regular crew of 108 officers and men, along with the embarked navy intelligence personnel and their gear, were stuffed inside the hull wherever they fit. Personal space was at a premium. Sailors and officers shared heads and showers.

With her hull of HY-80 steel, which was more than an inch thick, the *Blackfin* could dive to a test depth of 1,300 feet. Her pressurized water nuclear reactor working through two General Electric steam turbines produced fifteen thousand shaft horsepower good for sixteen knots on the surface and more than twenty-five submerged. Like all modern nuclear subs, she was faster submerged than surfaced.

Though stealth was the primary weapon used for the silent battle U.S. spy subs waged against the Soviets, submariners never knew when a torpedo might come in handy, especially when confronted with a situation like the one Hunter had faced in the attack simulator. Foremost an attack submarine, the *Blackfin* had four twenty-one-inch torpedo tubes and carried twenty-three wire-guided Mark (Mk) 37 torpedoes capable of sinking not only submarines but surface ships as well.

She also carried SUBROC (submarine rocket) ballistic missiles, each armed with a one- to five-kiloton W55 nuclear warhead. The missile was designed to strike targets beyond the range of Mk 37 torpedoes. Launched from a torpedo tube, the SUBROC immediately shot to the surface, then blasted off to hit a target, maybe a sub located earlier by sonar. Nearing the target, the rocket motor case detached from the rocket's main body, after which the warhead plunged into the sea and detonated. An unguided nuclear warhead didn't need great accuracy; landing anywhere close to a target, especially a submerged sub, would do the job. The *Blackfin*'s computerized torpedo fire-control system, the digital Mk 113, integrated the complicated elements—mathematics, geometry, guidance—that went into firing torpedoes or SUBROCs at, and getting hits on, a target.

The *Blackfin*'s torpedo room, located amidships below the control room, had four tubes aimed forward and canted slightly outboard port and starboard. Single-screw subs couldn't be fitted with after tubes, not just because there wasn't room for them but because it wasn't practical to time the firing of torpedoes to pass safely through the ship's spinning propeller blades. American and German aviators in World War I had fired nose-mounted machine guns through the spinning propeller blades of their Spads and Fokkers, but subs were different.

Mk 37 torpedoes, the *Blackfin*'s primary offensive weapons, had been designed in the early years of the cold war with a homing capability and wire guidance. The torpedo had a simple two-speed setting, its electric propulsion provided by a silver-zinc battery. Unlike older-style twenty-one-inch-diameter torpedoes, which had to be ejected by compressed air or a hydraulic ram system, the nineteen-inch Mk 37 "swam" out of its tube under its own power. That reduced its noise signature and also the submarine's since there was no roar of compressed air or hiss of hydraulics.

The submarine's fire-control system guided the Mk 37 to the target by sending guidance data down a long wire filament paid out from a supply reel at the torpedo's stern and plugged into the torpedo's "brain." At the appropriate point in the run the torpedo, regardless of whether it had been set for active or passive sonar search, signaled that it had acquired its target, after which the wire was cut and the tube secured.

While the Mk 37s were slow, making barely twenty-six knots at their high-speed settings, it gave them a usable range of ten thousand yards, or roughly five nautical miles. They could track targets to a depth of a thousand feet, where Russian subs were capable of operating. Since the Mk 37 was primarily designed as an antisubmarine weapon, it had a relatively small warhead consisting of a contact exploder and 330 pounds of HBX-3 high explosive, more than enough to punch through the double-hull plating of most Russian submarines. Because subs have so little reserve buoyancy, one hit from a Mk 37 was all it would take to sink one.

. . .

The *Blackfin* was a good-looking ship—a tad stubby, yet sleek when moving at high speed on the surface. Submerged, she was in her element, unimpeded by all of the forces the sea imparts to surface ships. There was no sense of forward motion or action of the sea around her, only the up or down tilt of her decks to indicate that there was any motion at all.

The operations center of the submarine, arranged over three levels, remained calm and quiet, save for the clipped orders passed between the OOD and the watchstanders in the control room as they put the *Blackfin* through a series of evolutions. The only other sounds came from the faint hum of machinery, the low whine of electronic gear, and the whisper of the ventilation system's air handlers and blowers. The manufactured atmosphere, despite all the machinery and electrical gear inside the ship, as well as a busy galley, was surprisingly neutral.

The crew's living and work spaces forward of the reactor compartment and engine room included the "goat locker"—the chief petty officers' quarters—the enlisted men's bunk rooms, various storerooms, diesel compartment, mess decks, and officers' staterooms. Men not on watch moved about the ship through narrow passageways sheathed in fake wood-grain plastic laminate and ascended and descended staircases with handrails. Everything else was trimmed in stainless steel and aluminum. Linoleum squares designed to absorb sound covered the decks. Heavy, thick water-

tight doors set into equally thick bulkheads between compartments stood open, ready to be dogged to isolate a compartment in
case of flooding or fire.

Interior communications (IC) aboard the *Blackfin* were maintained over several announcing systems. Numbered circuits, such
as the 2MC in the engineering spaces, provided communications
links for various engineering control functions, as did dial-up and
sound-powered phones. When Hunter wanted to address the entire crew to update them on ops or give them information, he used
the 1MC. There were also alarms for battle stations, collision, and
diving.

Aft, the ship's reactor compartment, auxiliary machinery space,
and engine room were crammed with noisy pumps, main engines,
turbines, and electrical generating sets. Here, sailors standing six-
hour watches oversaw the amazingly complex devices that propelled the *Blackfin* through the sea. More than half of her length
and diameter had been given over to this function. What space
was left over supported the crew who ran her. It also held the
computers, weapons, and sensors needed to fight or to collect intelligence. A submarine, especially a nuclear submarine, is one of
the most complex machines ever devised by man. Yet a glance at
the *Blackfin*'s heart, her nuclear reactor, told only part of the story
of how nuclear-powered submarines function.

4

SUBATOMICS: MAKING POWER

"ALL AHEAD FLANK," Hunter ordered, as he brought the submerged *Blackfin* around onto a new course to engage in a mock torpedo attack on the *Skylark*.

In the maneuvering room, the engineering officer of the watch supervised a petty officer seated at the main propulsion control console, facing two concentric spoked stainless steel rings looking very much like steering wheels. In fact, they were the throttles for controlling the main engines: The outer wheel controlled speeds ahead, the inner one speeds astern. The panel also had alarm and warning indicators for the steam and feedwater systems, rudder angle indicators, and an engine order telegraph, among other devices. When the engine order telegraph rang for, say, maximum speed, the petty officer, careful to avoid spinning the prop too fast, which would cause cavitation, slowly opened the outer throttle ring, sending power to the *Blackfin*'s engines.

Two other consoles connected to the main propulsion control console completed the arrangement. The middle console comprised the reactor plant control panel, with its array of gauges and all-important controls for raising or lowering the reactor's control rods. The right-hand console comprised the electric plant control console, with its AC-DC electric distribution panel and associated gauges and switches.

Power to drive the ship came from the fissioning of enriched uranium fuel in the shielded core of the *Blackfin*'s nuclear reactor, a vertical cylinder made of six-inch-thick alloy steel designed to contain fission by-products. Nuclear fission, the splitting of the U-235 nucleus, releases neutrons and other particles, such as alpha and beta particles, and gamma rays in the form of heat. The reaction, if not controlled, would quickly result in a runaway chain reaction not unlike that in a nuclear weapon. In a submarine reactor, however, purified water under high pressure is used as a primary coolant and moderator to slow down and control the reaction. The pressurized and radioactive coolant passing over the hot fuel rods heats to over 500° F. The hot water circulates via the main coolant pumps from the core through pipes to a steam generator, where heat from the coolant transfers to a separate pressurized system in which nonradioactive water (the two liquids are kept apart) vaporizes to produce steam. The smallest leak in any part of the system can result in radioactive contamination, loss of pressure, loss of power—perhaps even destruction of the reactor itself.

The steam produced in the secondary loop powers two steam turbines coupled to a set of reduction gears that slow the turbine's high speed output to a lower, more usable speed to turn the ship's propeller. A portion of the steam is directed into two other turbines that create power for the ship's electrical system. After exhausting its heat energy, the steam enters a condenser in which it's cooled by seawater and condensed back into water. From there the water returns to the steam generator, again via circulating pumps, for reheating by the primary coolant to start the process over again. The system resembles a shore-based, self-contained power-generating station and electrical grid. In fact, the *Blackfin*'s plant could have probably filled the power needs of a small city the size of St. Augustine, Florida.

Since the amount of uranium in the core exceeds the critical mass needed for fission, a set of control rods made of hafnium, a metal that absorbs neutrons, is inserted into the top of the reactor vessel. Normally the rods are raised or lowered into the core by a drive mechanism to speed up fission, slow it down, or stop it altogether.

In an emergency—say, an electrical power failure, a coolant leak, or a serious accident at sea—a submarine's reactor can be shut down, or scrammed, manually or automatically by discharging the electromagnets holding up the control rods. Gravity takes over and, with a powerful assist from a spring-loaded device at the top of each rod, the rods drop into the core, shutting down the reactor. One story goes that the word "scram" derived from the very early days of nuclear reactor technology, when a technician called the "safety control rod axe man" stood over the reactor with an axe ready to cut the rope holding up the control rods if the chain reaction threatened to run away. There are no safety control rod axe men aboard nuclear submarines.

Using nuclear power to run a submarine is an enormously complicated business. It demands constant monitoring of equipment and strict adherence to clearly defined and codified procedures to ensure safe operation. The operating rules for nuclear submarine reactors established by Rickover and the U.S. Navy before the *Nautilus* ever put to sea are immutable. Any violation of a submarine nuclear plant's operating procedures carries with it serious penalties.

One look inside the *Blackfin*'s machinery spaces would explain why such safety procedures were necessary. Mazes of piping, cables, valves, air lines, electrical buses, and gauges gobbled up every inch of available space. Everything needed to run the ship had been stuffed inside her skin of curved steel plates welded to hoop-shaped steel I-beams called frames. Where the hull plates butted, their edges had been cut to a V-shape and electrically welded, then X-rayed, inspected, and heat treated, a process that resulted in a tough, strong hull capable of withstanding enormous sea pressure. Like most submariners, the *Blackfin*'s crew hardly gave a thought to the forces the hull had to resist when submerged. Nor did it ever seem to trouble them that the sea was never more than inches away and that any failure of the ship's watertight integrity could spell disaster.

In any event, the crew didn't have time to think about these things. Nor did they think about the enormous forces unleashed by nuclear fission. They were too busy carrying out their duties, moving as their work required through narrow passageways and across catwalks, ducking under bundles of overhead cabling, squeezing past pipes filled with dangerous fluids and around steel housings containing the controlled chaos of rotating machinery. The sea was out there but not there. It was a presence, nothing more.

• • •

After completing five days of scheduled exercises, satisfied with the *Blackfin*'s and her crew's performance, Hunter lowered the periscope and said, "Officer of the deck, let's head for the barn."

"Yes, sir." The OOD gave the order. "All ahead full. Come to course north. Make your depth three hundred feet."

As the *Blackfin* crossed the hundred-fathom curve, she slowed to ten knots and came to periscope depth, or PD. Shortly the OOD toggled the 1MC and ordered, "Prepare to surface."

"Prepare to surface, aye."

The chief of the watch reported that all compartments were ready to surface. The diving officer planed up so the ship would just broach, then started the low-pressure blower to begin dewatering the ballast tanks.

From the OOD: "Surface! Surface! Surface!" The diving alarm honked three times.

The quartermaster scampered up the ladder from the control room to open the lower hatch leading topside and then up into the sail to open the folding clamshell covers that streamlined the bridge cockpit when submerged. The OOD followed the quartermaster topside to resume the conn on the surface.

Bow wave climbing her sail, sea cleaved by her hull, the *Blackfin* made for home. Astern, a wide bridal veil of froth, a chalk line pointing to the horizon, marked her passing. Ahead lay New London. The pleasure Hunter got from the power his ship possessed was undeniable. He wasn't a particularly sentimental man, but moments like this made submarining the most exciting profession on earth.

5

HIGH STAKES

THE FLIGHT FROM NEW LONDON to Norfolk was uneventful. Hunter, along with a group of his officers, arrived at the CinC-LantFleet (Commander in Chief Atlantic Fleet) compound. Left behind in New London were two nuclear-qualified officers to stand duty watches aboard the *Blackfin*. (The supply officer had stayed to count cans of beans and pork chops.) The group was escorted into the secure submarine operations center to attend a classified briefing about their upcoming Holystone mission, conducted by the staff intel officer of ComSubLant's intel group. Other staffers had brought along maps, photos, and visual aids, even some close-up aerial images of Soviet naval bases on the Kola Peninsula. These images might have been snapped from U.S. KH-8 spy satellites, though they weren't identified as such.

The briefer, a commander—a diesel guy, not a nuke—had no Holystone experience. Once again Hunter was struck by how the intel types had little practical experience in submarine espionage but plenty of ideas about how it was supposed to work. He was struck, too, by how informal it all was, like a bunch of guys sitting around having a bull session. That was okay, though, because it kept Hunter and his officers in a relaxed mood, which made for an easy give-and-take between them and the staff.

The *Blackfin*'s operation order arrived in the form of a bound booklet titled "Top Secret—Holystone," the cover stamped with a mission number. Typically op orders covered everything a CO and his officers needed to know, such as the rules of engagement, what procedures to follow in the event of a major casualty such as a reactor accident or flooding, under what circumstances the *Blackfin* could depart from her assigned area, and what naval activities or areas were of particular interest to those in charge of U.S. intelligence collection.

"Okay, your op area is the Barents Sea," said the commander. He pointed to the aerial photographs lying on one of the conference tables. "Your principal 'target' is the Severomorsk naval base on the Kola Peninsula." Not the actual target, he stressed, as Severomorsk was inland, but the ship traffic entering and departing from it via the Kola Inlet and the SIGINT—signals intelligence—emanating from the ships and surrounding areas.

Severomorsk was the main administrative base of the Soviet Red Banner Northern Fleet. Located ten miles north of Murmansk on Varlamova Bay in the Tuloma River, which emptied into the Kola Gulf, Severomorsk was home port to most of the Northern Fleet's surface ships. The Soviet navy had established its northern submarine base at Polyarnyy, while bases at Gadzhiyevo and Murmansk serviced icebreakers, and still others had full-scale shipyards and nuclear reactor repair facilities. Little wonder that what entered and departed from Severomorsk was a high-priority intel collection target. Polyarnyy, too.

The commander picked up steam. "There are two issues of political and strategic importance that will have an influence on your op." He discussed the Nixon-Brezhnev summit scheduled to take place in Moscow and the SALT negotiations currently under way, with the negotiators shuttling between Vienna and Helsinki. The fact that Nixon's visit to Moscow had been announced even while the administration was developing plans for a visit to China only confirmed the importance the United States and the USSR had placed on the Nixon-Brezhnev talks.

He continued. "As you know, we've been running Holystone ops in the Barents, always keeping in mind the delicacy of the Moscow summit and SALT talks. The ops are risky as hell but necessary." The commander didn't need to say that an "event" such as a confrontation between a Holystone sub and Soviet ships or submarines could prove disastrous for Soviet-American relations. If something nasty were to happen, it would cause a hell of an uproar throughout the operational chain of command and beyond. "Therefore, as of this moment," the briefer went on, "permission to penetrate the Soviet twelve-mile territorial limit has been withdrawn."

Though there was no ratified convention governing a nation's claims over territorial waters, the United States, unlike the USSR, claimed only a three-mile territorial limit. Nevertheless, while Holystone subs regularly penetrated the USSR's twelve-mile limit to collect intelligence, penetration of that country's three-mile limit was absolutely forbidden unless authorized by a higher authority.

Higher authority. Hunter understood what that meant: the president of the United States. Only intelligence of the highest priority would warrant Nixon's approval to collect it inside Soviet territorial waters. What kind of intelligence? Perhaps a videotape of a test launch of a missile from a new class of Soviet SSBN.

Also, it was known that the Soviets had new missile guidance technology, but how good was it? The collection of such intelligence would give U.S. SALT negotiators a real advantage over their Soviet counterparts. A submarine was the ideal platform to use for eavesdropping on Soviet naval operations and sneaking a peek at their missile tests, especially when orbiting satellites and naval radio intercept stations weren't always positioned to do the job. The *Blackfin* could get up close to the target—inside Soviet territorial waters if necessary—grab what was needed, then haul out undetected. Sure, it might be risky, but Holystone subs had done it before. All a submariner needed to do it was a pair of brass balls.

The briefer reminded Hunter's team that upon departure from New London, active sonar and any electronic gear capable of transmitting signals had to be secured and should not be activated during transit or while on station in the Barents Sea. It was a standard precaution all Holystone submarines exercised to maintain invisibility for the duration of their patrol.

While the briefer went over other minor details, Hunter thought about the Barents Sea, the *Blackfin*'s operating area.

Named after the Dutch navigator Willem Barents, the Barents Sea was in fact part of the Arctic Ocean north of Norway and Russia's Kola Peninsula. It had an average depth of just 750 feet though its bottom dropped away to over 2,000 feet in the Bear Island Trench south of Spitsbergen. Bounded by the Norwegian Sea, Spitsbergen, Franz Josef Land, and, in the east, Novaya Zemlya, an island that on maps looked like an inside out watermelon rind, the Barents was for all intents and purposes a private Russian lake. In early fall the northern half of the Barents was mostly ice-free, while the southern half, which included Severomorsk and Polyarnyy, remained ice-free year-round thanks to the

warm waters of the Atlantic Drift. While the Drift kept important Barents sea lanes open year-round, it also created the temperature boundary layers used as cover by spying American
submarines. Even so, the Barents was a rugged area in which to
operate. Storm-tossed, cold even in summer, and capped by skies
that were often overcast for weeks at a time, the Barents exacted a
harsh toll on men and ships alike. It was in a sense another adversary, one that could be even more deadly than the main enemy.

"Captain Hunter, take a look at these."

The briefer flashed slides onto a screen and pointed out important features of Soviet radar installations and communications
complexes located on the jagged northern coast of the Kola
Peninsula. Hunter observed that the radar installations were clustered mainly around the western frontier area near Norway, and
about twenty miles inland. Their current operating frequencies
and other characteristics were known, but Hunter would be looking for new installations with different frequencies and characteristics to collect. If war broke out they'd be on the Strategic Air
Command's primary target list for destruction by B-52s and
B-58s.

"The coordinates for these sites are noted in your op-order list
of primary collection sites," the briefer said. "Check them out.
We think the Sovs may have upgraded some of these radars, and
we need confirmation."

The briefing moved on to recent Soviet Northern Fleet deployments, specifically SSBNs, several of which had departed on
patrols into the North Atlantic. While the briefer didn't confirm
it, SSBNs were sometimes detected early on by SOSUS (Sound
Surveillance System), the U.S. Navy's network of cabled hydrophones designed to detect Russian submarines at very long
distances. Installed on the seabed off the east and west coasts of

the United States and in various choke points in the North Atlantic, it detected Soviet Northern Fleet submarines and Pacific Fleet submarines as they approached the United States. Sometimes they were picked up and shadowed by U.S. SSNs vectored into the area to keep an eye on their movements.

The briefer also had intelligence on Soviet subs that had been detected while trying to shadow American Polaris submarines as they departed from their base in Holy Loch, Scotland, on deterrent patrols. It hadn't been hard to find the snooping Russians; SOSUS had heard them coming, after which flights of navy P-3 Orion sub hunters equipped with sonobuoys pinpointed their locations. That gave the boomers plenty of time to slip away unheard and unseen and allowed the navy to dispatch an ASW team to harass the Soviets sneaking around outside Holy Loch.

SOSUS was a powerful ASW weapon. Its hydrophones, arrayed in clusters of two dozen or more and enclosed in large tanks on the seabed, were not only tuned to specific frequencies but so sensitive that they could hear rain falling on the ocean's surface and even aircraft flying overhead. With such extreme sensitivity SOSUS could track submarines halfway around the world and pinpoint their locations to within ten miles. The system fed into fixed shore stations that processed the collected audio data for transmission to U.S. intelligence agencies for action.

SOSUS had proven to be particularly effective in the North Atlantic, where it had been installed across the Greenland–Iceland–United Kingdom Gap (GIUK Gap) to detect Soviet submarines deploying southward from the Barents Sea. Much later, the U.S. installed a SOSUS network between Norway and Bear Island to detect Soviet submarines operating on the fringes of the western Barents. The Soviets, hemmed in by SOSUS, found it increasingly difficult for Northern Fleet submarines to deploy without being detected.

. . .

The briefing moved on to a question-and-answer session to clarify and define the fine points of the operation-order. The rules of engagement were particularly important, for they set out the parameters and limits of *when* and *if* the use of deadly force was authorized against Soviet naval units. As always, the situations a submarine might encounter dictated the response. There were caveats galore.

The op order gave Hunter the freedom to conduct operations as he saw fit given the environment in which he would be operating. Under certain circumstances—say, an unprovoked attack on the *Blackfin* in international waters, or any attack that put the ship in mortal danger—Hunter was authorized to counterattack. There were other parameters, too, all of which had attached to them certain requirements that had to be met before weapons could be fired even in self-defense. The paramount consideration in every case was to avoid a confrontation that could escalate out of control into a war with the Soviet Union. It was imperative that Hunter and his officers understood their orders and knew how to interpret them and, above all, how to respond to any situation they might encounter, especially mission-unique situations not covered by the op order.

While all of this information was presented in an objective and casual manner, Hunter and his officers were under no illusions that the Soviets had let their guard down or were unaware of how determined the U.S. Navy was to operate clandestinely in Soviet-controlled waters. They also knew that while the Soviets lacked the means to prevent incursions by U.S. subs, a mistake by the CO of a Holystone sub that led to counterdetection could put the ship and crew in jeopardy.

· · ·

The Northern Fleet existed mainly to defend the so-called Russian Northwestern Zone against attack by U.S. or NATO forces. As part of its regular duties the fleet conducted missile tests while it kept abreast of any current U.S. and NATO military operations anywhere near Soviet territory. Despite limited success against U.S. submarine incursions, the Northern Fleet conducted ASW exercises on a regular basis. One of the principal tools that the fleet employed was nuclear-powered antisubmarine submarines. Submarines constitute an effective means of locating enemy submarines, but they can't do it alone; that requires vast resources of ships, aircraft, and sensors and an interlocking network of command and control, all of which the Soviets lacked but were scrambling to provide. Moreover, due to the rigid and somewhat doctrinaire nature of their ASW operations and tactics and the lack of assets, the Soviets conducted operations only a few hundred nautical miles out from their coastlines. Constrained by this limit, the Soviet Northern Fleet was virtually powerless to prevent penetration of their northern waters by U.S. submarines. ASW amphibians like the twin-engine Beriev Be-12 Chaika (NATO designation Mail) were potentially capable of conducting long-range patrols from Soviet territory, but, loaded with heavy, outdated electronic search gear and without fuel drop tanks, the craft had limited range. In addition, the Northern Fleet had had little experience operating ASW helicopters from the decks of ships. Without an underwater detection system like SOSUS, without a large modern fleet of ships and helicopters dedicated to

ASW, and without a fleet of long-range ASW aircraft to patrol the enormous areas that had to be covered, more than one Soviet admiral had concluded that antisubmarine operations in the Barents were worthless.

Thus hampered, the Soviets were forced to limit their ASW patrolling to a series of ringlike defense zones radiating north from the Kola Peninsula like a fan inside of which, they believed, a small concentration of ships and planes might prove effective against U.S. submarines. The zones extended from near-shore to mid-range to roughly four hundred miles into the desolate northern wastes of the Barents Sea, an area where few ships ever operated. The search for U.S. submarines took place mostly inside these zones and within the marginal seas bordering it. According to the U.S. Navy's intelligence estimates contained in Hunter's briefing document, the Soviet Northern Fleet had approximately seventy destroyer escort–type ships and several hundred coastal patrol boats suitable for ASW work, most of them dating from the late 1940s to the early 1950s. They formed the nucleus of the inner zone defense force and of the transit zones into and out of harbors and bays. Accompanied by sub-hunting submarines, the patrol boats combed narrows and straits where the subs could focus their searches in smaller, carefully defined zones. This inner zone defense was layered and fairly effective, but as the zones radiated farther and farther from shore, and as ASW assets got spread thinner and thinner, the ASW defense grew weaker and weaker until it was almost nonexistent. Additionally, the limits on sound detection imposed by shallow coastal waters and the Soviets' inferior sonar hindered the search for U.S. submarines. Even under ideal conditions the best Soviet passive sonar systems could not match the sensitivity or the range of U.S. passive sonars, thus leaving the door ajar for Holystone submarines to slip through.

"Remember one thing," warned the briefer. "Just because you have good sonar and a good sub and they have crappy sonar and so-so subs, don't get overconfident."

Hunter knew better than to make that mistake. The Soviets might not have an ASW force comparable to that of the United States, but they had a hell of a big submarine fleet.

. . .

Nikita Khrushchev assumed leadership of the Soviet Union in 1953, after the death of Joseph Stalin. Khrushchev, a shrewd manipulator of the Kremlin's power and influence, had a keen interest in military affairs. He once said that submarines would be the only warships that mattered in a future war. Thus the rapid buildup of the Soviet submarine fleet. The first Soviet nuclear-powered sub, the *K-3*, *Leninskiy Komsomol* (Lenin Youth), designed and built at a breakneck pace, put to sea only five years after Khrushchev assumed power. It proved that Admiral Rickover knew what he was talking about when he predicted that the Soviets would waste no time trying to catch up to the U.S. Navy's nuclear sub fleet.

Unlike the U.S. Navy, which had a tightly organized and conservative submarine design bureaucracy, the Soviet navy utilized autonomous design bureaus to develop its submarines. This method fostered fierce competition between the bureaus and produced many highly specialized, innovative, and futuristic-looking submarines, both diesel-electric and nuclear-powered. Victor- and November-class subs (NATO used the phonetic alphabet to classify Soviet submarines and surface combatants) were not only good-looking ships; technically they were almost on a par with the U.S. Navy's best.

Nevertheless, Soviet submarine construction methods and safety features lagged far behind. During the cold war at least nine Soviet submarines sank, some going down with their crews and with nuclear-armed torpedoes and missiles. By comparison the U.S. lost only two submarines, the *Thresher* in 1963 and the *Scorpion* in 1968.

Paradoxically, despite their lagging behind the United States in sonar, quieting, and other technologies vital to submarine performance (problems with steam generators and deadly radiation leaks took them years to solve), the Soviets made impressive advances. On the high end of the scale, they were ahead of the United States in areas of communications, metallurgy, and reactor and hull design. For example, they built a submarine capable of diving to more than three thousand feet, a depth no U.S. combat submarine has ever reached. Yet on the low end, they couldn't solve problems with construction and maintenance.

Now, at the height of the cold war, with Soviet nuclear submarine construction under way in earnest, each of the four Soviet submarine-building yards was turning out five to ten boats a year. Starting in the early 1950s, by 1968 the Soviets had built 55 nuclear and 325 diesel-electric submarines. When the USSR collapsed in 1991, they had constructed close to 245 nuclear-powered submarines, more than all other nations combined.

All the while the Soviets strained to build submarines that wouldn't sink, catch fire, or irradiate their crews, they struggled with yet another vexing problem: the low quality of their personnel drafted into service. After all, the best ships and weapons are useless if the sailors who man them are poorly trained and lack motivation.

Unlike enlisted men, Soviet naval officers were well trained and highly skilled in their specialties, though not to the same degree as American officers like Roy Hunter. Sea tours and advanced education at the Grechko Naval Academy war college in Leningrad broadened their skills as shiphandlers and administrators, a necessity for command at sea, but the Soviet navy, with its inflexible rules and unwavering devotion to Communist ideology, crushed personal initiative and motivation. Few officers dared take risks or make suggestions about how to improve conditions aboard ship or training of personnel. To make matters worse, every submarine in the fleet had assigned to it a *zampolit*, or political officer, whose job it was to indoctrinate the crew and spy on the commanding officer. There was always a risk the captain might defect to the West with his ship and crew. Rather than instilling unwavering zeal for Communism, the *zampolit* had a demoralizing affect on everyone.

Soviet enlisted men were conscripts with limited education and goals and were usually competent in only one specialty. Consequently, they received low pay for hard work and long hours aboard submarines that were not always seaworthy. Advancement moved at a glacial pace with the result that there were few highly qualified senior petty officers in the Soviet submarine force. Still, it didn't take genius or skill to launch a torpedo or weapon at an intruding submarine. All it took was an "aye, aye, sir" and the press of a firing button.

. . .

"Any questions?"

Plenty, thought Hunter, even though he'd been through this before. Most of the questions he had would be answered once the *Blackfin* got under way for the Barents, others by reading the patrol reports of submarines that had been on similar missions. The reports might tell him what to expect and what to look out for since the last time he'd been up there and how not to screw up, even though Hunter had all the skill and confidence a CO needed to succeed.

Sometimes, though, skill and confidence only go so far.

No one had ever forgotten the tragedy that had befallen the USS *Cochino*, a World War II diesel-electric fleet-type boat which had undergone a GUPPY (greater underwater propulsive power) conversion. Modifications included better sonars and a snorkel for feeding air to her diesels while at periscope depth. Hastily prepared for intelligence collection and outfitted with experimental electronic gear, the *Cochino*, accompanied by the USS *Tusk*, another GUPPY, shoved off from Portsmouth, England, in late summer of 1949, bound for the Barents Sea. In addition to the *Cochino*'s regular crew, a civilian electronics engineer was embarked to handle comms intercepts. It was a classic pioneering Holystone mission to a part of the world few Western subs had any experience operating in.

On the hunt for telemetry from Soviet missile tests, or better yet, coded Soviet comms from Severomorsk, the two submarines hung around off Norway's North Cape, hoping to pick up something important. Rough seas and terrible weather had played havoc with the two subs for days, and it was hard for them to keep station on each other. The crews were miserable. The compartments of both subs dripped condensation. Bedding and clothing were sodden and smelled of mildew. It was like living in a slimy sewer pipe.

Off North Cape, submerged and snorkeling on diesels, seawater flooded the *Cochino*'s snorkel, cutting off air and suffocating the engines. Seawater that had poured into the forward engine room from the snorkel piping, after drenching personnel and equipment, drained through scuppers in the engine room flats into the bilges. Moments later an electrician's mate reported that explosive hydrogen gas was building up in the after battery well, a diesel boat sailor's worst nightmare.

No one was sure what caused it, but sparks from a short circuit touched off an explosion of the gas. The *Cochino*'s captain, fearing a disaster, ordered the submarine to the surface. Damage control parties fought to put out the fires raging in the after battery, but heat and smoke drove them back. Compartments had to be abandoned, and sailors lacking foul-weather gear were forced topside into lashing wind and waves. There was precious little room for them to huddle on the *Cochino*'s narrow, pitching deck. The men clung together as waves pounded the drifting submarine.

The *Tusk*, alerted to the emergency, came alongside the *Cochino* to help out but was driven off by heavy seas that threatened a collision. Then another explosion tore through the *Cochino*. Injured men, some of them badly burned, struggled to save the ship. Topside, men were washed overboard. Rescuers tried to get them aboard a raft, which then capsized. The *Tusk*, fighting howling winds and heaving seas, maneuvered to try to pluck the men from the water but almost ran them down instead. Men trying to save the drowning *Cochino* sailors got washed overboard from the *Tusk*. It was a nightmarish scene: a race not just to save the *Cochino* and her men but to rescue the rescuers. The water was cold; cold enough to kill. Some men had drifted away and were surely dead.

While the rescue unfolded topside, the *Cochino*'s engineers had managed, who knew how, to get two diesel engines running. Barely making headway, the *Cochino*, accompanied by the *Tusk*, limped toward port in Norway with her injured and half-drowned crew. It wasn't to be. Wracked by more explosions and fire, her hull damaged, the *Cochino* took on water. The battle to save her had been lost. Racing against time, her crew transferred to the *Tusk*. The *Cochino* settled deeper into the sea; the *Tusk* pulled clear and stood by as the ravaged sub sank stern first. The survivors, jammed together aboard the *Tusk*, mourned the loss of seven men: the *Cochino*'s civilian engineer and one officer and five enlisted men from the *Tusk*.

It was not the kind of beginning the U.S. submarine force had envisioned for what was to become Holystone. Clearly, better subs were needed; better snooping gear, too, and better training. It took time for the sub force to adapt its tactics to the requirements of espionage, especially in such a hostile environment as the Barents Sea. Of course, even after adapting there was still no way to prevent the unexpected.

Since the *Cochino* disaster no U.S. submarines or submariners had been lost carrying out intel operations. There had been some close calls—near-collisions with Soviet subs during which apparently neither side had realized how close they'd come to being hit. There were at least six reported collisions between Holystone subs and Soviet subs. Some were just a kiss and a brush-off; others had caused serious damage to both ships. In one of the worst known incidents, a Soviet Echo-class submarine rammed the USS *Tautog*, a *Sturgeon*-class boat like the *Blackfin*. Tape recordings made of the collision seemed to indicate that the Soviet sub had sunk. A report outlining the incident had reached President Nixon via his secretary of defense, Melvin Laird, who counseled that silence was the best policy—unless the Russians began asking questions. The White House hoped that if the Soviet navy had noticed that one of their submarines had gone missing, they might not say anything about it or admit such a thing could happen. They didn't, but years later, after the collapse of the Soviet Union, the Echo's retired CO came forward to prove that his submarine hadn't been sunk and that he was still very much alive.

The *Tautog* incident was history, albeit recent history, and while tactics and operations evolved slowly in the submariner's world, they often evolved in response to operational missteps.

Sure, stories like the *Cochino*'s and the *Tautog*'s made the hair stand up on the back of Hunter's neck, but taking risks was what submariners did for a living.

There were plenty of other stories to make the hair stand up on the backs of necks, stories that were buried in the patrol reports of submarines that had recently carried out intel missions in the Barents Sea. Hunter and his team read some of the bound copies kept on shelves in the briefing room. The reports contained material that sounded like it had been made up for a movie. It hadn't. Hunter could only shake his head in amazement.

One patrol report described how a Holystone sub had raised her periscope only to discover a helicopter hovering directly overhead, just a few feet above the scope. Another sub had had the same thing happen in the middle of an ASW exercise, then led the Soviets on a chase that lasted for hours. Still another sub had almost poked an intel collection mast up through the hull of a Soviet November-class sub that had been silently lying to on the surface, all her machinery shut down for some unknown reason.

One commanding officer of a Holystone sub described, in the lexicon of patrol report writing, how he

> had gained good position under a surfaced Foxtrot to commence examination of its hull through the raised 15D scope. Inched tip of scope to within twenty-five feet of the Foxtrot's hull. Had barely gotten comfortable when the Foxtrot suddenly vented ballast tanks and started to submerge on top of us. We dropped away just in time to avoid a broken scope and a crushed sail.

A close-run thing. Had the sub's commanding officer discovered that he was being dogged by a Holystone sub? If so, how? Had the captain of the U.S. sub made a mistake? It was something for

Hunter to ponder. A patrol report from another Holystone sub explained how they had

> commenced monitoring a torpedo-firing test. Low chop therefore using minimum scope exposure. Counted five ships, including a frigate-type vessel, participating in this evolution. Closed in on a torpedo retriever when I noticed a Russian sailor looking right at me. At first I didn't think he had seen our scope but changed my mind when he waved "hello." Dunked scope.

Then:

> Sonar reported heavy screw beats from all quarters. Took another look and saw that the torpedo test had been scrubbed and that the ships were scattering. Waver must have sounded alarm.

According to the U.S. sub commander, this was followed by

> two frigates and a Hormone ASW-type helo gunning for us.

The sub had dodged the frigate and helo, but once again, it was a close-run thing. Holystone subs had been detected before, and each one had managed to break out of the ASW cordons the Soviets had thrown up.

One of those subs was the USS *Gudgeon*, a *Tang*-class diesel boat that had been detected by Soviet ASW and rocked by grenade-type depth charges dropped from a frigate. The *Gudgeon* did the only thing she could: hunker down to wait it out. Running low on air, batteries nearly flat, she eventually had to surface and crawl away with her tail between her legs. But the hold-down had been another close-run thing, not something Hunter would want to endure. The detection of U.S. spy subs by the Soviets handed them not only a victory in the espionage war but propaganda points, too. More worrisome was the possibility, however remote, that the Sovs might decide one day to use real depth charges to show that they had tired of the cat-and-mouse game and wanted to change the rules. Even though the captains and crews of these Holystone subs were skilled operators, close calls were not uncommon, which proved that Admiral Zumwalt didn't knead his brow for nothing.

Hours later, fully briefed, operation orders in hand, Hunter and his officers departed Norfolk to return to the *Blackfin*. There was still plenty of work to complete before departure and not much time left in which to do it.

6

ON THE BEACH

"LISTEN UP. Now's the time for you married men to think about estate planning," the COB announced to a group of enlisted men from the *Blackfin*'s crew. "You single guys, too."

"Uh, Cob, are you saying we need to make out wills?" asked a young sailor.

"That's what I'm saying."

The men looked at each other. To carry out their mission, they'd be sealed up in their ship for sixty days or more. What kind of men would do that? What had induced them in the first place to want to spend huge chunks of their lives in cramped spaces, enduring physical and mental stress, and under constant danger from their own machinery and their adversaries, if not the sea itself?

Part of the answer is that the submariners' lifelong bond of brotherhood and camaraderie is like no other in the military service. Submariners have a certain mystique, as though schooled in some black art or arcane specialty. And why not? The submarine force takes only volunteers because the duty is so demanding. After undergoing the rigorous training submarining demands, the objective for each officer and enlisted man is to earn the designation "qualified in submarines" and to wear the Twin Dolphins insignia. Aboard a submarine each man is dependent upon his shipmates for the boat's performance as well as his own survival. The knowledge that he belongs to an elite service marks him as a man apart, a man who is special, even fearless.

In the old days, before World War II, it was dangerous to go to sea in a submarine, much less submerge in it. The old S-boats of the 1920s were rusty and leaked. Often their hatches didn't seal properly, and as seawater sluiced into the boat through gaps in the hatch's knife edge as wide as a man's fingers, sub crews had to rely on sea pressure to seat them. Then there was the stench of sweat and oily bilges, hundred-degree temperatures, a lack of air-conditioning, choking diesel fumes, and stopped-up heads brimming with waste. Conditions like these built character and fostered camaraderie, or so submariners of that era liked to say.

The submarines and submariners that fought the Japanese in the Pacific during World War II were altogether different. Compared to the German U-boat fleet of about 1,150 boats, the U.S. Navy's submarine fleet was modest: Roughly 240 boats with crews totaling about 16,000 men. Unlike the Germans, who lost more than 750 subs and thousands of men, U.S. submarine losses amounted to 52 boats and 3,505 men.

Since Japan required a huge web of supply lines and a vast fleet of merchant ships to deliver the raw materials, food, fuel, and ammunition needed to supply their conquered territories, U.S. submarines, operating from forward bases in the Pacific, such as Pearl Harbor, Brisbane and Perth, Australia, launched an all-out war of attrition against Japan's merchant fleet, not her navy.

United States fleet-type submarines were well designed for this offensive role. Unlike German U-boats, U.S. subs were big—over three hundred feet long and displacing 1,500 tons. They had a crew of eighty-one officers and men and were powered by four 1,600-horsepower diesel engines. Their enormous fuel capacity gave them a cruising range of about thirteen thousand miles. Equipped with air-conditioning for operations in tropical waters and refrigerated food storage for the best chow in the navy, and armed with ten torpedo tubes and 24 torpedoes, a fleet-type submarine could easily embark on a sixty- to seventy-day war patrol to hunt down and sink Japanese merchant ships.

As for spec ops, or what were then called "special missions," U.S. subs did it all. They infiltrated enemy harbors, evacuated men, women, and children along with gold bullion and silver pesos from the Philippines, reconnoitered Japanese-held islands, landed intelligence agents, delivered ammo to Allied outposts, bombarded shore installations, and, most daring of all, blew up a train highballing down an enemy coastline.

By war's end, submariners had proven, though it wasn't publicized, that there wasn't a thing they couldn't do. (See Appendix Two.)

What was true then was even more so during the cold war. The missions might be different and the submarines might be vastly improved, but it still took well-trained and determined submariners to carry them out. The *Blackfin*'s crew had known all along that their impending deployment was sure to be long and arduous, maybe even dangerous. Still, the COB's words had a sobering effect on them: There was always a possibility, remote though it was, that the *Blackfin* might not come back.

After a long silence one of the sailors spoke up. "Where're we heading, Cob?"

"That's classified information. I'll tell you where we were when we get back."

Scuttlebutt had it that they were headed for the Barents Sea, which to the *Blackfin*'s sailors, at least those who knew their geography, was such a remote part of the world it might as well have been on the moon. What if during her deployment the *Blackfin* met with an accident or, unlikely as it was, a deadly confrontation with the Soviets? Would it be hushed up or would the navy tell the men's families the truth? For submariners, long separations from families and loved ones were hard enough without the added burden of worrying about what would happen to them if the *Blackfin* were to simply disappear. Yet to do his job a submariner had to bottle up his feelings and not look back. Departure, then, often brought a mixture of emotions.

• • •

Separation from family and friends and the stress caused by long deployments were facts of life for submariners. Though Holystone deployments were generally shorter than those for sailors aboard some surface ships—two months or longer versus four to six months for carrier battle groups—Holystone submarine crews didn't make port calls or see the sun shining or, worse yet, receive letters from home. Familygrams, short personal radio messages, were the closest they came to having contact with loved ones during deployment.

During the cold war, the Navy used a VLF (very low frequency) communications system, broadcasting at twenty kilohertz, to communicate with submarines. This high-data-rate system penetrated seawater to a depth of about fifteen feet, where a submerged submarine could receive messages, including familygrams, through a floating wire antenna system without having to expose herself.

At first, familygrams were limited to three messages of fifteen words for each sailor. In time, as the VLF system improved, they were upped to ten messages containing fifty words, with extra familygrams authorized for birth announcements. Limited to I-love-yous and basic news from home, along with clever constructions and hidden erotic messages, familygrams were the only means deployed sailors had to stay connected.

Important as they were, familygrams couldn't ease the anxiety of separation when a submarine husband or dad was away from home. Marital separation during deployments, whether Holystone or SSBN deterrent patrols, was a serious problem for couples. It was also a problem for the navy because long separations affected a man's job performance and thus overall force readiness. Separation had a huge impact on a family's and an individual's quality of life and was one of the main reasons men left the navy.

Most submariners and their families lived in base housing or in apartments and rented houses close to their home port. Few couples owned their own homes. Those that did were faced with either staying put or selling and moving whenever the submariner was transferred. For families living on bases, life tended to be structured and insular, centered as it was on other submarine families and the profession of submarining.

Early in the cold war, base housing usually consisted of drab and drafty brick-faced units, many dating from World War II, when the government threw up housing as fast as it could to house the huge numbers of men with families entering the service. Too often the units, which were rarely remodeled, suffered from outmoded kitchens and a lack of space. Play areas for kids were limited to patches of crabgrass or cement. Recognizing the effect such housing had on morale, the navy built new, modern housing that encompassed all of the features and conveniences American families wanted.

During Holystone deployments, submarine wives and their children more often than not experienced a wide range of emotional reactions, from depression and anger to sadness and anxiety. Mothers often had to cope with changes in their kids' sleeping patterns, eating habits, and behavior, especially in school. Difficult as these problems were, the social changes sweeping across America in the late 1960s and early 1970s added to them and had a profound influence on the insular world of the navy's submarine community. The traditional line separating military life from civilian had started to blur, as more and more navy wives took jobs and as their children, influenced by the lifestyle of the counterculture, rebelled. Drug use in the navy, among dependents and in the sub force itself, was becoming a serious problem.

No wonder that when it came time to deploy, submariners worried that upon returning home they'd find that their kids had undergone serious changes in outlook and attitude. Submariners asked: How will my kids react when I come home, and how long will it take for them to adjust? Will my absence cause the very problems I fear most? No one knew the answers because little had been done by the navy to address these problems. No wonder that submariners often found it difficult to say good-bye to their children.

As for children growing up in a submarine family, they often felt as if they had only part-time fathers. Some grown children of submariners said that they never really knew their fathers, much less what they did. At home, during mealtime, Roy Hunter couldn't discuss his work. Though his wife had a pretty good idea what he did, the only thing his children knew was that he was the captain of a submarine who spent most of his time sitting around in the wardroom drinking coffee. A dependents' day cruise seemed to confirm this notion when one of Hunter's daughters spotted a bubbling Silex and coffee cups lined up on the sideboard in the sub's wardroom.

For Hunter's family, his putting to sea for trials and exercises was just another day at the office, one that happened with such regularity he wasn't even missed at home. His wife, used to his long disappearances, was so matter-of-fact about his comings and goings that around the dinner table, talk rarely centered on when he might go or when he might return.

Even when the day came for his return from deployment, his family felt little if any anticipation. Okay, maybe the house got an extra dusting, after which they'd all troop down to meet the ship at the pier. No surprise, then, that Hunter's children never really worried that their father might not return from a deployment. The adult daughter of a Holystone submariner said that as a child she had never given that possibility a thought until the day her friend's father got shot down in Vietnam. Only then did she begin to understand how dangerous a career in the military could be.

. . .

Just as with any naval deployment, when Holystone submariners deployed, normal family activities such as birthdays and anniversaries were shelved until the men returned. Nevertheless, thoughtful husbands made plans ahead of time for the delivery of flowers and gifts for special family occasions.

While their husbands were deployed, wives relied on friends

and social networks to help them cope with the problems that inevitably surfaced. Though it varied from ship to ship, during the *Blackfin*'s deployments, Hunter's wife, the executive officer's wife, and the wife of the COB were the ones to whom the wives of the officers and enlisted men could go for help when the going got tough or when a wife needed a confidante and buddy, someone to turn to in an emergency other than "mom." The three women acted as intermediaries between the navy and the submariners' families by providing assistance to those who needed help negotiating the often impenetrable thicket of bureaucracy that attends any military service.

Strong, stoic, self-sufficient, these three women not only had to deal with the families' day-to-day problems—financial, personal, even broken-down cars—they had to make sure the wives had lists of emergency phone numbers and information on how to contact a chaplain if needed, how to locate important papers like wills and powers of attorney, and even how to replace a lost ID card. Hunter's, the XO's, and the COB's wives' years of experience in these matters represented a shared understanding of the problems that can occur during separation, which helped the other submariners' wives feel a sense of belonging to a community coping with similar issues. In addition, telephone networks run by the submarine community on the base forged an important link between the wives. More than a communications link, the networks provided news and, most important of all, support for families of deployed submariners who needed it.

To cope with the frequent separations from their husbands, wives got involved in various activities. Some took full- or part-time jobs. Others took up hobbies. Those who did recognized the need to get involved and stay involved in something other than themselves, their children, and household responsibilities. It also made the separation pass more quickly than sitting around marking the calendar and waiting for the day when the *Blackfin* returned to port.

. . .

The reunion after a deployment could be just as stressful as departure had been. The wife had to readjust to her returned husband, the husband to his wife's role as head of the household. Sometimes a man returned home expecting an immediate "change of command" only to discover that his wife, having filled the role of a single parent shouldering all the burdens during her husband's absence, was not about to surrender her authority. Making adjustments was part of the reunion process.

Men usually needed time to decompress after living inside a crowded submarine with a hundred or so other men. For their part, wives had to resist overwhelming them with affection or, worse, handing them a list of things that needed attention around the house even before the sailor's seabag hit the floor. Some couples tried to adjust to living together again by having a honeymoon period to help them get reacquainted, one that might hopefully last at least until the first argument over who had it worse, you or me.

Married couples weren't the only ones who had to learn to adjust. Single men coped with problems of separation similar to those experienced by their married counterparts. Typical of most submarine complements, several officers and about half the enlisted sailors aboard the *Blackfin*, mostly younger men, were single. Ashore the officers lived in bachelor officers' quarters (BOQ) on the base, while enlisted men lived in barracks. Without families to care for, the lives of these men tended to center around their single shipmates and their ship. Frequent, lengthy deployments made it hard for some of these men to develop relationships with young single women, much less sustain a relationship for longer than a few months. For many of these men, their dating habits and relationships were awkward and unfulfilling. For some, developing the stability a good marriage required was virtually impossible.

At sea, enlisted men still in their teens or early twenties often experienced changes in attitude and behavior that parents and friends didn't always fully appreciate when the sailor returned home. Submarining was a demanding profession, and a young sailor's displays of vigorous self-confidence and maturity were often misinterpreted as a signal that his shipmates were the most important individuals in his life, that parents and friends no longer mattered.

Added to all of the problems single and married submariners and their families and friends faced was the issue of the secrecy that Holystone operations demanded. Men couldn't share information with their family and friends about what they did and where they went during deployments, which made these men seem different. It wasn't just their profession that made them different but also the secrets they had to keep. Perhaps more than anything else, the need for secrecy built a wall around their lives and personalities that no amount of love or intimacy could ever breach. To outsiders it may have seemed that submariners were cold and uncaring men, indifferent to the world around them. This wasn't true, of course, for submariners were just like every one else. They loved their wives and children, friends and girlfriends, cats and dogs. They did the grocery shopping and washed their cars on Saturday. They went to church on Sunday. The only difference was that from time to time they disappeared under the sea and did dangerous things that no one else knew about. It was what submariners did. It was their job.

. . .

The *Blackfin*'s COB was an old salt. He'd seen and done it all before. His lecture to the crew about making out wills was a precaution, of course. No one, least of all the COB, expected anything to go wrong on the *Blackfin*'s upcoming deployment. Even so, a prudent man always made sure that he kissed his wife good-bye and told her where he kept his will.

7

TO THE TOP OF THE WORLD

ON THE DAY OF DEPARTURE, as Hunter crossed the brow rigged between his submarine and the one lying next to it, the topside watch announced over the 1MC, "*Blackfin* arriving."

Looking aft, Hunter saw that the shore power connection had been disconnected, an indication that the ship's power plant was up and running. He sensed her urgency to get underway. Below decks, Hunter met the duty officer in the wardroom.

"We're ready to go, Captain."

"Very well. Station the maneuvering watch."

A moment later the announcement came over the 1MC: "Station the maneuvering watch."

Hunter, alone in the wardroom, smoked a cigarette and drank a cup of coffee while he reviewed a mental diary to be sure nothing had been overlooked aboard ship or at home. Everything had been topped off and loaded, and he'd kissed his wife and kids good-bye, had even given the family cat a chuck under its chin. Satisfied, he finished his coffee and returned the empty cup to the sideboard. Ready now, he donned his cap with the scrambled eggs on the visor and went topside.

On top of the sail, above the bridge cockpit where the *Blackfin* was conned while surfaced, Hunter looked out over the other submarines clustered in the nest alongside the *Fulton*. Linehandlers on the submarine she was moored to stood ready to take in her lines. Estimating currents and clearances, Hunter scanned the Thames River through binoculars and saw mist rising from its glassy surface. With the sun well up in the east, it was a fine morning for getting under way.

All hands were present and accounted for; seabags had gone down the hatches; a pre-under-way checklist had been completed and verified. Very well. With lines singled up, the hugs and tearful good-byes a memory, it was time to go.

Hunter took note of the current in the channel, then the squadron tug lying to, ready if needed to assist. Single-screw subs like the *Blackfin* had difficulty maneuvering on their own in restricted waters around other ships and piers even in slack water. A conning officer had to take care, for her big fiberglass sonar dome might not survive a collision with another sub's hull or a piling. Satisfied all was in order, Hunter looked at his watch and saw that they were on schedule. "OOD, get the ship under way."

"Aye, aye, Captain." The OOD leaned out from the cockpit and ordered, "Cast off all lines." As soon as this was done, the OOD ordered, "Helm, bridge. Rudder amidships, all back one-third."

Moments later, water boiling at her stern and with a blast from her whistle, the *Blackfin* eased out of the nest and backed slowly into the river's narrow channel. Hunter waved off the waiting tug and watched his OOD turn the submarine gently downstream for the mouth of the Thames and the Atlantic Ocean.

As she reached midchannel the OOD ordered, "Helm, bridge, all ahead two-thirds, left full rudder, steady on one-eight-zero."

"Bridge, helm, aye. Maneuvering answers all ahead two-thirds, left full rudder, come to one-eight-zero."

The *Blackfin* departed accompanied by a sputtering old LCM landing craft carrying the coiled STASS towed sonar array its crew would attach to the sub at the mouth of the river. Heading south, it didn't take long for the *Blackfin* to come abeam of the General Dynamics Electric Boat complex on the east side of the channel, then to steam past old Fort Trumbull and the landmark Pfizer pharmaceutical lab.

Where the Thames River ended at the New London Ledge Lighthouse, the OOD slowed to three knots for the LCM to come alongside for the STASS hookup. After it was attached to the stub on the *Blackfin*'s vertical stabilizer and fed out, and after a series of electrical continuity checks, the OOD ordered ahead full and steered a dogleg course around Fisher's Island and between Montauk Point and Block Island.

Here Hunter was truly in his element, aboard a nuclear-powered submarine tasked with a mission so secret that only a handful of people knew its details.

Somewhere, maybe at the Central Intelligence Agency (CIA) or the Defense Intelligence Agency (DIA), a meeting had been convened by members of some obscure subcommittee of the National Security Council to review ongoing intelligence ops. Maybe someone had circulated a document marked Top Secret, one that described Hunter's current mission. The subcommittee might have reviewed fresh intelligence on new Soviet SLBMs. SALT negotiators needed answers to questions. Did the missiles use liquid or solid propellants? How heavy was their throw weight? How far could they fly? Was the guidance system any good? If the Sovs decided to conduct a test, could that sub heading for the Barents capture telemetry data?

Or perhaps somewhere deep in the labyrinthine brain-maze of the NSA, an official had informed the agency's director, Vice Admiral Noel Gayler, that another Holystone sub, name unknown, had just departed New London for the Barents Sea. A nod or two and a "Keep me updated" from Gayler. If one of his "customers" over at CIA or DIA needed something, he'd talk to ComSubLant and have them dial up that sub. He'd administered the intel take from Holystone ops, which he'd inherited from his predecessor, ever since his appointment as the director of NSA in 1969. He didn't always know the names of the subs involved or the names of their COs, but he knew how risky Holystone ops were and recognized how much skill and dedication it took to carry them out. Gayler wasn't a worrier, nor did he knead his brow. He just sat back and waited to see what those unnamed subs departing their home ports came up with. Nine times out of ten it was something his analysts could use to fill in the blanks in the intel mosaic the nation had been building up since the beginning of the cold war. Soviet SLBMs were part of that mosaic. If the CIA or DIA was looking for fresh data on missile capabilities, they'd soon have another collection platform on station. Gayler would likely wager that the intel take from that submarine would probably be a good one. Those sub drivers hadn't disappointed yet.

• • •

Block Island lay far astern as the *Blackfin* approached the hundred-fathom curve, her diving point. During her run from New London, the *Blackfin* hadn't encountered a single Soviet AGI intelligence-gathering ship. Rigged to look like innocent fishing trawlers, AGIs bristled with ELINT—electronic intelligence—and SIGINT collection masts. Some AGIs had onboard intelligence officers and processing facilities to speed up the transmission of data to Moscow. Stationed just inside international waters, they monitored ship traffic entering and departing U.S. naval bases, and New London was one of their favorite haunts.

With the *Blackfin* on the surface, rigged for dive, the OOD watch had been transferred from the bridge to the control room. A bustle of activity broke out as the lookouts dropped down the ladder from the bridge to the control room, where the control room watchstanders at their stations anticipated the order to dive.

The two clamshell covers that streamlined the open cockpit when submerged had been swung into place and locked. The young lieutenant who'd earlier transferred his OOD watch to the control room now closed and dogged the upper and lower hatches in the sail. "Chief of the watch, bridge rigged for dive, last man down," he announced.

Hunter, standing aside in the control room, took note of the OOD, who had ascended the periscope stand and now had his eye pressed against the rubber buffer surrounding the scope's ocular and both hands on the grips, turning the scope for a full 360 look-around. A periviz slaved video monitor relayed the OOD's view out the periscope: There were no other vessels in sight or any reported sonar contacts.

"One minute to dive point."

The OOD turned to the quartermaster of the watch. "Sounding?"

"One-two-zero fathoms, sir."

Hunter looked around the *Blackfin*'s busy control room crammed with men and equipment. The operational heart of the ship, it was about the size of a kitchen in a modern suburban split-level.

On the port side of the control room looking forward, Hunter saw the ship-control station with its cushioned seats, control yokes, and instrument consoles. It could pass for the cockpit of a jet bomber. Like pilot and copilot, two men seated side by side facing the consoles controlled the *Blackfin*'s course, speed, and depth. The man on the left controlled the stern diving planes; because it was a critical function affecting the submarine's depth, this was the sole operation he controlled.

The man seated to his right had two responsibilities: He steered the ship, and he operated the fairwater diving planes, the control surfaces used to maintain depth at slow speed. He also operated the ship's engine-order telegraph, adjusting its speed settings as ordered by the OOD. Whenever the helmsman rang up an ordered change in speed, a bell rang on the engine-order telegraph in the maneuvering room aft to call attention to the change of speed order. After acknowledging the order, the throttleman in the maneuvering room turned one of the "steering wheels" on the main propulsion-control console to adjust the speed of the ship's main engines.

The diving officer, a chief petty officer, seated behind the two men at the diving station, supervised their actions. His job was to make sure that maneuvering orders had been followed correctly and that the ship was under control at all times.

The chief of the watch sat at the ballast-control panel, a console to the left of the diving officer. It accommodated the hull-opening indicators; hydraulic systems; trim and drain systems; the emergency blow activators—"chicken switches," they were called; mast controls; and monitors displaying the status of the *Blackfin*'s other vital operating systems.

Aft of the ship-control station, a low pedestal and handrail surrounded the two fore and aft in-line periscopes. Three additional consoles containing the central tactical display panels and their control switches stood to the right of the periscopes. A tempered glass–topped automatic plotting table for recording the *Blackfin's* track and for laying out courses and attack plots had been wedged in behind the periscope stand. Another table like it was positioned in front of the fire-control system.

The ship's inertial navigation system, or SINS (the gyrocompass was located in the torpedo room), and other navigation equipment filled up most of the remaining space on the control room's port side. SINS was vital to a submarine's long-range submerged operations. It allowed a submarine to navigate over long distances underwater without the need to come to periscope depth to get a fix. SINS kept track of a submarine's motion and position at sea at any given time from a known starting point. Without it long-duration submerged operations would be next to impossible. SINS, in reality a superaccurate dead-reckoning device, wasn't perfect, however, and as errors accumulated the submarine had to come to periscope depth for periodic updates from global positioning satellites.

Yet more equipment—radio receivers, video monitors, chronometers, and the like—nested in racks above the SINS and its components. The fire-control consoles and their monitors and repeaters took up every last square inch of space on the starboard side of the control room. The sonar and radio shacks filled up compartments of their own, partitioned within the confines of the overall control room layout.

A maze of cables, pipes, light fixtures, and ventilation ducts snaked across the control room's overhead and covered the ship's curved hull and vertical bulkheads. The maze pressed in from all sides. A man almost couldn't move without bumping into something or other, or knocking an elbow or knee into a console or a shelf loaded with technical manuals that were used when servicing all the equipment and electronics stuffed into the control room.

As she approached her dive point, heavy North Atlantic swells made the *Blackfin*, with her smooth round hull, roll like a cigar on a tabletop, more than a surface ship would under similar conditions. Submariners live under the sea, where it's always calm and tranquil, not on top, where the sea's rise and fall makes even the sturdiest of ships—and their crews—lurch and groan. The only cure for seasickness, the modern submariner's curse, was to submerge, where the world stood relatively still and a man breathed conditioned, scrubbed air whose temperature was constant.

"Officer of the deck, submerge the ship to four-five-zero feet," Hunter ordered.

"Aye, aye, sir, submerge the ship to four-five-zero feet."

The chief of the watch first sounded the diving alarm twice, a shrill combination of honking horn and shrieking siren, then announced, "Dive! Dive!" over the 1MC. Next, he snapped open the ballast tank vent switches. Instantly, eight lighted horizontal green bars displayed on the ballast-control panel changed to red circles. "Vents open," the chief confirmed.

The panel was a modern iteration of the World War II dieselboat "Christmas tree," with its rows of red and green lights indicating the status of the submarine's hull openings. Now, when the red circles flashed on, the sound of air venting from the *Blackfin*'s ballast tank vent risers fore and aft confirmed that the vents had opened and that inrushing seawater was forcing air out of the ballast tanks.

The *Blackfin* buried her blunt nose in the sea and started down, water chuckling around her hull and up her sail. The OOD, observing the dive through the periscope, had confirmed the venting and filling of ballast tanks and the gradual disappearance of the *Blackfin*'s hull underwater. There was none of the commotion associated with the diving of a diesel sub, no deafening roar of high-pressure air and its buildup on eardrums to confirm that the boat was airtight. Other than the creaking and popping of her shock-mounted decks under increasing sea pressure acting on the hull, there was little to indicate that the *Blackfin* was submerging. Except for the clipped exchange of orders, the decks tilting down at a ten-degree angle, and the watchstanders leaning away from the dive to compensate, the descent didn't feel any different than a ride aboard an elevator in an office building. Submerged, with far less resistance to overcome than when she was on the surface, the *Blackfin*'s mighty turbines drove her forward with hardly any effort. Able to manufacture her own atmosphere, limited only by the endurance of her crew and food supply, the *Blackfin* had no need for the world she was departing. She had entered a realm where everything she did from now on she could do submerged.

After the *Blackfin* had leveled out at her ordered depth and slowed to five knots, the OOD received reports that the ship's trim was satisfactory. "Very well," he responded. He toggled the 1MC mike and announced, "Rig ship for deep submergence."

Following standard procedure, a submarine heading out on patrol always made a deep dive to check for leaks, squeaks, and rattles. During this evolution, the *Blackfin*'s sonarmen listened for any sound shorts—noise coming from her internal machinery that might be "leaking" through her hull into the sea—and for any other noise coming from loose topside gear such as hatch covers or retractable cleats and bitts that might be detected by patrolling Soviet submarines or surface ships. This evolution always came early in the voyage so that in the event of a serious problem the submarine could return to port to have it fixed. If the problem was minor and fixable at sea, sea state permitting, repairs could be effected while surfaced.

After receiving reports that each compartment was rigged for deep submergence, the diving officer reported that fact to the OOD.

"Very well. Make your depth one thousand feet. All ahead standard."

The diving officer directed the planesmen, "Ten degree down bubble. Make your depth one thousand feet."

The helm answered bells for the ordered speed; the planesmen pushed their control yokes forward. The decks, adjusting to more pressure, snapped and cracked. The depth gauge wound past seven hundred feet, then eight hundred, then past nine hundred. Minutes later the *Blackfin* leveled off far below the surface.

After receiving a report on the ship's condition, the OOD informed Hunter, "Captain, all compartments report no leaks. Sonar reports no sound shorts. She's as quiet as a mouse, sir."

"Very well. Take her to test depth."

It took only minutes for the *Blackfin* to reach 1,300 feet.

Hunter said nothing until the OOD gave him a look. Hunter nodded. "Secure from deep submergence. Make your depth four-five-zero feet. All ahead full." Then, "Take us to the Barents."

8

ICE CREAM AND BLUE NOSES

HUNTER'S OP ORDER had specified a specific route to the Barents Sea. Transiting to the op area, Hunter had orders to maintain a course west of Iceland via the Denmark Strait. This route would take the *Blackfin* through the far western zone of the GIUK Gap, which if blocked by NATO forces in time of war would leave the Red Banner Northern Fleet bottled up in the Barents Sea.

Well beyond the hundred-fathom curve, the *Blackfin* struck northeast at fifteen knots. Normal transit time from New London to station took about two weeks, plenty of time for the crew, after setting a three-section watch, each watch six hours long, to get comfortable and settle into a normal underway routine. Everyone but Hunter and the XO stood watch. Transit was a time to deal with important matters such as OOD watch qualification, engineering officer of the watch qualification, submarine qualification of as yet unqualified officers and enlisted men, and watch station quals for enlisted men. Meanwhile, to fulfill the requirements spelled out in their qual cards, the ship's junior officers and enlisted men hunkered down like students cramming for college finals. When not standing watches, the men kept busy learning procedures and performing evolutions called practical factors, to demonstrate their knowledge and proficiency. This included tracing wiring and piping diagrams, studying the maneuvering and control room layouts, and much more.

Under way, the ship's clocks were set to Zulu, or Greenwich Mean, Time, but there were no clock watchers aboard the *Blackfin* because there was no such thing as time hanging heavy. Submarines are complicated and require constant maintenance and upkeep. Consequently their crews are always busy. In addition to operating their ship, the *Blackfin*'s crew conducted drills—fire, damage control, flooding, and more—and practiced high-speed maneuvers and stealth tactics that couldn't be conducted on station but were part of the ship's inherent capabilities and needed wringing out.

. . .

The *Blackfin* tore through the sea on a course that swept around Newfoundland and across the Labrador Basin. In a few days she would turn northeast for the cold waters of the Denmark Strait. The sea floor over which she passed had been sounded and charted so carefully that a deeply submerged submarine had nothing to fear from an undiscovered seamount looming in her path. Ironically, the greatest danger posed to her safe passage might be a Soviet submarine operating in the same area that had not been identified by SOSUS, but such a possibility was so remote that Hunter was hardly concerned about it.

Outside the *Blackfin*'s hull the temperature of the North Atlantic had steadily dropped since departing New London and would soon match the near-freezing temperatures found in the

Barents Sea almost year-round. The temperature inside the *Black-fin*'s hull, except in the noisy and hot machinery spaces, was maintained at seventy-two degrees, while the ship's atmosphere control system kept everyone breathing comfortably.

In the days of diesel-electric boats, little could be done to maintain a submarine's atmosphere other than using CO_2 absorbents, but those absorbents couldn't replace consumed oxygen or remove other deadly contaminants such as carbon monoxide. The atmosphere inside a nuclear submarine, which doesn't surface to replenish its air supply, is more complex. The four-part system that kept the air breathable aboard *Sturgeon*-class subs consisted of an oxygen generator that produced oxygen through the electrolysis of seawater, dual hydrogen and carbon monoxide burners, charcoal-filtered carbon dioxide scrubbers to remove CO_2, and electrostatic precipitators in the ventilation system to remove particulate matter.

In case something went wrong with the oxygen generator, the *Blackfin* carried enough oxygen for two weeks in high-pressure bottles like those filled with compressed air used for dewatering the ballast tanks. If all else failed, oxygen candles could be burned to produce oxygen in an emergency.

· · ·

Comfortable and relaxed, the *Blackfin*'s crew was nevertheless watchful and alert. As part of the daily routine, the radiomen copied the top-secret radio messages broadcast to the *Blackfin* continuously to update her on any intelligence relevant to her mission or any changes in orders. The broadcasts, copied via the ship's floating wire antenna, usually included a batch of "miss you already" familygrams, which the radiomen decoded and distributed to the addressees.

As good as the navy's VLF system was, there were still inherent problems communicating reliably with submerged submarines, often scattered around the world. Submarines have always operated independently, for the obvious reason that there is no effective way to control their movements without forcing them to reveal their positions to an enemy by breaking radio silence to report on their operations or request information. Radio messages from ComSubLant had to be broadcast and rebroadcast on a regular schedule so any that were missed while a submarine was submerged or engaged in ops could be picked up later. A better system would be one that could communicate with submarines while they were submerged, even at great depth. Something like that was under development, but it had serious technical shortcomings that limited its effectiveness.

While the *Blackfin* was at periscope depth copying ComSubLant's broadcasts, the navigator updated SINS from an orbiting GPS satellite to confirm the accuracy of their position rendered on both a navigation chart and the paper plot maintained on a plotting table in the nav center. At the same time, the commissarymen took the opportunity to discharge garbage overboard through the trash ejector, and, depending on what they contained, the OOD made sure that sanitary tanks were either blown or pumped overboard.

Hunter, a stickler for efficiency and cleanliness as well as material condition, made sure the ship's company kept up with the vacuuming, dusting, swabbing, and polishing of decks and fixtures. While some subs tended to slack off in the cleanliness department, Hunter believed it went a long way to maintaining high morale and thus a happy ship.

Hunter believed that sharpening the skills needed to torpedo ships boosted morale, too. To prove it was so, the *Blackfin*'s fire-control tracking parties practiced running mock torpedo attacks on unsuspecting merchant ships plying North Atlantic trade routes intersecting the *Blackfin*'s course. Her "torpedoes" sent to the bottom a variety of foreign-flagged cargo vessels, tankers, and ore carriers standing in for Soviet aircraft carriers, cruisers, and destroyers. These mock attacks were serious affairs, conducted with all the intensity and precision of a real attack.

As the *Blackfin* moved north, target traffic thinned out until one day there was just a vast expanse of empty, gray, cold ocean.

· · ·

"We there yet, Cob?" a sailor asked.

"Soon. Keep your pants on."

The first week of the voyage had flown by. The navigator marked the chart where SINS said the *Blackfin* would be by night-fall: a tad south of the Denmark Strait. Another week and they'd be in the Barents Sea.

When not occupied with fitness reports and watch station qualifications or evaluating drills and the like, Hunter, along with the XO and department heads, made a daily tour of the ship to check on her material condition. As a practical matter it was an opportunity to make sure that any balky or broken equipment got repaired before arriving on station. It also provided an opportunity to talk to the crew, to measure their preparedness and attitude. After each tour Hunter sensed a palpable change in the crew's daily tempo, in effect a gradual tightening of the main-spring and an eagerness shared by the men to get on with the mission they'd been sent to accomplish.

He'd sensed the same thing among the officers, who were putting in long hours of study to ensure they'd be effective while standing OOD watches on station. They'd studied everything from the geography of the Barents Sea and the Kola Peninsula to the complex science of underwater sound and the application of its acoustic parameters to the mission. They studied pictures supplied by naval intelligence of the types of ships and submarines they might encounter so that they could recognize and identify them quickly and correctly. They reviewed and discussed their op order again and again. It was imperative that every officer understand the order and know how to interpret it and what was expected of them in any situation they might encounter, especially a situation unique to the mission and not covered by the op order. To ensure that his standing orders would be followed to the letter, Hunter assigned himself and his executive officer the role of command duty officer, or "super OOD," to backstop operations.

Operational matters encompassed by these issues would in time appear in the *Blackfin*'s patrol report, basically a diary like those Hunter and his officers had read at ComSubLant headquarters in Norfolk. The report had to be more than just a recapitulation of the facts; it had to include essential insights gleaned from events while on station. After midnight each day, the executive officer gathered up the logs and data sheets kept by the quartermasters to prepare the past day's patrol report. This ensured that important information wasn't lost or forgotten in the flurry of ongoing operations. Once on station, the tactical intelligence collection prepared by the spooks would be integrated into the patrol narrative, while intel in the spook log would be treated as standalone packages. The *Blackfin*'s yeoman, busy as he was with that old navy curse, paperwork, typed up the daily narrative on stencils, which were proofed by the XO before reaching Hunter. Later, after submission to ComSubLant, the report would be studied and reviewed by submariners about to embark on future Holystone missions. If Hunter had been successful, his reporting would not only prove useful but also make the hair stand up on the backs of their necks.

. . .

Aboard any submarine, meals are the highlight of the day. The *Blackfin*, like all modern nuclear subs, had a galley that compared favorably to a kitchen in a gourmet restaurant. It included frozen and fresh food storage, ovens, a stove, an ice cream maker (very important), beverage dispensers, coffeemakers, even a seventy-second dishwasher—load it up and *zip*! Like magic, the dishes were done.

The *Blackfin*'s cooks had everything they needed to turn out the best meals in the navy, which was one of the reasons some men gave for volunteering for sub duty in the first place. The psychological effect of well-prepared and appetizing food aboard submarines was one of the most important factors in a crew's well-being and morale.

Roy Hunter had come from a family where nutritious and well-prepared food was part of his upbringing. After experiencing the pedestrian fare at the Naval Academy, he had vowed that if he ever had an opportunity to influence "naval eating," as he put it, he would—and he did.

Spam and canned fruit cocktail had been banned by the captain aboard the diesel boat Hunter had served in early in his career, so as an XO and CO he'd banned them, too. Since in a well-run submarine mess there was always more money in the ship's fund to buy food than could be spent, he not only made sure he always bought the best the navy had but also didn't hesitate to buy certain delicacies in civilian grocery stores ashore. Thus, from experience, Hunter made sure the *Blackfin* had an excellent lead commissaryman in the galley, complemented by a leading steward in the wardroom. The steward Hunter had brought with him aboard the *Blackfin* ran the wardroom like a private dining club complete with polished silverware and starched table linens for every meal. Before departure the steward, on his own initiative, had consulted with Hunter's wife, a gourmet chef in her own right, who gave him recipes for a host of menu items that she was sure would please every palate around the wardroom table. They did, too.

The op order had specified a food load-out sufficient for ninety days. The *Blackfin*'s supply officer, with Hunter's guidance, had procured the proper tonnage of high-quality fresh and frozen food from the *Fulton*'s stores, bearing in mind that the patrol might in reality last only sixty or seventy-five days. This approach to food procurement fit Hunter's requirement that the ship's complement eat well for the full time they were on station. If the patrol lasted longer than seventy-five days, they would make do with canned goods; that way they could eat, as he put it, "tastefully" if not "elegantly" for the remainder of the patrol.

Feeding a hundred or more sailors requires a lot of food, and its storage aboard a submarine takes up a lot of room. Aboard the *Blackfin*, canned and packaged foods along with staples like flour and sugar were stored in the food storage lockers. What didn't fit went into an auxiliary tank converted to a storeroom accessible through a man-way. Cartons and cartons of fresh eggs nestled inside one of the ship's escape trunks would keep for weeks, chilled by the waters of the North Atlantic flowing over the hull. Crates of lettuce arrived with the heads wrapped in plastic after they had been injected with nitrogen to keep them fresh so salad could be served every day for sixty days, another Hunter edict. No wonder that on their way to the Barents, Hunter and his crew feasted on eggs to order, pancakes, sausage, sweet rolls, fresh bread, steak, roast beef, chicken curry, chili, pizza, and, during movies, pop-corn.

After the evening meal, some members of the off-duty sections played poker before and after the daily movie. After midnight, those who wanted to watched another movie. The movies, remastered on 16 mm film, had been selected from the *Fulton*'s huge film library. They included new releases as well as popular older films like *Butch Cassidy and the Sundance Kid. The French Connection* was a favorite. The crew liked watching the car-subway chase under the elevated tracks in Brooklyn, and no matter how many times they had seen it, they cheered when Gene Hackman as Popeye Doyle wasted the French assassin.

Ops permitting, Hunter and his officers watched movies in the wardroom fortified by popcorn and Cokes, played poker on Saturday and Sunday evenings, and shot the bull at mealtimes and any other time there was someone to shoot the bull with. Sometimes, though, so many officers were busy poring over the op order and qualifications in the wardroom-cum-study-hall, it was hard to carry on a spirited conversation there without disturbing them.

The *Blackfin* was indeed a happy and well-fed ship as she eased north, toward the Kola Peninsula.

· · ·

Early one morning, the *Blackfin* entered the Denmark Strait, a 130-mile-wide strip of water between Greenland and Iceland. The strait formed a connecting arm of sorts between the Arctic Ocean and the North Atlantic. Stormy and forbidding, the Denmark Strait was famous in World War II naval history for the running gun battle in 1941 between the German battleship *Bismarck* and the British battle cruiser HMS *Hood*, pride of the Royal Navy.

The *Hood*, dispatched to find and destroy the *Bismarck*, was sunk minutes after being shelled by the *Bismarck*. Nearly 1,400 British sailors went down with her. The *Bismarck* later met her end in the North Atlantic west of France, when British planes found her and attacked, and the Royal Navy sent her to the bottom along with some 2,000 of her crew.

Transiting the strait, the *Blackfin* sped north. The crew had been primed by the tales the old arctic salts among them told of their mysterious ritual crossings of the arctic circle north of Iceland—and what terrible things might be in store for the uninitiated sailors in the crew when they did.

Crossing the arctic circle, the imaginary line separating the arctic zone from the northern temperate zone, didn't have quite the mystical and romantic significance seamen associated with a crossing of the equator, likely because the circle lay far away at the top of the world. Nevertheless, it was an old rite of passage for sailors and explorers alike who had not crossed the line before, one marked by an elaborately staged shipboard ritual known as a Blue Nose Induction Ceremony.

According to custom, Blue Nose inductees had to pay homage to the arctic's King Neptune. They did this aboard the *Blackfin* by kneeling and kissing the lard- and fat-smeared belly of a previously Blue-Nosed sailor playing the king's role, dressed in a tacky cardboard crown and bedsheet cape. There were other degradations, too, but none as distasteful as the belly-kissing routine. The ceremony provided an opportunity to humiliate one's shipmates in a good-natured way.

On every ship there were always a few men—officers and enlisted—who, not eager to kiss the larded belly of a grizzled chief petty officer, resisted induction or refused to participate altogether. Sometimes these craven mutineers tried to hide (where could they hide on a submarine?), though there were time-tested ways to enforce compliance with King Neptune's rules. One of the best ways was to dunk the reluctant inductee into a large bucket of ice water, which always made him instantly compliant. After a dunking even the hardiest soon-to-be Blue Nose holdout accepted his fate. With Hunter looking on, one by one the hold-outs were brought before King Neptune, where they meekly got down on all fours and gave the royal belly a slippery kiss.

Induction into the Order of the Blue Nose became a part of a submariner's permanent service record and entitled him to a colorful certificate commemorating the event. The ceremony was a lot of fun, and it gave the crew a needed break from their routine and for a time lightened the deadly serious nature of their mission.

. . .

The *Blackfin* was first and foremost a fighting ship headed for dangerous waters. As she approached the northern limits of the Denmark Strait she assumed a full wartime posture. Four Mk 37 torpedoes loaded in her tubes were ready for firing if necessary. The ship's nuclear-tipped SUBROCs were also ready for use, but, like all nuclear weapons carried aboard navy ships, they weren't armed and would not be unless their imminent use was authorized by higher authority, which would be only if World War III broke out. Informed that the ship was ready in all respects to engage the enemy, Hunter didn't have to be reminded that if war broke out, Holystone had failed.

9

COUNTERFORCE

A RECENT PHOTOGRAPH SHOT from a U.S. KH-8 Gambit reconnaissance satellite eighty-three miles above the earth had captured a picture of the Red Banner Northern Fleet headquarters at
Severomorsk. The photo revealed, down to the smallest detail
(KH-series satellites could resolve objects up to two feet long),
the roads, buildings, graving docks, and finger piers within the
confines of the sprawling naval base. The KH-8's special Kodak
lens system had even rendered the intricate matchstick pattern of
shadows cast by the coniferous taiga covering the Kola Peninsula.

Severomorsk, like the submarine base at Polyarnyy, was one of
more than a dozen "closed cities" in the USSR. Because these
cities contained military and nuclear facilities, Soviet authorities
had imposed strict travel and residency restrictions on their citizens and especially on foreigners, who were rarely permitted to
go near them. Severomorsk had been a military base even before
World War II. With the coming of the cold war, the sheer size of

the existing base and its requirements for more and more space soon overshadowed the city of Severomorsk itself.

Everything inside and outside the barbed wire fence surrounding the base was under constant surveillance and heavy guard by naval police and KGB border guards. Military personnel and civilian workers alike seeking access to the base came under sharp scrutiny. Civilians who lived full-time on the base, mainly the families of sailors, had to be self-sufficient since there was really no other place they could go if they needed things, except Severomorsk itself, which held little appeal and could be visited only under the watchful eye of the KGB. Life on a Russian military base north of the arctic circle was dull, sometimes harsh. Housing for families was dreary, as on many U.S. military bases, only more so, but unlike the U.S. Navy, the Soviets provided no support facilities on the base for wives to turn to for help. For a Russian sailor with a family, the pay was low. Food was scarce. Heating oil was expensive, and the weather in Severomorsk in winter could be brutal. Summers were warm but far too short.

Soviet military commanders exercised authority over all military and civilian personnel assigned to Severomorsk. They viewed any sign of discontent or individual enterprise among Soviet naval personnel with suspicion. Authority for the conduct of naval operations against the U.S. Navy in northern waters resided solely with the commander in chief of the Soviet Naval Forces, Admiral Sergei G. Gorshkov, headquartered in Moscow. Yet despite an ossified and top-heavy chain of command, the Soviet navy's Northern Fleet had managed, just barely, to keep pace with their main enemy.

The Kremlin willingly gave Admiral Gorshkov credit for his determination to build a navy equal to America's, one capable of dominating any maritime environment. He had overseen the huge naval buildup now taking place in Soviet shipyards turning out hundreds of surface combatants and submarines in a bewildering variety of classes and configurations. Under Gorshkov, new ships joined the fleet every month to assume major roles in his strategy designed to counter the West's growing sea-based strike force of ballistic missile–firing submarines, aircraft carriers, and attack submarines.

A close look at KH-8 satellite images by NSA intelligence analysts had confirmed that many of the warships tied up alongside the finger piers at Severomorsk, as well as those still under construction, made up a large part of Gorshkov's revitalized navy. The U.S. Navy had a special interest in the *Kashin-* and *Kotlin-*class destroyers and the *Petya*-class frigates. These ships, along with larger ones like the *Kresta*-class cruisers and new second-generation nuclear-powered submarines such as the Yankee SSBNs, Victor SSNs, and Charlie SSGNs (guided missile subs), had been built to fill a variety of roles that spanned strategic deterrence, anticarrier, and antisubmarine operations.

The need for ASW ships had grown in proportion to the threat from U.S. submarines. To counter this threat, the Soviets had recently started development of a new generation of orbiting satellites equipped with sensors capable of detecting the wakes of submerged submarines from outer space, or if not submarines themselves, the disturbances in deep ocean areas their passage was known to cause. Research on the principles behind this advanced yet unproven technology had been under way for years in the United States and the USSR but had stalled over the seemingly insurmountable technical hurdles associated with the technology itself. For now, some Soviet shipboard radars, such as the MR-600 Topsail, were said to be able to detect rising convection cells in the atmosphere, generated when a submerged submarine disturbed the natural layering of seawater in the ocean. Like so many other technical innovations, though, Topsail didn't always live up to expectations, and when funding in the USSR flagged, so did further development.

In the late 1960s, a spy ring operating inside one of the most sensitive and highly classified departments of the U.S. Navy provided the Soviets with the means to decrypt top-secret radio messages containing SOSUS reports on the locations of Polaris subs. The information proved valuable, but only for a short time, since as a practical matter the Soviet sub force lacked the ability to keep U.S. submarines under surveillance in open ocean areas—mainly because the Soviet sub force itself was the target of U.S. surveillance. The Soviets, aware of their deficiencies, simply kept ASW operations confined to their home waters.

In the main, Russian surface ships were fast, had good seakeeping characteristics, and were well armed. Armaments included ASW rockets, homing torpedoes, and powerful depth charges; for air defense, there were rapid-fire guns and surface-to-air missiles.

An important question U.S. intelligence sought to answer was, how many ships like these did the Soviet navy have that were capable of carrying out ASW ops, and how many of them were currently based at Severomorsk? Dozens of *Kashin* and *Kotlin* destroyers as well as *Petya* frigates had been photographed by satellites, yet NSA analysts had found it was hard to positively identify a particular class of warship from its topside configuration alone, particularly when Russian ships, even new ones, were constantly undergoing improvement and modification. Analysts who had pored over hundreds of photos couldn't deliver an accurate head count to the navy because, said one analyst, it was like looking down from an airplane and trying to identify individual fish swimming in a lake.

It wasn't just ships and submarines, either. The Soviets also employed ASW aircraft to patrol the Barents Sea. The versatile workhorse Ka-25 Hormone, a stubby, ugly helicopter—which, like other Soviet navy helos, had encountered serious problems operating from the decks of ASW ships—carried radar, dipping sonar, and a downward-looking electro-optical sensor for locating submarines. Some Hormone versions had a boxlike sonobuoy launcher scabbed to the fuselage. Dropped in patterns, sonobuoys had the capacity to listen for subs and, upon contact, radio targeting data back to the hovering helo. Hormones also carried a balky and notoriously unreliable Russian version of MAD, or magnetic anomaly detector, an airborne magnetometer used to detect minute disturbances in the earth's magnetic field, such as those caused by a submarine's steel hull. Hormone armament varied but mainly consisted of homing torpedoes and depth charges.

As noted earlier, the primary fixed-wing ASW aircraft in the Russian inventory was the Be-12 Mail gull-winged amphibious long-range patrol bomber equipped with MAD and sonobuoys. The lumbering twin-engine craft was easily identified by its "thimble" radome on the bow. Armament ranged from bombs and depth charges to homing torpedoes. The Mail was a crude package, its range, and therefore its effectiveness, hampered by a small payload and limited fuel capacity.

Nevertheless, Russian ASW weighed on Hunter's mind as the *Blackfin* approached her station. From experience he knew, despite their problems and shortcomings, not to underestimate the Soviets' abilities. He knew that while their ASW teams lacked the experience and know-how of U.S. ASW teams, a mistake on his part could lead the Soviets right to the *Blackfin*.

Counterdetection—detection of a submarine by an enemy— occurred for a variety of reasons. A collision with another submerged submarine or with a surface ship was the most obvious, of course. Collisions at sea like the ones described in the patrol reports Hunter had reviewed at ComSubLant most often happened when thermal gradients degraded or masked sonar reception of the noise radiating from a nearby submarine or surface ship. Couple them with an ineffective OOD, or a poorly executed sonar search prior to coming to periscope depth, or a heavy sea state, which could also acoustically mask the presence of nearby ships, and a submarine crew had a prescription for disaster.

A less dangerous form of counterdetection occurred when an overaggressive CO engaged in risky maneuvers that resulted from errors in judgment. The most basic mistakes—raising the ship's masts too high out of the water where they could be seen, using excessive speed at inappropriate times and places, or inattention at the periscope by the OOD—often led to counterdetection by patrolling Soviet ships or aircraft. It could also occur when acting on assumptions based on faulty data. In that regard, Hunter never forgot a mistake he'd made as the OOD on a previous patrol in the Barents, one he vowed never to repeat.

It had happened during an open-ocean trail of a submerged Soviet Type II submarine, either a Charlie or a Victor (Hunter never knew which). The target, out ahead of Hunter's sub, entered a heavy storm that had developed along its transit route. Wind and rain lashing the sea had seriously degraded sonar conditions, and for a while there was a possibility the Soviet sub might get away.

An hour into the trail the Russian slowed and turned off his base course to clear baffles, an evolution during which sonar listens to the cone-shaped blind spot directly astern for a trailing U.S. sub that might have been hiding in the Soviet sub's prop wash. Hunter veered away just in time, before his sub was detected. He had guessed correctly that the Russian captain had cleared baffles because he was headed for PD, perhaps to copy a broadcast from headquarters.

Hunter dropped back and slightly abeam of the sub, whose commander, despite having cleared baffles, was apparently unaware that an American sub had been sitting on his tail. The Soviet sub came to periscope depth, at which point Hunter lost contact with it due to the storm.

Determined to continue the trail, Hunter started over, searching for the target along its projected track until worsening sonar conditions ended any hope he had of finding it. Instead, Hunter gave orders to sprint ahead, to the Soviet sub's next likely position, which, based on data from his own dead-reckoning plot, he assumed was accurate. He hoped that by the time he got there sea conditions would have improved to the point that, waiting on the Russian's extended track, he could regain contact as he passed close aboard.

As Hunter's sub sped down the plotted track, sonar suddenly reported contact with the Soviet sub close aboard, its bearing moving rapidly and alarmingly close down the side of Hunter's own ship! *Christ, we've overshot him*, Hunter thought. He also realized that he'd made a mistake assuming that the Russian had sped up after copying his broadcast. Turning away and slowing down, Hunter heard a single *ping!* on the UQC speaker. It was coming from the Russian's active sonar, a sure sign that Hunter's sub had been detected.

Hunter opened out with his tail between his legs, convinced he'd been counterdetected. Not wanting to be outfoxed by the Russian captain, he waited a while, then slowly maneuvered back into position to try to regain contact and to determine whether he'd really been counterdetected or the Russian had only thought he'd heard something and gotten nervous. But what about that single ping? Had the Russian received a return echo, or had the ships been too close to each other? When things finally quieted down, the Type II resumed its former track. This seemed to confirm that the Russian CO hadn't identified his passive or active sonar contact, perhaps assuming it was an anomaly. Hunter, chastened but not deterred, regained contact and resumed the trail.

Hunter's present op order had emphasized that counterdetection was a cardinal sin. Let the Sovs pick up your scent, let them find you, and you've lost the game. He could just see the headlines in *Pravda* now: BELLIGERENT AMERICAN SUBMARINE CAUGHT SNOOPING OFF COAST OF USSR BY PEACE-LOVING SOVIET NAVAL FORCES. No, Hunter concluded, he and his crew would have to be on full alert at all times. They had to be ready to respond to every conceivable situation or contingency that might arise. The Soviets were a tough adversary and would show them no mercy if something went wrong.

· · ·

Hunter huddled with the navigator and quartermaster over charts of the Barents Sea and its western approaches. The charts provided a detailed picture of the *Blackfin's* op area and its boundaries, some of them marked by ship transit lanes into and out of the Kola Inlet. There were also clearly marked areas around the inlet where ships were permitted to anchor while waiting for permission to enter the Tuloma River. Soviet warships and merchant ships shared the Tuloma channel, but the navy had priority of movement. There were also many clearly marked exclusion zones where fishing and anchoring were forbidden.

Some of the transit channels outside the Kola Inlet doglegged northeast around Kildin Island, where the Soviets tested missiles, then into open water. Hunter knew the area around the inlet would be a good place to hang out—beyond the twelve-mile limit, of course—and to start the hunt for targets of opportunity.

The *Blackfin's* course approaching Norway's North Cape had ducked below the wavy line printed on charts that for seafarers represented the southern limit of the arctic pack ice. The late summer pack usually extended south of Spitsbergen to about 75° north latitude and to about 5° west longitude but could vary year to year, sometimes reaching as far south as the northern limit of the Atlantic Drift.

Normally the ice measured between four and five feet thick at the extreme edge of the summer pack, thickening to over twenty feet as it retreated north. Large icebergs, as well as smaller bergs calved off Greenland and driven southward by wind, were not an uncommon sight in the Norwegian Sea and its approaches to the Barents Sea. So far the radio watch hadn't copied any warnings about icebergs sighted by reconnaissance satellites. Though the greater portion of an iceberg's bulk is hidden beneath the sea's surface, it was reasonable for Hunter to assume that the *Blackfin*, submerged at 450 feet, would have little to fear even if a berg showed up.

For years U.S. submarines had been operating in and under the North Pole, starting with a submerged trip by the *Nautilus* in August 1958. The Soviets soon took a proprietary interest in the Pole, viewing it as a sanctuary where their submarines, hiding under the ice pack, could launch ballistic missiles over the top of the world at targets in the United States.

The North Pole wasn't on Hunter's agenda this trip, though. Rounding Norway, he gave the fringe ice a wide berth by shifting course southeastward into the warmer and now ice-free waters that kept the Kola Peninsula navigable year-round.

Once they were clear of the pack ice, the op order called for disabling the active portion of the BQS-6 under-ice sonar and the transmission capability of the UQC underwater telephone to prevent their accidental use to alert the Soviets that a U.S. sub was in the neighborhood. The UQC was a handy gadget to have when operating with friendlies, functioning as a kind of single-sideband underwater voice transmitter. It could also pick up Soviet underwater telephone transmissions from submarines and surface ships—the Russians liked to talk to each other over underwater telephones—which sonar used to home in on intel targets. When more than one Soviet ship was involved in these conversations, the onboard intel specialists had to work hard to sort out who was talking to whom.

Closing in on his op area, Hunter waited until sunset, then ordered the *Blackfin* surfaced to finish the last housekeeping chores. A quartermaster went topside with the OOD and lookouts to clean both periscopes' heated head windows. It was also the last chance to make any power plant repairs or fix minor steam leaks, which might limit power output.

"We're good to go, Captain," quipped the OOD as he spun shut the hatch locking wheel after all the chores were completed.

Satisfied with the *Blackfin*'s condition and her crew's state of readiness, Hunter gave the order to dive. Just hours away from her station, she was virtually in the red bear's backyard.

PART TWO

STEALTH

10

FORTRESS POLYARNYY

IT WAS AN INCONGRUOUS SCENE: dirty gray cement piers, a blue gray haze hanging over oil-stained waters and black submarines, a band complete with thumping drums and shiny tubas playing patriotic music, sailors in fresh naval uniforms with glittering brass buttons and braid. A ceremony to welcome the crew aboard a Soviet submarine. Despite an official ban against such displays, a few friends and relatives had been permitted to come wave good-bye and see the men off on patrol.

This was Polyarnyy, the Red Banner Northern Fleet's main submarine base on the Kola Peninsula and, like Severomorsk, a closed city. The city of Polyarnyy itself, population twenty thousand, lay northwest of Severomorsk and north of Murmansk. Established in 1935, the sprawling base at Polyarnyy had serviced naval vessels during World War II. With the advent of the cold war, Polyarnyy grew into an even larger facility for repairing and servicing nuclear submarines.

As in that Russian fortress Severomorsk, winters in Polyarnyy were brutal, summers short. Also as in Severomorsk, no one, least of all civilians, ever left the base without special permission, and then only under strict supervision. Military personnel, much less the families of submariners, weren't supposed to know when a submarine sailed for fear word might somehow leak to the West. The secrecy seemed pointless: Confined as they were to the base—like political prisoners, said one woman married to a submariner—who would they come in contact with to tell about seeing a submarine depart? Yet for today, just for a few hours, the rules had been relaxed.

Most members of the crew of the departing submarine consisted of experienced veterans. The new recruits joining them were almost all farm boys who had never, until they were drafted into service for the motherland, been away from their villages. Submarine command knew it was good for morale for both veterans and conscripts alike to have civilians present for a send-off, even if they were people the sailors didn't know.

The submarine's commanding officer, an overage Captain Second Rank, knew he'd have his hands full whipping the new boys into full-fledged submariners. Waiting to depart, he was witnessing a scene he was all too familiar with: Make the boys feel like heroes of the motherland, get them excited, then kick their asses belowdecks, dog the hatches, and shove off before they had time to get scared.

According to the admirals, an overage captain second rank had no business commanding a sub. Overage to them meant an officer who was only thirty-nine. The thinking went that a submarine captain's skills dropped off precipitously after that. The admirals believed that a man approaching forty wasn't fit to climb ladders like a squirrel climbing up a tree or to go without sleep for days at a time, that his efficiency and judgment suffered after years of breathing foul air and—this was a big secret—exposure to too much radiation. They believed this even though many COs had, by necessity, been kept on active duty in submarines to age fifty, even beyond. But with the hurried pace of submarine construction, the Soviet navy needed every man it could muster to crew the boats coming off the building ways to confront the growing U.S. submarine threat to the motherland. But age wasn't the sole criterion for command. The Soviet navy needed men with sound judgment, tactical know-how, and navigational and seafaring experience. They also had to have a sixth sense for judging the crew's mood and pulse, and the ability to train and indoctrinate subordinates in submarining. In other words, they needed all the "old men" they could get.

. . .

Many Soviet submariners believed their commanders were concerned only with their own survival in a corrupt political system and their advancement in a service riddled with incompetent senior officers. Too many of these senior officers were coldly indifferent to the welfare of the men who went to sea in submarines with improperly shielded nuclear reactors and contaminated with radioactivity, only to face fire, flooding, and all too often death.

Clearly a day in the life of a Soviet submariner was no picnic. Nevertheless, the officers and enlisted men were as dedicated to their service and country as were their American counterparts. They may have lacked the training and high morale U.S. sub crews enjoyed, but no one doubted that if war broke out Soviet submariners would fight to the best of their abilities.

It can be assumed that the Soviet adversaries with whom Hunter was playing cat and mouse had backgrounds similar to those of many Soviet naval officers of his generation. As the sons of heroes of the Great Patriotic War, as World War II was known in the USSR, they were guaranteed enrollment in the Frunze Higher Naval School in Leningrad. After graduation the captain continued his training at the Grechko Naval Academy war college, also in Leningrad, for advanced submarine training. From Grechko he went to the naval training college in Sosnovy Bor, about fifty miles west of the city, where the navy had three operational nuclear reactors like those installed in submarines. He worked hard to master the technology of nuclear propulsion, but in order to get new officers aboard submarines as quickly as possible, the course was shorter than it should have been. Hence he received far less training than he felt he needed. Reduced levels of competence in sub crews were simply a fact of life in the Soviet navy. Too many officers arrived in the fleet afraid of the very equipment they had been trained to operate. It was left up to them to learn on their own what they needed to operate a submarine reactor, or at least to not melt it down. His hard work paid off: Within a year he qualified as a top nuclear officer.

The problems plaguing Soviet submariners and their boats started in the shipbuilding yards. In order to surpass the United States in sheer numbers of attack submarines (the United States had a substantial lead in missile subs), builders were forced to work at a feverish pace constructing and launching submarines on a schedule dictated by the Kremlin's military planners regardless of shortages in manpower, matériel, and rubles. Not surprisingly, quality suffered. Accidents were all too common, both on the ways and at sea, and killed untold numbers of submariners who could not easily be replaced. As it was, recruiting for the rapidly expanding sub fleet had failed to meet its goals, resulting in scores of undermanned subs with poorly trained crews.

Another roadblock submariners faced was balky construction schedules. The navy had little patience with delays, even though delays were common in the construction yards. The submarines came off the building ways as fast as possible but with much of their construction left unfinished. Problems encountered with construction and fitting out had to be reported to the chairman of a government directorate whose job it was to meet with the builders' representatives to iron out the problems. If it hadn't been for a few daring submarine commanders who took matters into their own hands—again, personal initiative was a dangerous trait for an officer to possess—hardly any of the newly launched boats would have ever put to sea.

Looking back at his time as a junior submarine officer, the captain recalled how agonizingly slow the pace of promotion had been. Slower even than for enlisted men. Everyone knew that the promotion of officers was totally subjective, that it depended less on an officer's skill than on who he knew. Even though he had mastered the complex physics and technology associated with submarine reactors and their systems and had become an expert in submarine propulsion systems, promotion seemed to pass him by.

Then he saw an opportunity to advance in a specialty every submarine needed: navigation. It was a well-kept secret that most navigators in the Soviet navy, especially submariners, were not fully competent. He approached the study of navigation as he had nuclear propulsion: Learn everything there is to know, master the practical skills needed to navigate, then prove your competence aboard ship. With his mastery of navigation coupled to his expertise in nuclear propulsion, he quickly rose through the ranks, even passing officers with solid contacts in Admiral Gorshkov's headquarters. In no time at all, it seemed, he had command of a November-class submarine.

Like all other dedicated Soviet citizens, submariners were expected to put their collective interests above their personal interests. His ship's *zampolit* would see to that. He was assigned to look over the captain's shoulder, to monitor and sign every incoming and outgoing radio message, to supervise every move and every decision the captain made. As a captain third rank himself, he was technically the commanding officer's subordinate. Even so, the *zampolit* was in effect a second commanding officer, albeit one who knew very little about submarines.

The captain knew from experience how grim a patrol could be with a doctrinaire political zealot breathing down his neck. The crew would have to survive at least three hours a day of political indoctrination, this after standing watches and carrying out other duties they had been assigned. So be it. The captain had survived other *zampoliti* in the past, and he'd survive this one, too. Then, in a few more years—the hell with the Americans and their cold war—he might be able to retire.

It was true, he'd already acquired his lifetime's quota of radiation from serving aboard submarines with inadequate radiation shielding and from coping with reactor casualties that any sane man would run away from. It was said that American submariners accumulated less radiation serving aboard their submarines than they did living ashore. He wasn't bitter, just resigned to his fate: an early death from cancer.

So what could he look forward to? A one-room walk-up in Leningrad? A postage stamp–sized patch of garden he could plant for food? A broken-down, oil-burning Trabant to get around in? Hardly. That would be a slow death worse than cancer. Maybe it was better to stay in subs as long as he could.

He was concerned about the quality of his crew's training. Many of the sailors assigned to submarines had come from the surface fleet. Some were lazy and stupid. Ignorant farm boys. Well, he had to do the best he could with what he had. He was the CO, their leader, the man responsible for their and the ship's well-being. Character was important; he believed in leading by example, not by instilling fear. When he had to discipline or criticize a crewman, he did it so the sailor learned from his mistake.

Sometimes he felt sorry for them for their plight. A typical conscript's pay didn't begin to compensate for the responsibilities he had to assume. Worse, Soviet submarine pay barely supported a family. The navy promised to pay the men more but never did. There was no one for families who fell on hard times to turn to for help at Polyarnyy, either. They understood that they had to fend for themselves.

Soviet submariners worked on a three-watch rotation, and men not standing watch worked on maintenance and other shipboard duties. Sailors hot-bunked, meaning two crewmembers on rotating watches shared one bunk, a situation he knew was not uncommon in U.S. subs. Unlike their American counterparts, Soviet sailors faced water restrictions even on the newest nuclear subs, though cold-water showers were available at any time of day. What a thrill that was!

On another front, a shortage of spare parts meant that when vital equipment broke down it had to be jury-rigged. For example, atmosphere-control systems were notoriously unreliable. Pleas for more equitable spare parts allocation in the sub fleet went unheeded by the bureaucrats ashore. Some submarines had more spare parts than others, while some ships had none. No sub ever had enough, and the parts pipeline seemed to grow narrower and narrower under Admiral Gorshkov.

As if that weren't enough, the personnel shortages not only hampered effective operations but had also caused a serious lack of experienced men capable of dealing with emergencies brought on by worn-out equipment. Disaster can strike at any time, and a sub crew has to be vigilant and well trained to handle any emergency.

Like U.S. sub crews, the Russians never stopped training during deployment. Fire-control parties set up and practiced attacks against surface and submerged targets. Damage-control parties practiced firefighting and the control of flooding. Radiation-control units ran reactor and propulsion casualty drills.

The admirals liked to brag that the quality of food aboard Soviet subs was equal to or better than that served aboard U.S. subs. In fact, rations aboard ship were not the best, nor was there much variety, due to the lack of rubles to pay for the high-quality food those admirals consumed at headquarters. Sailors had gotten used to eating moldy bread and stringy meat in their goulash and hearing the *zampolit* lecture them on the necessity to conserve the food they had—but why bother, when too often food stores went bad or caused food poisoning? Submarine command issued directives on the proper care and handling of food aboard submarines, but to little effect.

Moreover, the rations available were barely adequate for a long deployment. Most of the food came from collective farms, where quality wasn't a priority. Frozen stores such as meat and poultry were in limited supply, and so were canned goods. Submarine supply officers had to scrounge for what they needed, and submarine cooks had to be inventive to stretch staples and come up with tasty meals to satisfy a hungry crew. Borscht and potato soup wouldn't do it, though to their credit, the commissarymen did their best with what they had. As on U.S. submarines, there were four meals a day: lunch, dinner, supper, and "tea," the equivalent of U.S. Navy mid-rats. Typical fare consisted of eggs, bacon, goulash, noodles, rice, salted fish, lamb, and caviar (the lesser quality sevruga, not the ultra-high-quality beluga the admirals enjoyed). The U.S. Navy did not permit alcohol aboard its ships, but the Soviet navy, for all of its strictures, did. It allowed sailors to have a half glass of wine at dinner.

Necessities other than food were hard to get. Soap had to be scrounged. Toilet paper, that scratchy gray pulp the navy bought from a state-run paper mill in Belarus, was rationed. Clothing allowances were nonexistent. Submarine sailors had to mend their own socks and shirts, sewing patches on elbows and cuffs. New sea boots? Impossible. Stuff cardboard inside and wrap them with electrical tape. Ashore, housing was a joke. Conscripts and petty officers lived together under one roof in drafty barracks with inadequate plumbing. Patriotism withered under such wretched conditions, and exhortations by the *zampoliti* that sacrifice built Soviet character fell on deaf ears. How much could the men take? Sometimes the captain worried about mutiny.

Right now, though, he was more worried about getting under way and out of Polyarnyy on time and on a slack tide. Also, the navigator wasn't the best, and naturally the captain had concerns about navigating out of Pala Bay and the Kola Inlet. Maybe he'd have to take over and plot a proper course to the Barents Sea. Fortunately he had filled the watch officer positions with the six most experienced officers aboard.

He was concerned, too, about how well the ship had been degaussed by yard workers. Degaussing—demagnetizing the submarine's steel hull by winding it with coils of wire, then energizing it with electricity—was necessary because Soviet magnetic-influence mines left over from the Great Patriotic War were still being found in bays, harbors, and the seaward approaches to several naval bases near the White Sea. Mine sweepers had found thousands, but there were thousands more out there waiting. Every so often a barnacle-covered mine, its horns festooned with kelp and old fishing nets, bobbed to the surface offshore. More than one fishing trawler had been blown up by one of these damn things. It wouldn't do to have a first-line nuclear submarine blown to bits by a mossy relic of the Great Patriotic War.

With an assist from a tug, the November eased away from the dock and the waving women and children standing apart from a knot of stolid-looking naval officers in greatcoats and peaked *propapka*s.

The captain waved good-bye to his wife and two children in the crowd, then, his breath puffing white steam in the cold, ordered, "Helm, both engines ahead slow."

The *starpom*, or executive officer, a captain third rank, acknowledged, "Aye, Kapitan, both engines ahead slow."

The submarine moved, ponderously at first, then slid away from the pier. Polyarnyy slipped away behind them. It wasn't the kind of place to call home, but home it was for the captain and crew. They wouldn't return for almost two months, time enough to miss what there was of home. Children growing up with fathers whose lives had been lived, it seemed, mostly underwater. Wives with husbands whom they hardly knew when they returned from patrols pale and gaunt. Perhaps, the captain thought, it would be better if submariners were bachelors. No marital problems, no unhappy, brooding wives, no arguments and recriminations. No locked bedroom doors. Better to be married to the service, to your ship and shipmates. How did American submariners deal with separation, he wondered?

"Course zero-four-four, Kapitan."

The captain looked at the huge bow wave rippling over the November's bulbous nose as she cleared the narrows into the

Tuloma River. Under way, he felt free as only a submariner could. And damn the *zampolit*. Give the new men time, he thought, and they'd discover that the lousy food, the cold showers, and the deprivations were worth suffering just to be free.

He hoped for contact with a U.S. submarine so he and his crew could test themselves against their main adversary. From time to time Soviet subs got vectored into areas where submarine command suspected U.S. submarines were operating. Maybe they'd get lucky and run up against one of those *Sturgeon*-class spy subs. Not likely, but if it happened it would be something to talk about with friends over a glass of chilled vodka.

Up ahead the captain saw the lighted buoy marking the start of the northbound channel. He felt the change in tempo as the big submarine speeded up. His weather eye noted the swift current roiling the channel. He marked the time, Moscow time: In four hours they'd be at sea.

11

STALKING SHADOWS

THE *BLACKFIN* CRUISED at periscope depth, on the hunt for targets of opportunity, what Hunter called "first blood."

Lacking specific intelligence about upcoming Soviet naval exercises, Hunter had positioned the ship near the Kola Inlet to track outbound warships and to sweep up SIGINT from them and stations ashore. Knowing U.S. subs might be hanging around the inlet, the Russians tried to time their departures to coincide with full dark or bad weather, but it wasn't always possible.

Weather, especially snow and fog, had an effect on visual target tracking but didn't interfere with the collection of SIGINT, which consisted primarily of electronic transmissions. Also, seasonal changes played a major role in intel operations. Late in the year, when there was very little daylight in latitudes north of the arctic circle, a submarine could virtually cruise all day at PD without concern that a plane or ship would spot a raised periscope or intel mast. While extended darkness provided excellent cover for intel collection, however, it limited visibility at longer ranges and hampered collection of high-definition periviz images on video-tape. Conversely, in summer, when the sun shone at midnight, there was always sufficient daylight for long-range surveillance but little or no way to hide raised periscopes. Consequently, scope exposure had to be minimized, which interfered with collection.

Russian ships most often spent weekends in port. Activity generally picked up on Monday, when they sortied for operations, after which they usually returned to port on Friday. Tuesday, Wednesday, and Thursday were active days at sea, although sometimes a ship returned to port early or departed to join operations. Submarines came and went any time of the week, almost always submerging as soon as they cleared the inlet.

Right now the periscope watch reported that other than seabirds, not a thing had been sighted, not even those ubiquitous AGIs disguised as fishing trawlers. The *Blackfin's* sonarmen, headphones clamped to their ears, listened intently to the cacophony of broadband static radiating for miles and miles around them but had nothing to report, though that could change in the blink of an eye.

Meanwhile, the crew went about controlling and monitoring the ship's vital systems. Consummate professionals, they knew their work was just as important as that of the spooks who augmented the *Blackfin's* regular radiomen, electronic technicians, and sonarmen. Few enlisted men aboard the *Blackfin* really knew what these men did or how they did it. Their job was to get them to their destination and bring them home safely. For that matter, some of the crew still weren't certain exactly where they were—somewhere up north, way north.

The *Blackfin* continued cruising submerged outside the twelve-mile limit with a single periscope raised. The naval bases at Severomorsk and Polyarnyy, and the areas around them, provided a rich environment for electronic communications collection. As the *Blackfin* patrolled, incoming signals lit up the collection gear. Receivers built into the 15D periscope swept up everything: ship-to-ship and ship-to-shore communications, encrypted and unencrypted radio broadcasts, even radar emissions.

Always in direct communication with the *Blackfin*'s OOD, the intel team, should the need arise, could ask him to raise a mast for the purpose of recording a bearing from a captured signal. The spooks then reported any information of immediate tactical interest to the OOD.

The ship's specially designed listening devices intercepted the signatures of Soviet radar and weapons telemetry systems and pinpointed their location ashore or at sea. The devices utilized electronic filtration systems not unlike those in submarine sonar systems to sort out and identify all the jumbled electronic signals, which to the untrained ear sounded like nothing more than a symphony of warbles, squawks, and squeaks. For instance, Soviet radar, like any radar, gave off electronic emissions that contained the unit's operating characteristics, which would be useful if a crisis erupted or if a war had to be fought in the arctic region.

In addition to their normal tasks, the intel team also performed near-simultaneous translations of intercepted uncovered, or open, voice communications broadcast over the Soviets' tactical radio net, which they used during training exercises and weapons tests. The translations helped Hunter decide which of these operations might be worth pursuing and which ones were likely to be a waste of time.

For communicating with the main fleet, the Soviets used a variety of covered systems. They broadcast messages to the fleet via an advanced communications network and an automatic encryption system that was almost impossible to penetrate. Unlike uncovered comms, covered systems made buzzing or hissing noises, which the eavesdroppers aboard the *Blackfin* were not equipped to decipher. All they knew for sure was that different transmission systems produced recognizably different noises, to which the intel team had given code names.

Covered or uncovered, the intercepts were recorded on tape for delivery to analysts at NSA headquarters at the conclusion of the patrol. It was all very hush-hush stuff. The spook team never discussed its work with other members of the crew. Even so, it wasn't hard to imagine how taxing it must have been to listen, hour after hour, day after day, to all that hissing and buzzing static, hoping to make something out of it. Still, that was the nature of intelligence work.

. . .

Created in secrecy, the National Security Agency came into existence in the last days of the Truman administration, on November 4, 1952. The NSA had two goals: interception and penetration of the Soviet Union's secret communications. Equipped with the most powerful computer systems in the world and code-breaking technologies almost beyond comprehension, the NSA set out to break the seemingly unbreakable Soviet cypher system. While over time the NSA turned its collection and code-breaking skills to other countries' encrypted communications, the Soviet Union was always its main target.

The encrypted SIGINT comms the NSA collected from all of its sources—land, sea, air, and space—which it then processed for code-breaking and analysis, included all Soviet communications around the world, wherever the USSR had its embassies and military bases. Collection of SIGINT by Holystone teams was just one

ABOVE: A typical *Sturgeon*-class SSN. *(Department of Defense)*

RIGHT: Attack center of a *Sturgeon*-class submarine. *(Department of Defense)*

BELOW: Submarine tender USS *Fulton* moored at New London, CT. *(Department of Defense)*

RIGHT: A view of the bridges spanning the lower Thames River. In the foreground a sub departs the submarine base at New London. *(Department of Defense)*

ABOVE: The ill-fated USS *Cochino* departing Portsmouth, England, July 1949 on a spy mission off Norway. (*Department of Defense/ Naval Historical Center*)

RIGHT: Adm. Hyman G. Rickover in 1967 wearing civilian clothes, which he favored over a uniform. (*Department of Defense*)

BELOW: The *U-3008*, a war prize, Type XXI U-boat commissioned into the U.S. Navy, undergoing tests in the Atlantic. Compare the similarity of her design to that of the USS *Nautilus* and USS *Cochino*. (*Department of Defense/Naval Historical Center*)

RIGHT: The USS *Nautilus*, the fulfillment of Admiral Rickover's vision for a nuclear navy. *(Department of Defense)*

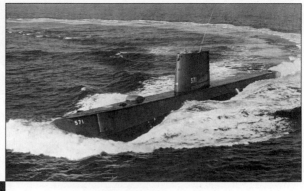

LEFT: Chief of Naval Operations Adm. Elmo R. Zumwalt, September 1970. A visionary who fought to modernize the Cold War navy. *(Department of Defense/Naval Historical Center)*

BELOW RIGHT: The USS *George Washington*, the U.S. Navy's first nuclear-powered submarine capable of launching intercontinental ballistic missiles. *(Department of Defense)*

BELOW LEFT: Soviet AGI intelligence-gathering ship posing as an oceanographic research vessel. *(Department of Defense)*

ABOVE: Soviet Charlie-class SSN. *(Department of Defense)*

BELOW: Soviet Yankee SSBN. Note how similar her design is to that of the USS *George Washington*. *(Department of Defense)*

BELOW: Soviet Victor-class SSN. *(Department of Defense)*

Soviet *Kresta* cruiser, identifiable by her tall, pyramidal midships tower.
(Department of Defense)

RIGHT: Soviet *Kashin-*
class destroyer with a
bone in her teeth.
(Department of Defense)

BELOW: Soviet *Kotlin-*
class destroyer.
(Department of Defense)

ABOVE: Soviet *Petya*-class frigate. *(Department of Defense)*

RIGHT: Soviet Delta-
class SSBN. *(Department
of Defense)*

BELOW: Soviet Be-12
Mail amphibious sub
hunter. *(Department
of Defense)*

LEFT: Soviet Kamov Ka-25 Hormone antisubmarine helicopter. *(Wikipedia)*

BELOW: Port side view of the USS *Seawolf*, one of the navy's newest and best submarines. Note her streamlined sail. *(Department of Defense)*

Cmdr. (later Rear-Admiral) Eugene B. Fluckey, submarine hero and Medal of Honor winner. *(Department of Defense/Naval Historical Center)*

ABOVE: Fluckey's submarine, the USS *Barb*, May 1945. *(Department of Defense/Naval Historical Center)*

RIGHT: Cmdr. (later Captain) George L. Street III, submarine hero and Medal of Honor winner. Four other World War II submariners won Medals of Honor: John P. Cromwell, Howard W. Gilmore, Richard H. O'Kane, and Lawson P. Ramage. *(Department of Defense/Naval Historical Center)*

BELOW: Street's submarine, the USS *Tirante* after her GUPPY conversion, circa 1954. *(Department of Defense/Naval Historical Center)*

small but important piece of the overall U.S. intelligence collection effort.

The half-million-square-mile Barents Sea area was ripe for SIGINT collection, especially from missile and weapons testing, one of the key components of Soviet military strength. Almost every weapon in the Soviet arsenal had undergone testing there at one time or another. For instance, in October 1961, the Soviets detonated the world's most powerful nuclear weapon, a fifty-eight-megaton thermonuclear monster, on Novaya Zemlya. At sea, Soviet ships conducted tactical weapons tests, and ASW squadrons tried out new tactics even while advanced Soviet submarines passed within hailing distance of prowling U.S. spy subs. The Barents Sea was the only place in the world where the United States could insert an intel team that could operate virtually without fear of discovery while monitoring the headlong buildup of the Soviet Union's might as well as its successes and failures.

The intelligence Holystone subs collected went directly to the NSA at Fort Meade, Maryland, for review and analysis by specialists. There, at Crypto City, as it was called, thousands of scientists, mathematicians, and deep thinkers studied the material looking for ways to extract its hidden data. The Soviets, aware that their codes were under attack by the NSA, used various techniques to armor-plate secret communications against break-in. One of their primary means of communicating was, of course, covered comms, or what the NSA called spectrum spreading, in which the primary signal was concealed by the noises that the operators on Holystone subs had recorded. Another was frequency hopping, with the signal jumping from frequency to frequency at blinding speed to hide encrypted data.

NSA technicians used sophisticated proprietary techniques

and high-speed computers to locate the encrypted signals hidden inside the SIGINT recorded by Holystone subs. After extraction, reconstruction, and classification, the signal went to the cryptanalytic division for further processing and, if possible, breaking, which was no sure thing. Some Soviet cyphers had resisted attack for decades even after applications of brute-force computer power. When a cipher proved breakable, the information extracted from it underwent further evaluation, after which it became part of the NSA's worldwide intelligence estimate, to which pieces were added every minute of the day.

The United States was not alone in the race to break into the enemy's coded communications. The Soviets had built one of the biggest SIGINT interception, processing, and analysis operations in the world, bigger even than the NSA's Crypto City operation, which, by any measure, was gargantuan. The Soviets were experts in every phase of intel collection and analysis. They had found ways to surmount the most sophisticated communications security techniques, even those protecting U.S. command and control systems, Defense Department data transfer systems and teletypes, and on rare occasions the executive branch's scrambler phones.

The NSA and other U.S. intelligence agencies were locked in a race to stay ahead of the Soviets in intel collection. Every scrap of data, no matter how insignificant, had to be wrung out for possible hidden meanings.

After the NSA completed its analysis of Holystone intel sweeps, the distilled information moved quickly through the intel pipeline to the NSA's "customers" such as the ONI (with whom the NSA had a close working relationship regarding Holystone), the CIA, the DIA, the secretary of defense, and possibly even the president. For example, information about a new Soviet missile's performance during a test flight might have an impact on the development of future U.S. weapons programs. Clearly it would have an impact on the SALT talks, in which intelligence acquired by Holystone subs on Soviet weaponry and its testing continued to play an important but unheralded role.

. . .

The *Blackfin* continued cruising near the Kola Inlet, her speed—three to four knots—consistent with the current sea state to minimize the feather produced by the raised periscope moving through the water. The OOD searched for visual targets, principally with the 15D, as its periviz system and built-in full-frequency signals intercept antenna ensured that anything detected would be recorded. Meanwhile, the trailing floating wire antenna kept the ship connected to the submarine VLF broadcast for any intel updates and directives that might influence current ops.

Given that antenna time was the principal reason the *Blackfin* was on station, the spooks settled in to monitor Soviet radio chatter. Comms intercepts, especially uncovered voice, would provide the first indication that an upcoming event such as a weapons test or missile launch was imminent. While the data included in a broadcast about an event was itself an important capture, it also gave Hunter a chance to preposition the *Blackfin* rather than be forced to tail-chase the upcoming evolution. This would allow more time to watch and collect intel.

An hour passed. Then two. So far, nothing. Not one ship had stood out of the Kola Inlet. Noon came and went. Still nothing. Radio reported hearing only routine chatter between shore stations: Someone had a parts requisition that needed a signature; a naval security team had a broken-down truck. Were the Sovs taking a holiday?

Hunter, chain-smoking, prowled the control room. He knew something had to happen soon. Call it submarine sense . . .

"Conn, sonar."

Hunter grabbed a mike. "Conn, aye."

"Captain, I have two contacts designated Sierra One and Sierra Two. They both appear to be surface ships, bearing one-six-zero, both drawing left."

Sonar had picked up a pair of ships, their high-pitched noise levels rendered as two rows of lines on sonar's paper printout.

Hunter took over the scope and toggled the triggers in the hand grips to activate the scope's torque motor. At periscope depth, even at slow speeds, manual periscope rotation was a chore; the torque motor made it easier to rotate the scope and for the OOD to put him on sonar's reported bearing.

Hunter searched the lowering horizon. "Got 'em," he said.

He saw a pair of pesky *Petya* ASW frigates standing out of the Kola Inlet. He identified them as *Petya*s by their blocky profiles and jumbled topsides. Hunter watched them sortie into grayish white fog even as sonar tracked their movements to the northeast.

"Radio, conn. Heard anything worthwhile from them?" asked Hunter.

"Not a word, Captain."

Things were off to a slow start and so far didn't look promising. He liked having a menu of activities to work on but was willing to take whatever came along. The *Petya*s weren't exactly the first blood he'd had in mind, but in a pinch they'd do until something better showed up, maybe a sub. Chasing after Soviet subs was a very high priority, but all he had so far was the two rusty frigates chugging toward a bank of sea fog—and maintaining radio silence at that.

Wait!

"Conn, sonar. Picked up a submerged submarine, bearing one-eight-five, drawing left. Designated Sierra Three. I classify the target as a submerged Type I."

Bingo!

Type I's were among the Soviet Union's earliest attack subs. Sonar had nailed this one departing the Kola Inlet. The sub's noisy broadband signal had been easy to pick up on the *Blackfin*'s bow and towed sonar arrays. Sonar continued tracking the sub as it exited the transit lane and turned north.

Hunter saw his chance—first blood—and issued a flurry of orders to the OOD. "Station the fire-control tracking party. All ahead two-thirds. Make your depth four-five-zero feet." To the busy watchstanders as much as to himself, he said, "The hell with those *Petya*s. Let's see what *this* guy's up to."

12

FIRST BLOOD

CHASING AFTER SUBMARINES usually resulted in a loss of valuable antenna time but was nevertheless a priority for intel collection, right up there with comms intercepts. For Hunter and the crew of the *Blackfin*, it could provide an opportunity to trail a sub and get comfortable with the technique this required. Not only that, trailing the Type I might lead to something interesting.

As the submerged Soviet sub pulled to the north, the *Blackfin* waited, then moved slowly into a trail position some fourteen thousand yards—seven miles—behind her, then increased speed to fifteen knots to keep up. Hunter began fishtailing around behind the sub, across her stern from port to starboard and then from beam to beam and quarter to quarter, to determine the target's course, speed, and range. As the trail got under way Hunter was thinking that it might lead to a submarine torpedo test or, if the target they were tracking were to meet up with another sub, an ASW exercise in which one of the Soviet subs would play the part of an American sub. In the latter scenario, how well they played their parts might demonstrate whether or not the Sovs understood U.S. submarine operations.

Running at fifteen knots, there was very little flow noise around the *Blackfin*'s sonar dome to degrade or mask the Russian's high signal-to-noise ratio. To Hunter, she seemed at least as noisy as the USS *Nautilus*, which he had once worked with and sometimes used as a benchmark for determining how noisy Soviet subs were.

"Sonar, what kind is he?" Hunter inquired. "Can you tell?"

"Definitely Type I, Captain. Possibly a November, but I can't be sure," he was told.

Hunter frowned. A November wasn't a high-value target; a Victor would be more like it. Still, the potential possibilities it held made the trail worthwhile. Later on, if a high-value target appeared, one that was a good candidate for an ASPL evolution, they'd be ready. For now, Hunter was content following along behind the Soviet sub while the tracking team sharpened its trailing skills on a real Soviet target, not a friendly merchantman.

A tape recorder located in the sonar room had been running ever since the *Blackfin*'s departure from New London, its tape reels capturing everything sonar had heard so far. The value of the recordings lay not so much in the data reported by the rotating sonar watches as in the acoustic information itself, in other words, the actual sounds made by, say, a distant underwater explosion or a single ping from a submarine or its high-frequency under-ice sonar. Some of these sounds were easy to identify, but those that weren't could have Hunter and the attack team scratching their heads and asking, *What the hell was that?* Replaying the tape usually provided an answer. It was a valuable tool that could be useful during a trail evolution, when the unexpected sometimes sprang a surprise.

. . .

The Soviet sub churned steadily north, the *Blackfin* trailing. Hunter noted that her course line, if extended out, would eventually end up at the North Pole. She had a long way to go to get there, and unless something important happened well before then, continuing the trail would be a huge waste of on-station time, to say nothing of having diverted the *Blackfin* out of her op area. Even so, Hunter counseled patience and settled down to wait and see.

The watch changed. At midnight, off-duty sailors gathered in the crew's mess to watch a movie. Hunter, meanwhile, occupied his time reviewing qualification paperwork and editing the patrol report. He kept in touch with the OOD, but nothing had changed: The Russian hadn't varied his course or speed. The OOD kept track of him by fishtailing off his quarters.

Hunter mulled this over for a while, then returned to the control room. They'd been in trail for over four hours, and there was no indication that the sub would alter course anytime soon. It had Hunter thinking, *Wild goose chase.*

One look at their present position on the chart of their op area convinced him of it. "OOD, break off the trail," he ordered. "Take her up to PD. Get us a satellite fix and pick up the broadcast, see what we might have missed."

The *Blackfin* turned south, back toward the Kola Inlet, where pickings might be better. Minutes later, after the radio watch had combed through waiting traffic, including familygrams, beamed to the *Blackfin*, the XO handed Hunter a message flimsy.

"Priority, Captain, ComSubLant."

Hunter read that SOSUS had been tracking a Soviet Type II submarine, possibly a Charlie or Victor, northward from an area west of Ireland. Here was Hunter's high-value target. ComSub-Lant believed that the sub was returning to Polyarnyy and wanted Hunter to try to intercept her and if possible identify her. No surprise there. He knew that SOSUS could, with reasonable accuracy, identify Soviet subs by class, and that the navy wanted to confirm they had this one's identity nailed down, too. ComSub-Lant's message had included the sub's known track and possible ETA in the *Blackfin*'s op area.

"We can do that," Hunter said as he huddled with the XO over charts of the Barents.

Trouble was, the *Blackfin* was up in the northern part of her op area, while according to intel from ComSubLant, the incoming Soviet sub was inching her way around Norway's North Cape. The idea was to intercept the Russian CO as he entered the *Black-fin*'s op area. One important advantage Hunter had was that the returning Russian CO probably didn't know for sure if he'd been picked up by SOSUS and, therefore, would have no reason to suspect that an American submarine would try to head him off. Plus, if he took his time heading for the barn, which the Sovs sometimes did to conserve their nuclear fuel, it would make interception easier.

There was plenty of time for the *Blackfin* to get into position ahead of the Russian, so Hunter moseyed onto a southwesterly course toward the western boundary of the op area. The run north hadn't been a waste of time after all, Hunter thought. It had tuned everyone up, and now they were primed. Hunter ran the numbers in his head, course, speed, distance. He visualized the geometry of their tracks and the Soviet sub's. He was confident they could intercept it with plenty of time to spare, maybe even get in an ASPL recording as well. If they could, it'd be akin to yanking the red bear's tail.

While the *Blackfin* eased toward the intercept box, Hunter settled down to wait. It gave him time to think about the Soviet submarine they'd tracked north and about the one they were trying to intercept.

. . .

Two examples serve to demonstrate the type of problems the Soviet navy encountered as it struggled to master the technologies inherent in the operation of nuclear-powered submarines.

The *K-3*, the *Leninsky Komsomol*, the first nuclear submarine built by the Soviets, put to sea in July 1958, just three years after the *Nautilus*. In certain respects, mainly speed and operating depth, she was more advanced than the *Nautilus*. Naturally the Soviets were quick to use the *K-3* as a propaganda tool and to tout their achievements in science and technologies that were applicable to sea power projection.

Following a string of successful early operations, poor-quality design and construction caught up to the *K-3*, a November-class sub. She suffered a string of crippling power plant failures that kept her tied up in port for months in the early 1960s. After repairs she went to sea, only to have another series of breakdowns. Repaired again, the *K-3* was on patrol in the Norwegian Sea in 1967 when her luck ran out, ironically not far from where the *Cochino* had gone down nine years earlier.

A vicious fire fed by hydraulic fluid broke out in her torpedo room and threatened to set off the torpedoes' warheads. Flooding the torpedo room saved the ship, but forty sailors, including the commanding officer, had died. Over the years the *K-3* suffered other disasters common to her class, yet survived to the end of her service life. Her unlucky sister ship, the *K-8*, caught fire and sank off Spain in 1970. Fifty-two men, including her CO, were killed.

The fate of the submarine *K-19* proved how dangerous nuclear reactors could be when not properly designed or maintained. A Hotel-class submarine, the *K-19* was the first Soviet nuclear-powered submarine designed to fire ballistic missiles. She had a surface displacement of four thousand tons and an overall length of 374 feet, about the same configuration as a U.S. Polaris SSBN, which the Soviets had virtually copied. Unlike Polaris subs, which had single reactors, the *K-19* had twin VM-A reactors, each capable of producing seventy megawatts of power. Like many submarines of her class, she was plagued by leaky steam generators and could stay at sea for barely thirty days, hardly enough time to arrive on station before having to turn back for needed repairs.

The *K-19* had been built to launch the R-13 Sark SLBM. The big missile weighed fifteen tons, carried a one-megaton nuclear warhead, and, like all early Soviet ballistic missiles, was liquid-fueled, unlike the solid-fueled U.S. Polaris missile. The Soviets' reliance on liquid propellants for their seaborne missiles posed enormous safety and handling problems aboard ships, especially submarines. Explosion of liquid propellant not only doomed many a Soviet missile test but often set fire to or sank the ships that had launched them, to say nothing of killing members of their crews. Nevertheless, the Soviets had the distinction of launching the world's first nuclear-armed SLBM during a test conducted in the Barents Sea in October 1961. Launched from a specially modified diesel-electric Golf-class submarine, the R-13's one-megaton warhead detonated on Novaya Zemlya. There is no known record of its launch and strike having been recorded by a Holystone submarine.

Ironically, it was a damaged nuclear reactor, not a propellant fire, that almost sank the *K-19*. In July 1961, barely a year after commissioning, a rupture in her reactor's primary coolant loop spewed steam and highly radioactive material into the ship's compartments. Her men fought like demons to repair the leak and saved the *K-19*, though eight men died in the process. Many more suffered serious burns and radiation sickness. Thirteen men died later from exposure to high levels of radiation. Not surprisingly, the *K-19* became known throughout the Soviet fleet as "Hiroshima."

Soviet submariners like those on the *K-19* were shockingly ignorant about radiation and its effects on humans. Sailors were taught that there were only two possible responses to radiation's unseen perils: fear or scorn. Submarine commanders were woefully uninformed about the workings of nuclear reactors, much less nuclear physics. They gained experience the hard way, by coping with accidents and the human casualties they caused.

Accidents like those aboard the *K-3* and *K-19*—improbable in the U.S. sub force—were treated as routine occurrences as the Soviet navy rushed submarines with faulty operating systems and inexperienced crews into service. Undaunted, Soviet submariners pressed on.

Though accidents aboard their submarines were hushed up by the Soviets, word that they were having problems eventually reached the West, where submariners like Hunter had long ago developed a grudging respect for their Russian counterparts and understood only too well the plight they faced. After all, the submarine brotherhood cut across ideological lines, and no man wanted a brother submariner to die of radiation exposure or anything else. The Americans used their enormous technical and tactical superiority to outwit and outmaneuver, even demoralize, Soviet submariners, not to kill them. Hunter didn't underestimate them, but he was keenly aware of their limitations and of the almost insurmountable advantage he had now, as the *Blackfin*, silent and virtually undetectable, sped toward the incoming Soviet sub.

"Coming up on our expected intercept point, Captain," said the OOD. "Almost there."

Hunter slowed the *Blackfin*'s headlong rush across the Barents to start patrolling on a course perpendicular to the estimated track of the approaching Type II. As the *Blackfin* drifted slowly southwest, her sonarmen searched through the broadband noise spectrum, eager to find the Type II's distinctive tonals.

As usual, Hunter prowled the control room and sonar shack, waiting for word of contact. The interception point where the two submarines' tracks should meet, assuming the Russian CO hadn't diverted or changed his speed of advance, lay about fifty miles off the coast of Norway. It was there, near the north-south transit lane to the Kola inlet, that Hunter hoped to perform an ASPL, then, when the Soviet sub surfaced to begin her approach to port, he'd make a visual ID. Everything depended on the Russian CO adhering to standard operating procedure, which called for him to surface well outside the twelve-mile limit. If he did, Hunter would make a sound recording and get a look at her before she slipped inside the protection of the territorial limit. All Hunter needed now was patience, patience, patience.

13

EYES AND EARS

"SONAR, ANYTHING?"

"Negative, Captain. Just garbage."

Several hours spent in and around the intercept box had turned up a Norwegian fishing fleet but not much else. Hunter sat tight, thinking. Had they missed him? Had the Russian somehow slipped past them? Not likely. Sonar would have heard the sub's tonals for sure. They'd won the race but so far had come up empty-handed. The Russian's track, according to ComSubLant, had him dialed in for arrival right now. So where was he?

The *Blackfin* drifted, waiting.

A sense of anticipation gripped the OOD, the tracking party, and the sonarmen. Hunting another sub was exciting, sure, but it was also a challenge and a test of skill and patience. There was a lot of ocean out there to mask a submarine, many cubic miles of noisy seawater to comb through to find one tonal among all the others that said "submarine." Tuned in to the deep beyond the *Blackfin*'s hull, the sonarmen on watch assumed a trancelike state as they listened for the Soviet sub; they looked like they were trying to will it into existence.

Hunter, meanwhile, studied the plot and chain-smoked.

At length one of the sonarmen stirred. "Got him."

A moment later Hunter heard, "Conn, sonar. I have a three-hundred-hertz tonal contact. Bearing three-four-zero, bearing drift right. Designated as Sierra Thirteen." The numerical Sierra classifications used for ship contacts had been piling up. "Classified as a submerged Type II."

Hunter's hunch had paid off; the incoming sub was north and a little west of the *Blackfin*.

The fire-control team went into action. Interception and a positive ID depended on getting an accurate solution on her course, speed, and range, then closing in. Hunter, a step ahead of the tracking team, had worked out rough estimates in his head, pleased that their prepositioning estimates had turned out to be correct.

Minutes later the submerged Soviet sub loomed up, and as she went on by the waiting *Blackfin*, Hunter swung in behind to trail.

Things were looking good until sonar warned, "Sierra Thirteen's slowing—clearing baffles."

Hunter didn't hesitate; he pulled to one side to avoid being detected. Moments later the Soviet sub came to PD.

As if reading Hunter's mind, sonar reported, "Sierra Thirteen's blowing ballast tanks."

Sonar reported, too, that there were no other ships in the vicinity. Hunter, eager to make an ID, ordered the *Blackfin* to periscope depth. Waiting as the ship rose, he reached into the overhead and turned the scope's hydraulic lift ring to the right. A thump and the scope started up. As soon as the optics module appeared, Hunter crouched, put his eye to the ocular, and grabbed and snapped down the training handles while the scope was still rising. He slowly rose with it to a standing position, his view aimed upward at the underside of waves. He spun the scope, searching for the bottoms of any ships whose noisy machinery and props might have been missed by sonar, but no ominous dark shadows loomed overhead. All he saw before the scope's head pierced the surface was the bottom of a rumpled carpet of seawater.

"Scope's clear." Hunter spun it 360 degrees twice. The control room had fallen silent, waiting for his next report. "No close contacts."

Hunter steadied up on the last reported bearing of the surfacing sub. "There she is." He watched the submarine's streamlined sail break the surface first, then her sleek, sharklike hull. "Target's a Victor. That was a hell of a catch for SOSUS. Too bad we couldn't get an ASPL on this guy. Maybe next time."

Hunter watched the Victor resume its southerly course toward the Kola Inlet. Visual confirmation that the submarine SOSUS had followed across the North Atlantic was a Victor would aid in the future identification of Soviet submarines and of this one in particular. For now, Hunter had done all he could. It was time to move on.

• • •

Hours later the *Blackfin* crawled along the northern edge of the thumblike protrusion of the Kola Peninsula, just outside the twelve-mile limit, collecting SIGINT while looking for something to do. The spooks copied frequencies of interest, though when there was nothing going on they sat there looking like bored passengers riding in a bus. In parallel with the signals collection business, the ship's regular radiomen stayed busy with housekeeping—sweeping up VLF broadcasts, familygrams, intel updates, and news.

Sniffing for targets of opportunity, the intel team kept up a dialogue with the OOD, delivering reports on what they were hearing on uncovered comms of tactical significance. The take was pretty thin. Hunter, impatient for some action, would have welcomed a missile test, something to get hold of like a dog with a bone, something more to show for their efforts than ID-ing a Victor.

Hunter had a meal, then checked out the movie in the wardroom. He didn't like *A Clockwork Orange*, so after tending to paperwork he turned in. He'd just nodded off when the command duty officer roused him. "Captain, sonar has a submerged sub contact."

Hunter hurried to the already busy control room to pick up the details. Based on the contact's three-hundred-hertz tonal, it was likely another Type II, a Charlie or another Victor, heading west in a transit lane parallel to the coast and on a steady course and speed. The look on the XO's face mirrored Hunter's thoughts: This guy might be a candidate for an ASPL recording.

Just as with the Victor they had trailed and identified earlier, the sound signature of this present submarine was as unique as a set of human fingerprints. Once recorded, her signature, like that of the earlier Victor, could be used to identify her at some future date. The goal of ASPL was to measure a submarine's emitted sound levels to determine how noisy or quiet various classes of Soviet submarines were. In addition to having a set of "fingerprints," ONI might be able to determine how the Soviets' submarine quieting program was progressing and how effective it was. Such information was valuable to submariners because it gave them a quantitative figure that predicted the maximum range at which various submarines could be detected, depending, of course, on the temperature gradients present in the waters in which they were operating.

To an untrained ear, a recording of a submarine's sound signature might sound like nothing more than white noise. In the NSA's sound labs, technicians using special tools and techniques had ways of picking out and identifying the individual components that made up the ship's rotating machinery, such as shafts and gears. Another piece of intel the technicians sought in a recording was the turns-per-knot ratio, that is, how fast the submarine's propeller turned in relation to its speed in the water. Determining that ratio provided a means for discriminating between different classes of subs, each one of which had its own individual characteristics.

A really good ASPL was akin to a lab test, and the validity of the data was directly proportional to the accuracy with which the data was recorded. Sea state wouldn't be a problem, since both the *Blackfin* and her target sub were submerged.

Another factor that influenced an ASPL's accuracy was the target's signal-to-noise ratio and its effect on sonar reception. As observed in the earlier unsuccessful trail of the November headed toward the North Pole, high underwater speeds create flow noise around the sonar dome that can mask sound reception. Like the sub that was heading north, this new sub that Hunter had in his sights was also cruising at only fifteen knots, and flow noise would have almost no effect on sonar's ability to hear her audio fingerprint. As for what type of submarine Hunter had in his sights, a Victor or a Charlie, it really didn't matter. The *Blackfin* was a collection device; it would be up to an analyst to make the determination from the ASPL tapes and accompanying data package Hunter delivered.

ONI already knew that Victors were comparable in many ways to the U.S. *Sturgeon*s. Information about them was sketchy, given the secrecy surrounding their construction, starting in 1967, at the Admiralty Shipyard in Leningrad. Nevertheless, intel about their capabilities, along with data from their trials conducted in the Barents Sea and the White Sea, had reached the West.

The Victors, designed as ASW submarines, had a twofold mission: Locate and dog U.S. SSBNs; protect Soviet missile-carrying submarines from American SSNs. Streamlined and double-hulled, the Victors displaced 4,780 tons submerged. Their overall length of 305 feet and beam of 34 feet 9 inches almost mirrored that of the *Sturgeon*s. Powered by twin VM-4P reactors producing thirty-one thousand horsepower (twice as much as a *Sturgeon*) and driving a single screw, the Victors could reach twelve knots surfaced and thirty-three submerged, eight knots more than the *Sturgeon*s. Like the *Sturgeon*s, they had a test depth of 1,300 feet. Typical complements ranged from seventy-six to eighty men. Armament consisted of six 21-inch bow torpedo tubes and twelve reloads. Had they not lacked modern sonar and quieting technologies such as rafted decks with special sound insulators and sound dampening coatings on their inner pressure hull to reduce noise transmission to the sea, they might have been a match for any U.S. submarine.

The Charlie-class SSGNs were the first submarines built by any nation that were capable of firing antiship missiles while submerged. Eight Amethyst SS-N-7 missiles housed in vertical launchers in the ship's blunt bow were intended for use against U.S. aircraft carriers. The Charlies' main armament consisted of four 21-inch and two 15.75-inch torpedo tubes. Built with streamlined double hulls but only single reactors, the Charlies displaced about four thousand tons. They could reach speeds of twenty-four knots submerged and dive to 1,300 feet. Charlies, too, were in most respects similar to the *Sturgeon*s.

Debating the merits and capabilities of submarines was an academic exercise that put Hunter to sleep. He was a doer, not a rivet counter. Satisfied that the Russian was holding a steady course and speed, he wiggled the *Blackfin* back and forth while closing in to make an ASPL recording of the Type II.

To ensure that the data about to be recorded were precise and to avoid counterdetection—and collision—during the evolution, it was essential that the maneuvers Hunter employed were at all times based on an accurate determination of the target's distance, or range, from the *Blackfin*. Later, archived range values would be important in the analysis of ASPL data packages and provide an essential point of reference when setting up future ASPLs. Real-world experience coupled to accurate data made risky evolutions such as ASPLs possible.

How far away a target was had a huge influence on the accuracy of recorded decibel levels, as did the effects of sound scattering and absorption. Generally, a benchmark range of a thousand yards gave the best recorded results. It was also a matter of pride for Hunter to get it right. He didn't want analysts poring over the recordings his crew had made to find discrepancies that would degrade the recordings' usefulness.

The sonarmen got to work setting up their taping equipment to capture the noise radiating from the Soviet sub's machinery and propeller cavitation. Hunter, meanwhile, kept fishtailing around behind the target so the fire-control tracking parties could refine TMA data.

Passive sonar can determine a target's bearing but can't calculate the critical dimension of range. Range can be determined only by engaging in a series of maneuvers that alter the trailing submarine's position relative to the target and recording the changes that occur over time in the target's bearing and bearing rates. Zigzagging behind the target at ten-minute intervals caused the target's bearing relative to the *Blackfin* to undergo the kind of rapid changes needed to produce an accurate TMA solution.

As the *Blackfin* maneuvered, target bearings flowed into her Mk 113 fire-control system's three major components: the target motion computer, which calculated the target's course speed, and range; the target motion display, which showed the *Blackfin*'s heading, bearing, and distance from the target; and the weapons-control panel with its torpedo readiness display, firing key, and wire-guided torpedo control, which was always on standby when dealing with a potentially hostile target.

Installed next to the Mk 113 system was a signal-to-noise meter, which displayed sonar signal strength, yet another critical quantitative measurement essential for automatic target following. In this mode, with sonar locked on the target and providing a continuous flow of bearing information, a dramatic change in signal strength would alert the fire-control tracking party that the target had suddenly started maneuvering, speeding up, changing depth, or dipping in and out of the temperature gradients that affect or degrade sonar reception. Absent such a warning, the chances of collision and counterdetection increased dramatically.

To follow the action as it unfolded in real time, the *Blackfin*'s attack center had a dead-reckoning tracer (DRT) incorporated into a two- by three-foot table topped with tempered glass, which the tracking team used for fire-control plotting. A lighted device resembling a bug moved around under the glass. When viewed through translucent plotting paper, the bug reproduced every move the *Blackfin* made as she maneuvered. The plotting scale was adjustable from two hundred yards to the inch to several miles to the inch. For the upcoming ASPL, plot shifted to a short scale, which provided a more detailed visual assessment of the unfolding evolution.

In Hunter's view, the earlier trail of the sub heading north had definitely proved its worth: Everything for this ASPL had come together easily and quickly.

"Okay, we're in good shape," Hunter announced. "Let's do it."

With an accurate range solution in hand, Hunter eased the *Blackfin* into position two thousand yards abaft the port beam area of the target. Then he began sliding around back and forth across the target's stern and up and down either beam.

"Sonar, start your tapes," he ordered.

Alert, ready to break contact in the event the Russian CO maneuvered unexpectedly, Hunter reached for one of four cigarettes burning in ashtrays scattered around the control room. If all went as planned—this was where all the training and prep paid off— the Soviet submariners plugging along up ahead would never know they were being trailed and recorded. All Hunter had to do now was try to relax and enjoy the ride while the tape recorders copied the sub's noisy, whirring machinery.

· · ·

Russian submarine designers had not yet solved the problems inherent in silencing submarines, which was one of the last technical frontiers left to conquer. Admiral Rickover had said that silencing nuclear submarines was a bigger headache than nuclear propulsion itself. He meant the noisy pumps, engines, and turbines that propelled nuclear subs. They required innovative solutions and advances in engineering and acoustic science to quiet.

Early on in the development of nuclear submarines, the navy realized that its subs, capable as they were, produced a lot of noise from their large hull-mounted machinery components. For example, the *Nautilus*, an SSN, and the USS *George Washington*, an early Polaris SSBN, were so noisy that SOSUS arrays strung along the eastern seaboard of the United States tracked them clear across the Atlantic. If the Soviets had had SOSUS, they'd have tracked them, too.

A submarine produces noise from four main sources: internal machinery, propeller rotation, transient disturbance, and crew operations. Each source requires its own quieting solution. Machinery can be silenced by installing it on rigid platforms, or rafts, which are sound-insulated on flexible supports connected to the ship's hull. This technique reduces radiated noise levels but can't reduce the source of the noise itself, so proper raft insulation is critical. Improperly installed rafts create sound shorts, direct paths across the insulators and hull through which sound enters the sea, where it can be heard outside the sub's hull by sonar. While rafting helped reduce transmitted noise levels, engineers still had to redesign pumps, bearings, gears, and other rotating equipment for quieter operation. Some types of machinery were redesigned to make them quieter and even more reliable, but some components, such as the pumps used in nuclear reactors, defied solution because they had to be mounted directly to the hull to strengthen their resistance to depth-charging.

Another source of noise, propeller blade rate, made its appearance in the early 1960s. A ship's rotating propeller blades make noise when they slice through the turbulence created by the flow of water past the hull. Each time the prop rotates, the blades vibrate, creating noise that can be detected by sonar. Intel analysts use recorded blade rates to determine operating parameters and to identify individual ship types.

Attempts to solve this problem with larger or smaller props, contrarotation, and even prop shaft gearing failed. Instead, the solution to the problem lay in a redesign of the propeller blades themselves into the now familiar scythelike shape seen on modern subs. The scythe profile cut into the wake-water turbulence more gradually than did conventionally curved blades. Early scythe blade construction for U.S. subs required advanced computer-controlled machining equipment that was available only from Japan, and the United States kept it under wraps. It took years of work and the help of spies working for them in the United States for the Soviets to obtain the technology to develop their own scythe-bladed propellers. Meanwhile, for the Soviets, U.S. submarines had slowly but surely become so quiet that they seemed to have disappeared altogether.

Transient noise was yet another problem. The best example was the noise created by the opening and closing of torpedo tube doors, the famous "He's opening outer doors!" heard in movies. Transient noise is also produced by the movement of diving planes and rudders projecting into the flow stream, which can produce cavitation at high speed. Transient noises generated by submarines as part of normal operations at sea are often of short duration yet can be heard by a pursuing enemy sub.

Transient noise created by the activity of a submarine's crew— the opening and closing of hatches and watertight doors, heavy footfalls on decks, a dropped tool or the rattle of dinner trays, plates, and silverware—can be controlled to some degree by rigid adherence to noise reduction procedures aboard ship. That's why Hunter made sure every man aboard the *Blackfin* never forgot that they were in the *silent* service.

The sub force studied another vexing source of noise caused by the flow of water over hull appendages and openings and its degrading effect on sonar reception. Engineers and naval architects solved the problem of this hydrodynamic flow noise by paying greater attention to the exterior design of a submarine's hull. The navy reconfigured and relocated submarine sails fore or aft as needed and streamlined all hull openings and control surfaces. They even adjusted the height and finish of weld beads and the fit of covers over retractable deck cleats and mooring fixtures.

For their part, the Soviets, preoccupied by the problems they were having with reactors and other vital shipboard components, had paid little attention to submarine quieting, though they were apparently aware of the complex undertaking necessary to develop silencing technologies. Their inattention may have been caused by the poor quality of their sonar, which masked the issue for years. It wasn't until an American spying for the Soviets revealed how easy it was for the United States to track their submarines that the Soviet navy tackled the problem in earnest. The results of their belated effort were first seen in new submarines whose design incorporated rafting, scythed props, and absorptive interior hull coating technologies.

Right now, however, the submarine Hunter had in his sights was noisy, and that was okay by him and by the sonarmen at their tape decks. They had been recording for about twenty minutes. Everything was running smoothly. It was one of the best ASPLs Hunter had ever set up. He relaxed and lit a cigarette. . . .

"Conn, sonar."

"Conn, aye," Hunter acknowledged.

"Target's slowing, turning to clear baffles."

"Break off contact," Hunter barked. "All ahead one-third; come to course zero-nine-zero."

As the Soviet sub maneuvered, the *Blackfin* swung away in a long, slow, lazy arc, opening the range to avoid a collision or counterdetection.

"Conn, target's blowing his tanks, gonna surface."

Chances were good that the turbulence caused by the blowing of ballast tanks would mask any noise the *Blackfin* made as she slinked away to await developments. Hunter, like a dog with a bone, wasn't about to let this guy get away.

"Bring her to periscope depth," Hunter ordered. "See if we can identify what type this guy is, figure out what he might be up to."

When the sub surfaced, Hunter looked her over through the scope and identified her as a Victor, but he could only watch as she headed south for the Kola Inlet.

14

THE COVETED PRIZE

A PROBLEM WITH the submarine's power plant delayed final departure from Polyarnyy. Now, after a four-hour run up the Tuloma River, the Victor at last stood out from the Kola Inlet.

An hour later the OOD reported, "At our dive point, Kapitan."

"Depth under the keel?" the captain called to the *starpom* in the central command post.

"Two hundred forty-five meters, Kapitan."

"Prepare to dive. Lookouts below. Clear the bridge."

The snapping red, blue, and white hammer-and-sickle naval ensign came down, too. The captain ducked into the hatch trunk and went below, followed by the lookouts. The OOD had a final look around, then followed them down after securing the bridge hatch.

The chief of the watch, a *michman*, greeted the captain with, "The ship is ready to dive, Kapitan." The duty sailor in each compartment had reported to the chief of the watch that preparations for diving had been completed.

The captain looked around the central command post, or CCP, a compartment similar in size to the control room of a U.S. *Sturgeon*-class submarine and equally crowded with watch-standers and equipment. Like the *Blackfin*'s control room, the Victor's CCP contained periscopes, radar consoles, gauge panels, plotting tables, communications gear, sonar repeaters, and more. Two men seated in the forward end of the CCP gripped the control yokes that actuated the ship's rudder and diving planes. Experienced men, the captain noted, not farm boys. If the trim calculation was accurate—the *starpom* was responsible for making it so—the boat would submerge without any hesitation, and with the two veterans at the helm and planes, she wouldn't overshoot her mark.

"Status?" asked the captain.

"Green board, sir," replied the *michman*.

The captain saw for himself that the hull opening indicator showed a double row of green lights indicating that the submarine was rigged for dive. He relieved the *starpom* at the periscope, then ordered, "*Pogruganye*." Dive. "Make your depth forty meters."

A loud buzzer, the diving alarm, sounded twice, followed by the *michman* bellowing orders. "Make your depth forty meters, aye! Flood main ballast tanks! Five degree down angle!"

With a release of air from her ballast tanks, the big submarine pitched down and began to submerge. The captain watched the spectacle through the periscope. Sea foam rode up and over the bow, then the sail, then the scope. The ship was under. There was no hesitation. The *starpom*'s trim calculations were on the mark.

"Down periscope. Retract all masts."

The periscope, radio antenna, and radar and ESM masts hummed into their wells.

Minutes later the deck leveled out at one hundred meters.

The captain ordered, "Helm, come to course two-nine-zero. Full speed ahead."

Now it was time to go to work.

. . .

The captain, seated in the commanding officer's pedestal chair in the center of the CCP, a *kashtan* microphone in hand, addressed the crew. Following Soviet navy protocol, he gave the crew a pep talk, a canned exhortation to devote themselves to the goals of the Communist Party for the good of the motherland, then briefed them on the ship's operation orders. Knowing what they were going to do and looking forward to it would be an antidote to the inevitable boredom that would set in about a week after sailing. Yet the captain never doubted that his crew, even the new boys, had the fighting spirit needed to carry out any order. On a submarine, an order to launch weapons is one order among many that sailors obey without a moment's hesitation, and to consider the consequences that might result is the last thing on their minds.

Their mission boiled down to one word: *razvedka*—reconnaissance. Collect and evaluate data on the enemy. Specifically, locate and, if possible, trail a U.S. Polaris missile submarine. The captain didn't tell the crew that the Soviet navy still believed that the best way to locate Polaris SSBNs was to detect their noise output. Of course, he knew better. Except for the earliest versions, Polaris submarines were too quiet to detect with sonar. Once they departed their base in Holy Loch, Scotland, they simply disappeared. No one could find them. Even if a Soviet sub were to make contact, there was no way an SSN, even *two* SSNs working as a team, could hope to trail a U.S. SSBN. Try telling that to the admirals ashore. Or the *zampolit* standing smugly at the captain's side, listening to every word he uttered. To do so might be tantamount to treason. Tactical recon by submarines was just part of the overall Soviet global recon system geared to finding U.S. SSBNs, a system that included AGIs, merchant ships, trawlers, SIGINT, and HUMINT. But the system was virtually ineffective; contact with a U.S. SSBN was a rare event.

The captain's operation order included a secondary but no less important task: Detect and, if possible, track U.S. SSNs entering Barents Sea operating areas for the purpose of collecting intelligence on the Northern Fleet and its capabilities, specifically submarine sound signatures and electronic intercepts. The op order urged caution to avoid counterdetection by U.S. submarines. A tall order. The Americans were good at hiding in underwater thermal layers, or thermoclines, that were dragged into the Barents by the Atlantic Drift. Such layers made sound waves bend in unpredictable ways and made submarines very hard to detect.

In deeper, colder waters, American subs could pick up Soviet subs at great distances. Still, sometimes the Sovs got lucky and made sonar contact with a U.S. sub running at high speed or at close range. It had happened before and, with luck, could happen again. Making sonar contact with a U.S. sub was a prize every Russian submariner coveted.

The captain was a dedicated professional. Despite his cynicism, he believed that what he was doing would prevent the USSR and the USA from launching a ruinous nuclear war. Far better to play a simple game of cat and mouse with submarines in the Barents, where a man's skill could be tested and his ego broken. Better to do that than to play a much more dangerous game of brinkmanship—threatening to launch intercontinental nuclear missiles at U.S. and Soviet cities. He'd have done his job if he did nothing more than prove to the stubborn admirals running the navy that Soviet submarines lacked the ability to find and neutral-ize U.S. submarines. If he could, it might make them think twice about which side would win a nuclear war. Then he could retire to his walk-up flat in Leningrad and tend his vegetable garden. Of course, he knew that was a dream. Neither side would ever be sat-isfied with the status quo. There were always bigger and quieter submarines to build, and better sonars and weapons to deploy.

He had no indication, either in his op order or from any pre-departure briefings (he assumed that Moscow had spies planted in the U.S. Navy's headquarters in Norfolk, Virginia) that an Amer-ican submarine had entered the Barents Sea. If one had, he'd try like hell to find her. He was no different from the others; he cov-eted the prize, too.

Two reactors online, the Victor sped north.

The tension and excitement that was so evident during the de-parture phase of the deployment, discounting the breakdown, had slowly diminished, replaced by the rhythm of shipboard routine. The captain ordered drills early in the day, knowing from past ex-perience that most casualties aboard submarines happened early in the morning when the crew was less alert, anticipating watch changes, thinking about breakfast.

This morning he held a damage-control drill. "Fire in com-partment five!" The crew reacted instantly to the alarm. First they grabbed firefighting equipment. Then they donned emergency breathing masks, plugging the air hoses at the ends of the masks into ports connected to the ship's central air service lines in the "affected" compartment. The breathing equipment was awkward and barely adequate to keep a man alive in a cramped, smoke-filled compartment. Fortunately this was a drill, not the real thing.

The captain and the damage-control officer, a senior lieutenant who was also the assistant torpedo officer, looked on as the men suppressed a "fire" in an electrical panel. Had it been a real fire, the compartment's forward and after watertight doors would have been sealed, and the men stationed in that compartment would have been fighting the fire all alone. No one would be able to help them or rescue them without endangering the ship.

After concluding the drill, the captain evaluated the evolution and pointed out what had to be done to improve the men's damage-control skills: They had to improve their reaction times; it took too long to get organized, plus people got in each other's way, impeding fire suppression. Afterward the men resumed their duties while the captain made his daily inspection of the ship's seven compartments. He was pleased to see nothing but asses and elbows, showing that the men were turned to for field day, cleaning and scrubbing the ship. The work in each compartment was overseen by a *michman* who knew how to train young submariners and keep them sharp. The captain lamented that the navy sorely needed more *michmen* like these, not more *zampoliti*.

The captain enjoyed participating in one of the rites of passage for all submariners. Several young sailors were summoned to the CCP, where the captain awarded them their qualifications in submarines and pinned the Soviet navy's submarine insignia on their uniforms. Then, in accordance with submarine tradition, each sailor drank from a tankard of seawater drawn from the Barents and swallowed a bite of hardtack. Each man had his picture taken with the captain and was presented with a scroll commemorating the event. While not as raucous as a Blue Nose ceremony, it livened up the deployment and solidified the camaraderie shared by the entire crew.

Twice a day the submarine came to periscope depth to receive messages from headquarters that concerned the deployment. Like

ComSubLant, Soviet submarine headquarters used the VLF band to communicate with submarines. VLF messages could be picked up just below the surface with a deployed floating wire antenna. The Soviets, like the Americans, retransmitted broadcasts to patrolling submarines several times a day to allow submarines that had been engaged in activities a chance to snag their messages. Failure to receive a regularly scheduled broadcast might be a signal that something serious had happened ashore—maybe war had broken out—in which case the submarine had to deploy an alternate means of communication and await further orders.

The broadcast contained no special instructions. While at periscope depth, the radio watch copied the latest news from around the world broadcast by the Voice of Peking or the BBC. Oddly, Radio Moscow was hard to receive. News from home was sketchy at best.

News broadcasts were copied and posted on a read board outside the messroom for the crew, which on a typical Russian submarine reflected the ethnic diversity of the USSR itself. Without news from home, food, money, and women were the main topics of discussion.

. . .

"Kapitan, a problem." The *starpom* looked grim. "The oxygen generator has gone out."

"Can it be fixed?"

The assistant mechanical engineer was deep into the generator's innards. A few days earlier there had been a problem with a circulating pump clogged by the discharge of garbage in a prohibited fashion. The garbage had been loaded into the garbage ejection tube loose instead of in the weighted waterproof bags intended for that purpose. The culprit had been punished, restricted when off watch to a small auxiliary compartment for a week on reduced rations, but the damage had been done. Now this. Like food, spare parts were in short supply.

The assistant mechanical engineer had worked a miracle on the pump, and the captain had confidence he'd fix the oxygen generator, too, but not without difficulty. The generator was already on borrowed time; some of its parts had been remanufactured by the ship's engineering gang. The generator was one of the most vital pieces of equipment aboard ship, and without it the deployment would come to an end. The thought of having to report a casualty that couldn't be repaired at sea gave the captain a chill. The assistant mechanical engineer would have to fix the generator, that was all there was to it.

"Report to me when it's fixed."

"Aye, Kapitan."

The air inside the ship seemed a touch stale when the captain received a decoded message from headquarters, ordering them to search an area for a possible unfriendly submarine contact. Unfriendly? What headquarters meant was that it had intelligence that a U.S. *Sturgeon*-class sub was prowling around inside the Barents. How such intelligence, whether from spies, satellites, AGIs, or a combination of all three, ended up at submarine headquarters wasn't the captain's business. His business was to locate the intruder, try to identify him, and run him out of the Barents. Better yet, embarrass him by proving he wasn't as clever—or silent—as he thought he was.

The area to be searched was close to a productive northern fishing ground used by Soviet as well as Norwegian and Finnish fishing fleets. The fleets were forbidden to enter waters in which Soviet submarines operated, but sometimes they ignored the rules. The captain, alerted to their presence by sonar, wasn't all that surprised to find them working in his op area, yet he swore; the presence of trawler fleets would complicate the search for the U.S. sub merely by the need to avoid getting caught in their trawl nets and deepwater tackle, to say nothing of the masking noise they put into the water with their engines. Well, fish go where they please and the fleets follow them, no matter what the rules are. If a *Sturgeon* was in the same area as the fishing fleet, it, too, would have to beware of their nets.

The captain chose to approach the op area from the east, assuming the intruder might be moving from the west, deeper into the Barents, aiming for the U.S. submarine op area off the Kola Inlet. The captain maneuvered slowly, sonar listening for anything suspicious. Was it possible to get the drop on a U.S. sub before he knew he had been detected? Not likely, but such a possibility was exciting.

A periscope view revealed trawlers flying the flags of several nations.

"Sonar?"

"Kapitan, just fish and trawlers."

"Keep listening."

The men were on edge, hoping for contact with an American sub. But how would they know they'd made contact? The trawlers made too much noise. No one, not even the captain, had ever heard a real U.S. submarine, only tape recordings of them used for training. Now that he thought about it, where had those tapes come from?

"Kapitan . . . possible sonar contact bearing two-eight-zero, faint."

"Blade rate?"

The sonarman shook his head no.

"Keep trying."

The Victor was pointing due west, which gave her bow sonar receiver unrestricted coverage of the area in question.

The captain paced the CCP.

"Nothing, Kapitan."

He took a seat in the pedestal chair and waited. Was it a sound anomaly or a real submarine? The layers played tricks on sonar. Was the American submarine out there listening to them? A *Sturgeon* even now might be close aboard and the Victor's sonar might not know it. He was tired of always playing the underdog. He saw now that he should have hit the contact with active sonar. If it had turned out to be a U.S. sub, it would send a message that the American submariners weren't invisible after all. If nothing else it would have made his own crew feel good, that they weren't spitting in the ocean for nothing.

"It's gone, Kapitan. I have no contact."

The contact had been on a westerly bearing. Maybe it still was. "Helm, new course two-eight-zero. Let's see what we can find."

15

DOWN UNDER

HUNTER, his mind working like a computer, lit yet another cigarette even though he had others burning in ashtrays scattered around the control room. So where was all the action? Had they overlooked a Soviet holiday? No, radio would have picked up chatter about it.

The bug under the plotting table had moved with the *Blackfin* to a position about twenty nautical miles north of the Kola Peninsula. Hunter had been on a racetrack course there most of the day waiting to snare whatever might exit the transit lanes. At 1300 an ESM sweep picked up something, a radar, a weak one, bearing due south of the *Blackfin*'s position.

Fifteen minutes later the 27MC squawked: "Conn, sonar. Got another sub."

Looking through the periscope the OOD reported visual contact with what appeared to be a surfaced Victor, classified as Sierra Fifteen. Hunter saw an opportunity to make a close-up underwater hull inspection of the Russian submarine, another evolution they had practiced prior to departure from New London. Back then the U.S. sub standing in for a Soviet one had made it relatively easy for the *Blackfin* to close in and make a hull survey. This was the real thing, and there was no guarantee the Soviet sub would hold still long enough for Hunter to complete an inspection.

Another element Hunter had to factor in was that shallow underwater visibility in the Barents Sea, even on a sunny day, was only about twenty-five to fifty feet. He would have to get up close and intimate with the Victor to videotape the sub's underwater body configuration, her propeller blades, and other vital parts through the periscope. Hunter knew this was cowboy stuff, that it was a high-risk evolution. Sure, it made great reading in the patrol report and sounded terrific in postpatrol debriefings, but it was still cowboy stuff. Moreover, since the opportunity didn't often present itself, it was seldom attempted or encouraged by ComSubLant. The decision to do it was left up to individual COs.

One motivating factor for Hunter was his curiosity about the Victor's features. In an earlier foray into the Barents another SSN had gotten a brief look at the underside of a Victor and the small propeller pods known as "spinners" fitted to the sub's stern diving planes' structure. Question was, what were they for? An emergency propulsion system? For maneuvering during mooring and docking? A secret silent drive mechanism? Conditions for surveillance had been poor, and they'd missed a chance to count spinner blades and accurately estimate their size and shape.

Another unanswered question was whether or not the rubberized anechoic tiles that covered the hulls of Victor-class submarines, to absorb active sonar, extended all the way to their keels. A videotaping might provide an answer.

Underwater surveillance of a submarine's hull demanded extraordinary shiphandling skills. Running submerged underneath a moving, surfaced sub—friend or foe—was a brass-balls evolution. One mistake—loss of depth control, too much speed, getting too close, or getting out of position—could result in a collision with the target or counter detection. A sub's spinning prop was like a giant buzz saw and could do a lot of damage. It went without saying that having a prop chew into steel hull plating would surely reveal the trailer's presence.

Hunter issued orders for the crew to cease any activities unrelated to the upcoming maneuver, especially any routine maintenance or adjustments to the power plant that might interrupt propulsion. Only the most essential activities were permitted.

Though the initial visual contact had provided the fire-control tracking party with a rough course, speed, and range estimate, Hunter maneuvered in behind the unsuspecting Victor and, as he had during the ASPL, began fishtailing to collect accurate data. Once he was satisfied he had an excellent solution on the Victor's motion, he inched up, slowly closing the gap between the *Blackfin* and the target. At two thousand yards Hunter ordered the *Blackfin* to periscope depth for a final visual check of the Victor. Flipping to high magnification, he saw men on the bridge; that was a good sign, an indication that she probably wasn't about to submerge.

"Okay, here we go," Hunter announced.

He ordered a change of depth to 120 feet and, with the scope all the way up, closed in.

The Victor's draft was a touch over twenty-three feet. With the *Blackfin* at 120 feet, the tip of her periscope would be less than forty feet away from the Victor's keel; not much wiggle room there.

Hunter put a control room telephone talker in direct contact with the throttleman at the ship's reactor controls back in the maneuvering room. Via the talker, Hunter started coaching the throttleman through a series of speed adjustments an rpm or two at a time, until the *Blackfin*'s speed matched the Victor's. Now came the tricky part. Hunter slowly increased speed an rpm or two at a time and, careful not to overshoot the target or get out of line, steered the *Blackfin* directly up the target's track.

As the range closed inside three hundred yards, sonar's depression-elevation angle rapidly increased until sonar bearings became so erratic they were next to useless. Now position control was critical. If Hunter overshot he'd have to fall back and start over, risking detection. Then there was that damn spinning prop, to say nothing of accidentally kissing the Victor's hull with the scope and snapping it off.

It was a challenge to keep the *Blackfin* in position relative to the target. Holding her there required incremental throttle adjustments. The throttleman had to rely on a sluggish and imprecise analog rpm indicator to adjust his speed. All it took was a light touch on the throttle to make the indicator jump up or down, or for the *Blackfin*, with her huge inertia, to slow down or plow ahead too fast. It was like two NASCAR racers drafting nose to tail at Daytona, the drafter six inches away from the draftee's back bumper.

Hunter might have felt like a cowboy, but he knew his business. His sub driver's skill was rewarded by the sight through the scope of a huge corkscrew of bubbles curling off the Victor's spinning prop. The sub's underwater hull showed up on the periviz video monitor as a long, dark, narrow shape, but it was too dark to see details like whether or not the anechoic tiles on the sub's hull extended to her keel or if any of them were missing. On close inspection the spinners that had caught his attention earlier looked to be an emergency maneuvering system and nothing more, not a secret silent drive mechanism.

Hunter, who had just completed a pretty neat trick, held position while sonar started archiving material at point-blank range. He made a mental note not to hang around under the Victor too long. No sense in overdoing it, especially if the Soviet submarine captain decided to submerge on top of the *Blackfin*. If he did, it would sure as hell ruin Hunter's day.

. . .

Under-hull surveillance of Soviet ships wasn't new. Nor were cowboy tactics. The British had played cowboy years ago when they sent a diver—a frogman, not a submarine—to surveil the hull of the Soviet cruiser *Ordzhonikidze* during her visit to England in April 1956. At the time, the plan seemed foolproof enough, but in typical fashion, it ended in disaster for Britain's MI6, who had concocted the scheme on their own.

Nikita Khrushchev and Nikolai Bulganin had arrived in Portsmouth, England, aboard the *Ordzhonikidze* for a series of meetings with Prime Minister Anthony Eden. MI6 believed the *Ordzhonikidze* had an advanced sound-canceling antisonar device installed on her hull, and propellers designed to mask her sound signature. Despite Eden's explicit orders that MI6 was not to undertake any clandestine operations that if discovered would embarrass the British government, they recruited Commander Lionel "Buster" Crabb, an overage former Royal Navy diver, to inspect the cruiser's hull.

Crabb and an MI6 controller worked out of a room in a hotel overlooking Portsmouth harbor, where the 14,500-ton *Ordzhonikidze* was moored. Crabb made a dive but had problems with his equipment and returned exhausted. He made a second dive the next day and was never seen alive again.

The British press soon broke the story. Though the British denied it, the Soviets were outraged that they had spied on them during their visit. A chagrined MI6 assumed that either the Soviets had discovered Crabb poking around under the *Ordzhonikidze* and killed him or that he had drowned.

Apparently Crabb had indeed been spotted by a sentry on the ship, but how he died remains a mystery. Speculation centered on his electrocution by antiswimmer devices. Investigators said no, that he was killed in a struggle with a Soviet frogman. The most likely explanation is that he died of heart failure.

A year later, what remained of Crabb's headless and handless body, still in its wetsuit, washed ashore. The Soviets eventually sold the *Ordzhonikidze* to the Indonesian navy, and MI6 agents finally had a chance to look her over; she turned out to be just another conventional warship with no special sonar gear or propellers.

• • •

How times change. It took only about a half hour for Hunter to make a full under-hull inspection of the Victor and to collect visual and audio data. Finished, Hunter slowed and dropped back to a safe distance behind the Soviet sub. Naturally the question arose: Where's this one headed, and what's it up to?

Hunter saw two possibilities. He could keep an eye on the sub and what might develop, perhaps a torpedo test or an exercise involving other ships in the immediate op area. Or, if the sub departed the op area and headed west, possibly for the North Atlantic, he could set up a trail that might provide useful information.

The trail option had drawbacks. If the Victor headed for the North Atlantic, Hunter would have to break radio silence to inform ComSubLant, who would then have to decide whether permitting the *Blackfin* to depart her op area would yield intelligence of sufficient importance to justify her absence. After all, she might be off on a trail mission of several days' or weeks' duration, and anyway, SOSUS would probably pick up the Victor, as they had the one Hunter had ID'd returning to the Barents, and trail her south.

Hunter knew the USS *Lapon* held the record for a trail of a Soviet sub, a Yankee she'd followed for an amazing forty-seven straight days without being detected. The *Blackfin* was unlikely to break the *Lapon*'s record, so Hunter scrubbed the trail idea. Better to break off and move on to better pickings.

"Captain, the Victor's slowing down," sonar reported. "Barely making steerage."

Surprised, Hunter ran the scope back up to discover that the sub had hove to. Hunter watched the Victor, lolling on the surface, apparently in no hurry to go anywhere. He saw men crammed into the cockpit atop the sail, sunbathing and smoking, shooting the breeze. Apparently the sub had arrived in its assigned area and was waiting for orders. Something was definitely up. Hunter moved away from the Victor so he could keep the scope up and surveil from a distance without being seen while monitoring radio, visual, and electronic data.

In a little while Hunter heard, "Conn, radio. He's waiting for someone, Captain. Possibly another sub."

"Torpedo exercise?"

"Yes, sir, might be, but can't confirm it yet. It's hard to grab anything definitive."

At length sonar reported another vessel approaching from the south. Then: "Hey, we're picking up chatter on the UQC," said Hunter. The *Blackfin* had intercepted underwater telephone comms between the sub and the approaching ship.

"What are they saying?"

"A torpedo firing exercise. The Victor's the shooter. There's another sub out there somewhere, probably the target."

Sure enough, Hunter spotted what looked like a *Poluchat-*I-class torpedo retriever. A diesel-powered craft equipped with a torpedo recovery ramp aft and a crane amidships, it approached and circled the surfaced Victor.

The Soviets, Hunter knew, expended a lot of effort and rubles on torpedo testing—and with good reason.

• • •

British engineer Robert Whitehead invented the torpedo in 1866. He called it the devil's weapon. In 1906, Admiral H. J. May, RN, said, "But for the Whitehead, the submarine would remain an interesting toy, and little more." True enough, but it was also true that Whitehead's invention bedeviled every navy that adopted it for use in their submarines, especially during World War II, when the United States and Germany were plagued with torpedoes that wouldn't explode when they hit targets.

The problems afflicting both German and U.S. submarine torpedoes centered around three main defects: faulty depth control, premature detonation of the warhead by the magnetic influence exploder, and a faulty contact exploder mechanism that produced duds. The Germans, banking that their U-boat campaign would defeat England, recognized as early as 1939 that their torpedoes had problems. Even so, it took almost two years to correct them. The standard torpedo employed by U.S. submarines, the Mk 14 steam torpedo, was plagued by the same problems, and it took the better part of two years to solve them, too.

The technical problems inherent in the Mk 14 were compounded by the refusal of certain senior commanders, both in-theater and in the Bureau of Ordnance, to acknowledge that the problems even existed. Instead they blamed them on what they said was the submariners' lack of training and skill. ComSubPac (Commander Submarines Pacific) Vice Admiral Charles Lockwood disagreed. He knew his submariners weren't at fault and that when they had reliable torpedoes they sank ships. Instead, they were risking their lives to fire duds. Lockwood, an innovator and problem solver, assembled a group of savvy submarine officers to fix the Mk 14's problems once and for all and to do it fast. The Japanese, after all, still had plenty of ships that needed sinking. After extensive testing, including live torpedo shots, the officers uncovered a nest of interrelated problems. It took them many more months of trial and error, including an extensive redesign of the Mk 14's depth-control and exploder mechanisms, before submariners finally had a weapon worthy of their skills and confidence.

As a footnote, in the 1950s, Hunter, then serving in a diesel sub, had had the opportunity to meet one of Germany's famous U-boat aces, Otto Kretschmer. Kretschmer, who had sunk forty-four Allied ships, admitted that German torpedoes had been plagued by the very same problems that had plagued U.S. torpedoes. Comparing notes with Kretschmer, Hunter also learned that U-boat operations and procedures had been strikingly similar to those in use in the wartime U.S. sub force, proving that all submariners are indeed members of a special brotherhood and that the differences in submarines themselves are only skin deep.

Also, the Soviets had torpedo problems similar to those plaguing the United States and Germany. Early on they had acquired a number of Whitehead torpedoes for their nascent submarine fleet. Using Whitehead's design, by World War I the Russians had manufactured thousands of their own torpedoes. During the interwar years they not only made improvements in basic torpedo design but also built torpedoes equipped with sophisticated magnetic triggers and wakeless electric drive. They even built an acoustic homing torpedo, a technology quite advanced for its time.

Early in the cold war, the Soviets concentrated on designing bigger and better torpedoes. While these torpedoes conformed to the Western standard twenty-one-inch specification, some carried heavier conventional warheads, and others had longer usable ranges than most U.S. and NATO torpedoes. The Soviets also developed a large, especially lethal wake-homing antiship torpedo. Fired from a submarine into the wake of a large warship like an aircraft carrier, the torpedo was designed to follow up the target's wake and detonate in its stern, destroying props and rudders and disabling the ship. It appeared that the only defense against this weapon was to station an expendable frigate behind each carrier.

Naturally the Soviets encountered problems with their torpedoes, which required extensive modification and constant refinement. A robust testing program was necessary to root out design flaws and malfunctioning components. Such a program had to be conducted at sea, an environment that was ideal for intel collection by Holystone subs.

· · ·

The fire-control coordinator informed Hunter that he had both the sub and torpedo retriever dialed in.

"Sonar? Anything on that other sub, the target?"

"Negative, Captain. Haven't located it yet."

Hunter concluded that the Victor's missing partner, potentially Sierra Seventeen, had to be a diesel sub running silent on batteries. "Keep looking," he urged.

The Soviets had a multitude of torpedoes in their arsenal. Most of them were older steam-driven torpedoes like the U.S. Navy's troublesome Mk 14. By contrast, their wire-guided STEST-68, with a hundred-kilogram warhead of Torpex or H-6, was one of their best weapons and therefore a high-priority target for intel collection. The spooks had their hands full recording unencrypted chitchat between the retriever and the sub while also trying to identify what type of torpedoes the Sovs were planning to test.

Hunter poked the periscope up to see what the torpedo retriever and the Victor were up to. Nothing much, it seemed, except waiting. "Down scope."

Sonar broke in. "Victor's submerging."

"Up scope!" Hunter grabbed the training handles and rode the scope up. "Where the hell's that other sub?" he bellowed as he watched the Victor's rounded sail vanish beneath the surface.

"Conn, sonar. I only have contact with Sierra Fifteen, the submerged Victor, bearing zero-seven-zero, and with Sierra Sixteen, the retriever, bearing zero-eight-five."

Hunter wanted contact with Sierra Seventeen, the mystery sub. He wasn't comfortable that another submarine was out there somewhere, still undetected. He wasn't thinking counterdetection but collision!

The *Blackfin* moved slowly on a course diverging from the submerged Victor to avoid counterdetection. If the Russian made a sudden, unexpected move toward the *Blackfin*, Hunter would have plenty of time to react. He knew only too well how dangerous it was to stick your nose into a nest of Soviet ships conducting exercises and how bad luck or a wrong move could turn the tables in the Soviets' favor.

Hunter had no sooner thought about this than sonar broke in with *"Torpedo in the water!"*

A loud roar from the UQC confirmed that a torpedo fired by the Victor was charging through the water at forty knots! But at whom?

This wasn't the attack teacher in New London, this was the real thing! Hunter's pulse rate soared. *It's only a firing exercise!* ran through his mind. *Unless . . . unless we're the target* . . . Before he could voice that thought, sonar broke in again: "Torpedo bearing one-three-five, moving right, opening out."

The torpedo was speeding *away* from the *Blackfin*, not toward her. Hunter heard a collective sigh of relief, saw the looks on the men's faces. He reached for a lit cigarette, inhaled deeply, then wiped his face on a sleeve.

After the torpedo had run its course and popped to the surface, the retriever hooked on and winched it aboard. Hunter decided to hang around at a safe distance to monitor the ongoing torpedo tests and sweep up comms on the unguarded Soviet voice circuits. *Just don't get counterdetected*, he reminded himself. *And don't eat a torpedo.*

Sonar finally had contact with the target submarine, Sierra Seventeen, a diesel boat on batteries just as Hunter had suspected. The two subs rendezvoused, then spent the next several hours tracking each other and firing dummy practice torpedoes. Most of them were older gas-turbine hydrogen-peroxide-fueled 53–65 active-passive acoustic-homing torpedoes. Others were unidentifiable. Several torpedoes failed to run properly, their sputterings and warblings duly recorded by sonar.

Later in the day the two subs and the retriever headed for the barn. Hunter had been on his feet for hours and needed a breather. He'd drunk a gallon or two of strong navy coffee and smoked two packs of Lucky Strikes. He needed a shower and a fresh poopie suit. (Officers and some enlisted men wore lightweight cotton-polyester coveralls called poopie suits; the engineering gang wore dungarees, which were cooler.) Tonight's movie was *Bullitt*, one of his favorites. He liked Steve McQueen and the car chase through San Francisco. He could taste the popcorn already.

16

SNOOPERS

IT WAS FRIDAY AFTERNOON. After the torpedo test, Soviet activity had slowed; ships returned to port for the weekend, their sailors hungry for liberty even though Severomorsk had little to offer. Hunter took advantage of the lull and pulled back about fifty miles from the coast to give the crew of the *Blackfin* a breather. Though the ship was still on full alert, the men had a chance to catch up on housekeeping, sleep, and maintenance while continuing to monitor comms, hoping something interesting would show up. Hunter and the XO spent time reviewing the patrol report to date, making sure nothing had been overlooked in the heat of conducting operations. As always, the ship's quartermasters had done an excellent job of keeping their logs current and accurate.

The crew also enjoyed some good meals, the cooks serving up shrimp and pork dishes and one of Hunter's favorites, chicken adobo. The adobo and the corned beef served aboard the *Blackfin* could not be equaled anywhere ashore or afloat, Hunter declared.

Yet Holystone sailors could remain inactive for only so long. Late Sunday afternoon, the *Blackfin* was back in position near the Kola Inlet, the intel teams' tape recorders ready to record SIGINT from ship and shore radars and from ship and aircraft comms. As always, SIGINT was the primary take. Hunter was itching for something more—a fleet exercise would do just fine—but after the torpedo exercise, come Monday morning, the Soviet navy seemed to have pulled a disappearing act. As he watched and waited, not a single ship sortied. An area that had been so busy had suddenly gone cold.

Around noon of the *Blackfin*'s second day back on station, sonar picked up heavy screw beats in the direction of the inlet. The OOD reported that a medium-sized oceanographic research ship had hove into view. Hunter monitored its movements for a while, but when the ship turned northeast, toward Novaya Zemlya, he broke off contact and resumed patrolling around the Kola Inlet. Two hours later, long-range contact with a Be-12 Mail amphibian patrol plane's search radar drove the *Blackfin* deep. Later still, a trio of destroyers in company with a provisions ship appeared just inside the twelve-mile limit steaming west, apparently from the White Sea. The *Blackfin* swung onto a long racetrack course while Hunter studied the navigation charts looking for possibilities.

The coastline of the Kola Peninsula was studded with harbors and inlets. The Soviets had a base at Varzino for auxiliaries and coastal patrol craft, but not major combatants or submarines. Gremikha had dry docking and ship repair facilities but lacked military installations of the type that had powerful search radars and comm centers. Hunter reminded the spooks to look for unidentified sites that might be emitting signals that were new and different from those that had been recorded by other Holystone subs.

At noon on a day that had so far been unproductive, the crew sat down to a meal of curried chicken and rice, another of Hunter's favorites. Rested, relaxed, Hunter was in the mood for a few hands of poker.

The wardroom phone chirped.

"Captain," said the OOD, "sonar's picked up echo-ranging. Sounds like a surface ship, bearing two-six-zero."

Hunter, glad to be distracted from a lousy hand, said, "Anything else besides echo-ranging on that bearing?"

"Picking up three-hundred-hertz tonals on both sides of the surface ship. Sounds like more than one ship. Might be a couple of Type IIs out there."

Hunter folded. "Very well, I'll have a listen."

As Hunter arrived in the control room, the OOD reported that the targets' range had closed: The pinging had gotten louder. Hunter listened to it, then said, "All right, let's find them and take a look."

It didn't take long. The OOD made visual contact with a large warship on a northeast heading. He identified the ship by her profile as a *Kresta*-class cruiser. Sonar identified the other two targets as submerged Type II submarines.

Kresta-class cruisers were handsome ships with raked knifelike bows and low freeboard, their uptakes, stacks, and radar towers massed amidships. Designed on a crash schedule for an ASW and sea power projection role, they never received the weaponry they needed to be effective in that role. Still, they carried potent antiaircraft and antiship missiles.

After watching the *Kresta* through the scope and studying her two submerged consorts' tracks, which plot had been updating ever since making initial contact with them, Hunter concluded that the trio was engaged in a demonstration of some sort, or possibly a rehearsal for anticarrier operations. The Soviets had understood early in the cold war that U.S. aircraft carriers, with their deep-strike capabilities, posed a serious threat to targets inside Soviet territory as well as seaborne operations. While a U.S. carrier battle group had the speed to outrun and evade attacks by Soviet diesel submarines, the advent of nuclear subs with their higher speeds changed the picture drastically. Soviet nuclear submarines armed with antiship missiles could now keep up with a fast-moving carrier battle group. Even though carriers were well protected by their escorts of surface ships and attack submarines, a fast hostile sub could position herself far ahead of the carrier's track, wait for her to arrive, then attack even if detected by the carrier's escorts. If such an attack failed, it was always possible that a determined Soviet sub commander willing to make a suicide run could bore in, pierce the escort screen, and launch torpedoes.

The threat to U.S. carriers from Soviet submarines had grown as the U.S. Navy found itself engaged in operations off Vietnam and focused on the tempo of its air ops and the priority funding those ops demanded. Investment in ASW no longer had the urgency it once had. The Soviets, quick to take advantage of the situation, saw an opportunity to exploit the U.S. Navy's vulnerabilities and began to concentrate on developing more effective anticarrier tactics for their submarines, some now armed with wake-homing torpedoes.

What Hunter was watching and what the spooks were recording might give intel analysts at NSA and ONI an insight into what kind of anticarrier tactics the Soviets had developed and how to neutralize them. As the trio moved steadily northeastward, however, it proved extremely difficult to track three widely dispersed targets at the same time and also to stay out of their way while trying to make sense of what exactly was unfolding.

Running a TMA plot via sonar on the two slow-moving submerged subs, with their correspondingly low bearing rates, was a real test for the fire-control tracking party, whereas with the *Kresta*, they had visual bearings and ranges to go on. The active Soviet sonars, one each from the subs and another from the *Kresta*, were an aid to target tracking, though Hunter found it was easier to keep track of them on the plotting table as he had earlier than by looking at data displayed on the fire-control system.

As he and the fire-control team watched the exercise unfold over the course of several hours, the two subs practiced moving into positions behind the *Kresta*, standing in for a U.S. carrier, then made mock attacks from astern and from either beam. Hunter observed that there were no air operations to direct the attacks and seemingly no coordination between the two subs. It all seemed rather haphazard, the subs trading places and maneuvering around willy-nilly, each sub needing more than two hours to gain position and carry out an attack—an extremely cumbersome set of exercises. It hardly seemed possible that the tactics the Soviets were practicing could pose a threat to a real U.S. carrier battle group. Nonetheless, if nothing else, it proved that the Soviets were committed to anticarrier operations, which they treated as the cornerstone of their overall defensive posture at sea.

Even as the spooks monitored the *Kresta* op, like a big ear they swept the Soviets' other operational frequencies, on the lookout for any upcoming events of interest. Late in the day the radio watch picked up something interesting translated from plain-language Russian.

The intel team's officer in charge explained. "Captain, sounds to me like a version of a notice to mariners to stay out of that missile test area the Soviets use around Kildin Island," he said.

"So's not to become a target," Hunter added.

"That's my guess."

The quartermaster of the watch plotted the coordinates for the area identified in the message to be avoided by ships and aircraft, both commercial and military. It encompassed a region fanning northward for three hundred miles from Kildin Island through an arc of some seventy-five degrees.

Hunter waved the message. "This missile test, it's due to commence in forty-eight hours."

The team officer read the message again to make sure. "Yes, sir. It says forty-eight hours."

Hunter toggled a mike switch. "Radio, conn. Break out some fresh tape reels."

. . .

Hours after a slow transit out of the area where the *Kresta* and the two submerged submarines had been conducting anticarrier ops, Hunter came to PD twenty miles off Kildin Island. Home to yelping seals and flocks of squawking gulls, Kildin was a rough-hewn lump of rock hard on the coast approximately twenty-five miles east of the Kola Inlet. The air around it virtually stank of desolation. Looking and listening, Hunter watched a small flotilla of ships heave into view on the horizon.

Missile testing of any kind, tactical or strategic, was always presaged by heightened communications on circuits used by the Soviets for that purpose. As the time for the missile test drew near, the volume of comms increased the way it did prior to an Apollo launch at Cape Kennedy. Listening in, the spooks confirmed that the Sovs were going to test surface-to-surface missiles fired by submarines. Hunter, a step ahead of the spooks, had already visually identified three submarines moving into position: a diesel-electric Juliet SSG and two nuclear-powered Echo II SSGNs, all capable of launching P-5 and P-6 antiship missiles. The missiles had to be fired while the subs were surfaced, not submerged, which meant the entire launch sequence could be captured on videotape.

Hunter eased on in.

It wasn't necessary to get right on top of the test since the intel the spooks wanted was primarily missile telemetry data and, secondarily, video of the launch and the launching submarines themselves. Sometimes the spooks got lucky and ended up with data they didn't expect to get—or to understand, but when analyzed and correlated to various parts of the recorded event, it would make sense.

Hunter cautioned that everyone had to be alert not to miss anything. From experience he knew how easy it was to miss a launch. For one thing, there were so many covered and uncovered circuits that the spooks might not know which one was transmitting the countdown until it was too late. When the missile took off, Hunter didn't want to be caught in the middle of taking a spin with the scope to make sure the *Blackfin* hadn't been counterdetected. Without a heads-up, he might not even see the launch. Compared to an SLBM, which lumbers relatively slowly into the air, surface-to-surface missiles are airborne in seconds.

As Hunter moved in, he saw planes and helicopters buzzing over the test range. If he wasn't careful and allowed his enthusiasm about gathering intel to overcome prudence and good judgment, there was a damn good chance they'd be counterdetected. How far in did he dare press? He had to balance scope exposure time, which permitted greater signal capture, against risk of counterdetection. As it was, it was hard to keep track of all the aircraft he could see, much less search for those he didn't see. The periscope's ESM had been lit up like a Christmas tree ever since arrival, but it couldn't detect aircraft overhead with their radars shut down. Hunter wiped his face; he felt like he had a three-ring circus on his hands, one second searching for aircraft, another second monitoring a missile test, another listening to intership and underwater telephone comms, all at the same time he was trying not to get counterdetected.

So far so good . . .

"Conn, sonar; we have a launch!" The spooks had picked up the launch cadence over an uncovered circuit.

Hunter spun the scope around, almost buzzing past a spurt of flame. An instant later a dartlike object shot from one of the raised paired missile canisters aboard one of the Echo IIs, enveloping the sub in a billowing cloud of white smoke.

In quick succession the sub fired three more missiles. They accelerated so fast that Hunter had a hard time tracking them with the scope as they arced out of sight over the horizon, presumably heading for a target barge at the northern terminus of the restricted zone.

The test of missiles designed to attack surface targets, coupled with the earlier mock anticarrier exercise against the *Kresta* cruiser, clearly confirmed the Soviets' intention to build a credible strike force to counter U.S. aircraft carriers capable of launching nuclear attacks on the Soviet Union. Fresh intel on the latest P-5 and P-6 missiles' speed, range, thrust, and guidance package would add to the growing body of data the United States needed to develop weapons needed to counter the threat they posed.

The missile tests continued until late afternoon, when the subs and surface ships headed for home. The intel take had been voluminous. Through adroit shiphandling and prudent mast exposure, and by not pressing his luck, Hunter had avoided counterdetection. If the Soviets had suspected an intruder was snooping on the tests, they'd have pounced.

Satisfied with the take, Hunter cleared the area to regroup and give everyone a breather. It had been a draining experience tracking all the targets and recording the missile launches. A lot of information had to be prepared for inclusion in the patrol report, and the spooks had to consolidate their take and log it all in. All hands welcomed another break in the action, but there was still a lot of work to do.

17

CAT AND MOUSE

ABOARD THE SOVIET VICTOR, vigilance and quick thinking averted disaster. A sailor had discovered an overheated transformer and took action to prevent a fire. The engineers shut down the transformer and made repairs. An inspection indicated that had the sailor not acted immediately, the transformer would have burst into flames. The captain was delighted that the sailor, a crew member for only a short time, hadn't hesitated to act. He congratulated him and informed the others that they had a hero in their midst. Later, he wrote up a report recommending the sailor for a medal.

The days wore on. For relaxation, the crew took turns watching a movie on a screen set up in the crew's lounge. The lounge, apart from the mess, was cramped but better than those found in older submarines, especially diesel boats, where movies, in the rare event there were any to show, had to be screened in the torpedo room on a bedsheet hung between the tubes. The sailors liked Western movies, especially American cowboy films.

The captain, meanwhile, faced a new problem: food. More than half of the meager supply of scarce fresh produce had rotted. This after a detail of the ship's conscripts had spent time, before sailing, gathering produce from one of the few collective farms in the north. What else had gone bad? The precious but limited quantities of fresh milk? How about the eggs and cheese? The boneless chicken breasts? It called for a good chewing out of the senior supply warrant officer. The cooks, too, shared the blame for improper stowage and handling of food stores. The captain contained his anger but wondered, *What next?*

What next? His thoughts turned to the ship's twin nuclear reactors in their shielded compartment amidships, aft of the CCP. The Soviets used two reactors for reliability and to produce more power. Like those on American submarines, they were fueled with enriched uranium. The level of enrichment was lower than U.S. naval reactors, which were enriched to over 90 percent. Soviet naval reactors worked on principles similar to U.S. naval reactors, though with fewer safety features. Coolant leaks and near-meltdowns of the reactors' cladded fuel pellets were all too common. Equipment failures were also common—witness the faulty transformer—which is why the captain had taken steps to ensure his crew knew how to react to casualties and make repairs. At one time or another he'd had every officer aboard ship, regardless of his duties, enter the reactor compartment when it was safe to do so, to get a better understanding of its piping, valves, and controls. For those officers not nuclear trained, it scared the hell out of them, but they gained instant respect for, as they put it, "the machine that makes the submarine go."

Still, he had serious concerns about his officers' qualifications in nuclear propulsion. Like himself, too many of the officers under his command were overage, having been mired in the strangled promotion bureaucracy. The good ones had been trained early and now were almost too old to undergo the rigors of sixty-day patrols at sea. Men to replace them had been pulled off of nuclear-powered icebreakers and put aboard submarines with little special training.

Well, this was a new Project 671 submarine, a Victor, not some old tub with a failing reactor and a leaky hull. Maybe she wasn't the equal of a *Sturgeon*, but close. The new Project 671RTs on the building ways would be better than a *Sturgeon*, so he had heard. All the same, the captain made a mental note to double up on the reactor casualty drills just in case.

. . .

The elusive sonar contact first reported around the fishing grounds never materialized. The captain continued patrolling the area he'd been assigned earlier by headquarters, alert to possibilities. According to his op order, the area wasn't known to have been seeded with American SOSUS hydrophones. Whether or not that was true, no one knew for sure. There had been speculation that the United States had submarines capable of laying cable and SOSUS nodes on the sea floor. If so, SOSUS could be tracking them now, which might account for the loss of the earlier contact. Then again, maybe not. So much was unknown. It was like two blindfolded men swinging baseball bats at each other, hoping to hit something.

Passive sonar hadn't picked up a thing for days, not even a merchantman. Sometimes the periscope watch spotted a NATO P-3 Orion sub hunter, one of those land-based four-engine turboprop aircraft with sonobuoys and a MAD stinger in their tails. On a few occasions sonar heard a NATO ASW ship on patrol south of Bear Island, but that was an unusual event, as NATO warships rarely strayed out of the Greenland and Norwegian seas.

To break the boredom, the captain held more drills and training for junior officers and conscripts alike. The training stressed proficiency in watchstanding skills and how to deal with emergencies—like the overheated transformer—and real-world problems that demanded informed decision making.

During one of these drills, sonar reported contact with a freighter headed south. The drill immediately broke up as men took their positions in the CCP to work attack problems on a real "target." Nevertheless the drills had paid off, for the next day sonar picked up a NATO ASW ship towing a sonar array. The captain kept his distance while the attack team practiced firing "torpedoes" at it.

At midnight in the mess room, a sailor marked another day off the calendar: There was still a long way to go before returning home.

•   •   •

Next morning, the captain received a radio message with orders to cease patrolling the area they were in and proceed to a torpedo test range north northwest of Kildin Island, an area off the Rybachiy Peninsula, a mass of fog-shrouded black and gray rock that was home to seal rookeries and flapping gulls.

The captain felt he was on a short leash. One minute submarine command needed a unit to track and find U.S. subs in the Barents, the next minute they needed a unit to participate in a torpedo firing exercise. It was the consequence of operating so close to home, where the admirals thought nothing of moving their assets around like chess pieces on a board. Go here, go there. The captain was just getting comfortable scouring the area they were in for U.S. submarines, now this. In fact, he'd become convinced that a U.S. sub was out there dogging them, and with time and patience, he believed, he could find it. His reports to headquarters of a possible contact with an unidentified submarine had so far gone unanswered. He envied the American sub commanders' freedom of movement, their confidence, their cowboy tactics. Of course, they didn't have a *zampolit* looking over their shoulder.

The navigator shaped a course for the torpedo test range, a run of just a few hours' duration but one requiring a careful sonar search of the area they would pass through. The captain issued orders to clear baffles every hour. It would slow them down but had to be done; an American submarine could be on their tail and they might not know it. He also called away the attack team with instructions to tune up on the Victor's fire-control system. No one wanted to stumble during a torpedo exercise that would likely have several high-ranking officers critiquing the results. Bad enough the *zampolit* would report any miscues.

Arriving in the test range, they rendezvoused with two destroyers and a torpedo retriever. Another submerged submarine stood by to participate in the exercise. Comms between ships over underwater telephones and uncovered tactical radio frequencies were kept to a minimum, but still there was enough chatter for a snooping U.S. sub to pick up if one were in the test area. Helicopters patrolled overhead, but they had limited means of keeping intruders away. If a U.S. sub wanted to snoop on them in international waters, the captain knew, there was no way to prevent it.

The attack team didn't embarrass themselves or the captain. They conducted a series of torpedo tests that pleased even the *zampolit*. Best of all, they avoided detection by the destroyers playing the roles of U.S. destroyers, which as such had to endure the embarrassment of having their hulls bruised by repeated impacts from dummy torpedoes.

The captain observed, but didn't say, that the prescribed attack procedures they were using proved too cumbersome and rigid. They relied too heavily, as did most Soviet naval tactics, on unproven theories and assumptions about how U.S. warships would react when under attack. The captain knew from practical experience, gained during earlier patrols as a junior officer aboard a diesel submarine during the Cuban missile crisis, that the U.S. Navy's tactics were flexible and unpredictable. He knew that a real confrontation would require the use of antiship missiles and that it would be difficult if not impossible to penetrate an American ASW screen and press home a conventional torpedo attack on, say, an aircraft carrier—unless, of course, the sub commander was willing to engage in kamikaze tactics. Nevertheless, the fact that there had been no complaints by the task force commander or the *zampolit* meant he and his crew had done well. Tonight there'd be a double ration of wine for the men with their dinner. The cooks had promised to prepare a special meal topped off with a favorite dessert, canned strawberry-filled *piroschki*.

There was little time for self-congratulation, though. Another message from headquarters: The submarine had been shifted to an ASW exercise a hundred miles east of the torpedo exercise range. Soviet ships and planes needed a stand-in for a NATO submarine trying to penetrate an ASW barrier. Headquarters provided the coordinates of the exercise area. No acknowledgment required.

The submarine reached her holding area the next day at noon and awaited further orders. The radio watch rode the bands for news and possible action updates on other frequencies used by surface ships for some inkling of what the ASW team was up to.

"Kapitan, sonar."

"Submarine contact?"

"Yes, I think with an American. Faint, not close. Comes and goes."

The captain wasn't surprised. Had they been followed? For how long? Baffle clearing every hour hadn't picked up the American. He didn't want to be blamed for allowing an intruder to ride his tail into an ASW exercise. As it was, the *zampolit* was fuming over the contact. *The hell with him*, the captain thought. *Let's see if we can find this American and nail him with active sonar, watch him haul out.* Then the ASW team would have a real target to practice on, not a stand-in.

"He's gone, Kapitan. No contact."

The captain weighed whether or not to alert headquarters that they'd had another possible contact with an American submarine. After mulling this over, he decided not to report it. Too iffy. Unless he had proof it was a legitimate target, he'd only ruffle the admirals' feathers and make himself look bad. Plus, he'd have to clear it with the *zampolit*, who would pull a sour face.

The *zampolit* made the decision for him. "Alert the task force," he ordered.

It was like shoving a stick into an anthill. Pandemonium broke out as the task force dispersed, their active sonars lit up. It was a mad melee of ships and helos careening this way and that, on the hunt for an intruder.

One that got away.

Hours later all that the sonar watch could do was report—nothing. Just pinging from their own ships, and even that had died down. Even the *zampolit* admitted that they had been bested.

By morning the task force had regrouped. The helos were low on fuel. So, too, was one of the *Petya* frigates. Plus, the weather had closed in from the north. Blinker signals from the flagship calling off the exercise went out to all the ships: Return to port.

Told they were returning to Polyarnyy, the crew didn't try to hide their delight from the *zampolit*, who growled that such a shortened cruise had been wasteful—wasteful of food stores and, as he called it, atomic power. The ship could have easily stayed on patrol another forty or more days.

. . .

The submarine entered the Kola Inlet accompanied by seagulls. A tug waited at the berth in Polyarnyy, ready to give an assist warping in. This time there were no thumping drums and booming tubas. Just the waiting families, some with children in prams— who had told them the ship's arrival schedule?—and a group of burly linehandlers. The captain saw his wife and children and waved. Even though they had been to sea for only a short time, it was a joy to be home, even if home was Polyarnyy. But how long before he would be waving good-bye again? And what was waiting for him ashore? New orders? A reprimand? He'd done the best he could, carried out his duties as ordered. Was it enough? What could he say about the phantom submarine contact? Had she gotten away, far away? Or was she still out there waiting for him to return and start the game all over again?

18

FIRE IN THE DEEP

"**CAPTAIN.**" The executive officer caught up to Hunter in the wardroom. "Priority from ComSubLant."

Hunter scanned the message.

////INDICATIONS SOV ICBM TESTS UNDER WAY
IN BARENTS SEA ////

There was more.

According to ComSubLant, a new type of ICBM was scheduled to be launched from a modified Yankee SSBN operating in the Soviets' missile test range north of Kildin Island. SLBMs were launched in a southeasterly direction, toward the Soviet nuclear test site at Semipalatinsk, on the steppe in the Kazakh SSR, a distance of approximately 2,100 miles. According to ComSubLant, the missile to be launched was possibly solid-fueled, not liquid-fueled, and therefore had a very high data-collection priority.

Hunter was to stand by for a clarification of the launch schedule and for further orders.

This was an important operation. Hunter knew that though the Soviets continued to rely on unstable liquid-fueled missiles, should they deploy a long-range, solid-fueled ICBM similar to the U.S. Polaris, with its greater safety and reliability, to say nothing of its quick-launch ability, it could alter the current strategic balance between the two countries and give the Soviets a powerful new position from which to bargain during the SALT talks. It could also have a serious affect on the Nixon-Brezhnev summit.

. . .

For years U.S. intelligence agencies had watched the development of Soviet SLBMs. They paid special attention to the liquid-fueled SS-N-6, a single-stage submarine-launched weapon that had been introduced in 1968, shortly after Yankee-class SSBNs, from which they were designed to be launched, started entering the fleet. The SS-N-6 had a one-megaton nuclear warhead and a range of 1,300 nautical miles.

Hunter, an expert on Soviet missiles, knew from prior intel briefings that the Soviets had been racing to develop a solid-fueled long-range SLBM. Now it seemed that they had succeeded. It made sense that if they were planning to use a modified Yankee as a launch platform they would test a solid-fueled variant of the SS-N-6 that had the range necessary to reach Semipalatinsk or, by comparison, America's heartland. If so, the United States needed all the intelligence it could get on this new missile's capabilities, particularly its reliability and accuracy. Satellites and ground stations couldn't collect all the needed launch data or videotape the launching from inside the missile test range. That was a job for the *Blackfin* and her crew.

Waiting for more intel from ComSubLant, Hunter pored over charts of the Barents Sea missile test range at Kildin. A brass balls op, if ever there was one: Slip in under the Sovs' noses and don't get caught doing it; snatch what you were ordered to snatch and haul ass out. One look at the charts made it clear that this time the *Blackfin* would have to slip inside the USSR's twelve-mile territorial limit to do her work.

Waters around the amoeba-shaped Kildin ran to about six hundred feet, plenty of room for submerged operations by Holystone subs. Nevertheless, Hunter would be operating in an area dangerously close to the forbidden three-mile limit, where a simple error of navigation could spell trouble. Certainly the mission would test Hunter's seamanship. Avoiding counterdetection would be paramount. If the *Blackfin* were detected inside the twelve-mile limit, much less the three-mile limit, all hell would break loose. He could just picture all the ships pouring out of the Kola Inlet and the ASW blanket they'd throw over the area. Hunter didn't need to review his op order's rules of engagement; he had that part memorized: Use of defensive weapons was authorized only if absolutely necessary to repel an attack. Hunter, looking at the chart, couldn't help think that nosing around Kildin could be like entering a loaded bear trap.

However, he could count on the *Blackfin*'s inherent stealth to give him the same advantage submarine aces Günther Prien, Gene Fluckey, and George Street had had in World War II. (See Appendix Three.)

In a classic example of submarine stealth, on a moonless night in October 1939, Kapitänleutnant Günther Prien sneaked the surfaced *U-47* into Scapa Flow, the British Home Fleet's main base of operations inside the Orkney Islands north of Scotland. Skillfully avoiding the dangers posed by treacherous currents and primitive antisubmarine defenses, Prien torpedoed the HMS *Royal Oak*, a 39,000-ton dreadnought. The ship exploded and sank, taking down with her 833 British sailors. Two hours after entering Scapa Flow, the *U-47* had escaped without a trace into the North Sea.

The loss of the *Royal Oak* was a huge blow to the Royal Navy. In Germany, Prien—hailed as the Ghost of Scapa Flow—and his daring crew were welcomed home as heroes.

Not to be outdone by Prien, in early 1945 U.S. Navy Commander Gene Fluckey, the daring CO of the USS *Barb*, tracked two Japanese ships into the shallow and mined Namkwan harbor on the coast of China. Using a fleet of junks for cover, Fluckey, employing stealth, surprise, and luck, found a convoy of more than thirty ships at anchor, a solid wall of targets ripe for torpedoing!

Fluckey fired away. Ships erupted in flames and sank. Pandemonium broke out as Japanese gunners opened fire at a fleet of phantom bombers winging over the harbor. Meanwhile the *Barb*, later known as the Galloping Ghost of the China Coast, untouched and broken-field-running through the junks, hightailed it out of the harbor to deep water, leaving behind a scene of utter devastation. For his exploit, Fluckey was awarded the Medal of Honor.

Like Fluckey, Lieutenant Commander George Street, CO of the USS *Tirante*, saw an opportunity to wreak havoc of his own on the Japanese. In April 1945, using stealth, surprise, and determination, Street took the *Tirante* up a thirty-mile-long channel into an anchorage deep inside Quelpart Island off Korea that was teeming with Japanese ships. Under cover of darkness, Street selected his targets and fired torpedoes. Explosions and blinding white flames lit up the night; Japanese guns opened up all over the harbor, sometimes shooting at each other.

Like Fluckey in the *Barb*, Street turned the *Tirante* on her heel and, dodging patrol boats, sped for deep water, leaving behind a harbor filled with flaming, sinking ships. Once again Street had proved what a submarine and her crew could accomplish under even the most difficult circumstances. Like Fluckey, Street was awarded the Medal of Honor.

Given what Hunter was attempting, no one would have blamed him if instead of thinking about Prien, Fluckey, and Street, he thought about U-2 pilot Francis Gary Powers. But Hunter believed in action, not hand-wringing. Success, not failure. If ever Hunter was faced with a daunting challenge, this was it.

. . .

In a holding pattern waiting for more intel, Hunter continued the mission. He picked up another sub in the Kola Inlet–White Sea transit lane, a candidate for an underwater hull surveillance. Hunter tucked in and gave the Victor a good once-over from below, mindful that he was pushing his luck with this evolution. He completed two more ASPLs, one on a Yankee, another on a Charlie, before the radio message with information he was waiting for arrived.

> ////SLBM TEST IMMINENT//LIKELY A.M.
> TOMORROW EARLIEST//AFTER LAUNCH DATA
> IS SECURED BLACKFIN WILL TERMINATE
> OPERATIONS AND DEPART OP AREA////

Just as important as having intel on the missile's performance and throw-weight specifications was knowing whether or not the missile launch itself had been successful. When a test launch of a Soviet missile went awry, when it blew up on the launch pad or veered out of control, sometimes even hitting populated areas and killing civilians, Soviet officials nevertheless claimed that the USSR's ballistic missile program was a total success and that new ICBMs, even those that had failed or didn't exist but were only in the early stages of development, were about to be deployed. All the more reason for the *Blackfin* to witness and record the upcoming missile test.

If Hunter hadn't had more important things on his mind he might have pondered how information about a top-secret Soviet missile test had gotten into the U.S. intel pipeline in the first place. How it did wasn't his business, of course; his business was to collect and deliver intelligence, nothing else. Still, it was a question of more than just passing interest.

. . .

Collecting usable intelligence from deep inside the Soviet Union's military complex was an immensely difficult task. Unlike the passive collection of SIGINT and ELINT, penetration of the Red Army's and Soviet navy's inner sanctum required action on the ground by spies working for the United States. In the spook business, these agents were known as HUMINT—human intelligence. Spying on the Soviet Union was dangerous, sometimes deadly, work, and it took a lot more than just airdropping trained agents into the USSR or slipping them over controlled borders to count ships, planes, and tanks. It took time (lots of time) and patience (lots of patience) and money (lots of money) to recruit an official working inside the Kremlin with detailed knowledge of the Soviet military to spy for the U.S.

The USSR was a closed society with a ruthless secret police network and a political system that imposed severe restrictions on movement by citizens and noncitizens alike. Even before the cold war, most penetrations of the USSR by agents posing as native

Russians and working for U.S. intelligence—the old OSS and, later, the CIA—had failed; the agents were caught, were killed, or disappeared without a trace. The few who evaded detection and survived to carry out their missions often had little to show for their efforts simply because it was too difficult for them to penetrate the wall of secrecy surrounding every aspect of Soviet life, much less its sprawling military machine.

During the cold war, HUMINT ops directed at the USSR had been run on a parallel track with intel collection from the aircraft, ships, and satellites that overflew or ringed the Russian landmass. Intel collection by technical means had proven successful, but the collected data often lacked the insights necessary for analysts to make informed decisions about Soviet intentions. In other words, it lacked the detail and specificity that only a person on the ground can offer. While much of the intel delivered by spies working inside the Soviet Union proved of limited value, every now and then a breakthrough occurred, and highly valuable information worked its way out of the dark heart of the USSR to those in charge of Holystone.

So where did the best HUMINT intel come from? Hadn't the KGB run to ground just about every spy the United States ever had in Russia? Even the CIA admitted that their HUMINT failures far exceeded their successes. Nonetheless, there was a small number of dedicated and intrepid Western spies in Moscow whose cover had not been blown. Perhaps one of them was a trusted upper-level bureaucrat working in the GRU—Soviet military intelligence—or a midlevel KGB operative who'd been turned and was working under deep cover for the CIA. Perhaps the GRU bureaucrat had come across information about an upcoming Soviet missile test in the north. Perhaps the intel had found its tortured way to a dead drop, where it had been retrieved by someone working for the United States and willing to risk arrest. Landing on a desk at the CIA, NSA, or ONI, the intel began its trip up the pipeline and eventually to the *Blackfin*.

. . .

Full dark.

As the *Blackfin* approached the twelve-mile limit north of Kildin, Hunter manned the scope searching for the Soviet patrol boats sonar had picked up. There! Red and green navigation lights marked a pair of *Petya*s maneuvering at a distance from the *Blackfin*.

Easing toward the test range, sonar picked up the buzz of more ships and their screws. Away toward Kildin, Hunter saw navigation lights, some moving, some not. Radio reported hearing chatter about the missile test over open voice comms but nothing that nailed down the exact time and location of the launch.

Near dawn, with sonar contacts on almost every compass bearing, Hunter, ears and eyeballs alert, poked the scope up and saw more *Petya*s patrolling in a haphazard fashion, apparently unconcerned about the possibility of uninvited snoopers.

Hunter eased the *Blackfin* deeper into the test range at walking speed. The watchstanders in the control room, some with sweat-darkened poopie suits, felt the tension build; Hunter himself was on a third pack of Lucky Strikes.

Minutes passed. So far so good. The crypto team was eavesdropping on the riot of voice and radio signals buzzing around the launch site, confident that something was going to happen soon. Their priority intelligence sweep was going to be video and unencrypted launch telemetry; the secondary take would cover intership communications and underwater telephone chatter from the missile-launching sub.

For Hunter, the challenge now was to remain invisible while

capturing data, no small trick what with sniffing *Petya*s, plus those helos flying around over the launch area with their radars off, which prevented them from being tracked with ESM. Hunter had no choice but to bore in. To get good coverage of the missile's initial launch phase, the *Blackfin* had to be close to the action. To avoid detection, Hunter had to balance periscope exposure to maximize data capture against the risk of exposure. It was getting lighter, and a periscope sticking out of the water kicking up a feather was a prescription for counterdetection. The ESM receiver in the scope was squawking and chirping in response to all the electronic transmissions emitted by various Soviet search radars, an intel bonanza for the ESM and radio operators. Hunter reminded himself not to let his eagerness to get ELINT data overcome prudence and good judgment.

While Hunter was preoccupied with counterdetection, sonar sifted through multiple contacts looking for submarine tonals. The tracking party knew that at periscope depth, and with *Petya*s and helicopters covering the test area, there was no margin for error or for inattention or confusion. Everything depended on remaining invisible.

With the *Blackfin*'s bow-mounted spherical sonar array's two operating stations, it was like having two separate sonar inputs to the Mk 113 fire-control system, which could track two targets simultaneously. In addition, the BQR-7 conformal array provided a third sonar input, which the attack center used to track three targets simultaneously: one for plot and one for each of the fire-control computers. The sweating fire-control tracking team looked like they were trying to manage one of Hunter's out-of-control three-ring circuses, the elephants here, the clowns there.

"Conn, sonar. I have a Type II, bearing west. Sounds like our Yankee."

"That's our boy," Hunter said. "I'd bet on it."

The surfaced missile-firing Yankee, on an easterly course into the test area, chugged on by the waiting *Blackfin*. Hunter watched the Yankee rendezvous with a *Kresta* cruiser, her huge tracking radars leaving little doubt that she was the flagship.

Hunter halted their advance. So far so good. He had worked the *Blackfin* into position and had not been caught. Now all they had to do to cover the launch was keep tabs on the Yankee while the intel team snatched data that once again might provide ample warning of the launch so they wouldn't miss the most important part of the event. As with the surface-to-surface missile test witnessed earlier in the patrol, there might not be any advance warning that the SLBM launch had entered the final countdown stage. Dawn was a gray murk, and though Hunter doubted the Sovs would launch until full daylight, he cautioned that all the spooks might get in the way of a heads-up would be a sudden flash of brilliant yellow light as the missile's boost stage ignited and the ICBM rose skyward atop a tail of flame.

• • •

It took several hours for the Soviet ships to form up and move into firing position. The *Blackfin*, positioned astern of the ships, trailed at PD as the missile launch team took up their final positions near the three-mile limit off Kildin.

Hunter saw the Yankee and the *Kresta* exchange blinker signals, then the *Kresta* two-block her signal flags. "We're on," Hunter reported. "The Yankee's diving,"

The UQC underwater telephone speaker in the control room echoed with the sounds of venting air and seawater filling ballast tanks as the Soviet submarine submerged. The *Kresta*, tracking the Yankee with pinging active sonar, took up station off the sub's port quarter. The spooks got ready. Ship-to-ship chatter on the launch network and the sharp plain-language transmissions between helicopter crews indicated that the launch had neared its countdown stage.

Hunter was at the scope, watching, checking on *Petya*s and helos, waiting for the missile launch, hoping to hear the countdown warbling from the Yankee over her underwater telephone.

Instead, he and the watchstanders in the *Blackfin*'s control room heard a strange sound, then the booming voice of a panicked Russian sailor.

"Quick," Hunter barked. "What's he saying?"

"It's an emergency, Captain, something about the missile . . ."

The UQC roared like an angry Russian bear.

"Conn, sonar. That Yankee launched his bird."

Hunter, eye pressed to the scope, saw the sea erupt, first a white dome, then a giant fountain of spray. The missile broke the roiled surface, hung there for an instant fully exposed, then blew up with a huge orange-red ball of flame, black smoke, and a thunderclap that rocked the *Blackfin*.

"Misfire," Hunter said calmly.

The control room watch gaped at the periviz spectacle of flaming debris pinwheeling from the destroyed missile body and warhead, pattering into the sea like falling rain. A moment later the Yankee, apparently undamaged but shaken up, surfaced.

"Back to the drawing board," Hunter muttered. He stepped back, snapped the training handles up, and said, "Down scope. We'll pull back and monitor the situation, see what's what. Make your depth four-five-zero feet. Come to course north. All ahead two-thirds."

For the spooks, it was a gold mine of intel. For the Russians, it was a whole lot of rubles down the toilet.

19

SNEAK AND PEEK

OVER A THREE-DAY PERIOD the *Blackfin* monitored four more missile launches from the Yankee. None was as dramatic as the first one, but two missiles blew up in the early stages of their flights, perhaps deliberately, when they drifted off course. Another spun out of control back into the sea. Only one launch was successful, the missile disappearing downrange toward Semipalatinsk.

During each missile launch, sonar and fire control kept track of where the Yankee and its escort were at all times. More than once sonar reported contact with *Petya*s, but, not finding anything suspicious, they remained well clear of the *Blackfin*.

On the fourth day, with light fading early, the *Kresta* and the Yankee had moved into position for another launch. As usual, a helicopter darted to and fro over the area, its crew chattering about the launch on open radio circuits. The UQC was busy, too, with prelaunch chatter between the submerged Yankee and the *Kresta*. *Any minute now*, thought a weary Hunter. The last seventy-two hours had been stressful and exhausting for everyone, what with having to monitor missile launches and avoid counterdetection.

Radio broke in on Hunter's ruminations. "Captain, Sovs are reporting that a helo has contact with an unknown object in the water."

Shit! Hunter knew what that unknown object was: the *Blackfin*'s periscope! He issued a flurry of orders. "Down scope! Make your depth four-five-zero feet. Right full rudder, all ahead two-thirds. Rig ship for ultra quiet."

Men jumped to their tasks. As the *Blackfin* slinked away, sonar reported, "He just launched."

The UQC picked up the noise of a missile clearing one of the Yankee's missile tubes but not the above-surface boost phase kick-in or the thunder of ignition. Hunter was too busy breaking contact and heading for wide-open water to pay it any attention. He regretted missing the launch but had other things on his mind—like not getting nailed by a *Petya*. He grabbed a mike. "Sonar, conn. How're we doing?"

"Captain, I have active sonar from the *Petya*s and *Kresta*."

Now what? Go hide in an out-of-the-way place somewhere along the coast until things quieted down and the Sovs concluded it was a false alarm? Would they mount a search and then attack? Best to get the hell out of there. Fast. Which Hunter did.

• • •

He took a trick at the scope. Arctic night had arrived, and with it, rain squalls marching across the sea's surface. The squalls provided more cover for the *Blackfin*, maneuvering in dangerous waters. Plot was trying to keep track of the ships scattered across the Barents hunting for the *Blackfin* after they had come pouring out of the Kola Inlet. Hunter marveled at how fast the Soviets could react to an emergency. It seemed as if they were there in minutes; of course, it took longer than that. There were a lot of them, too, and now two frigates, white foam curling away on either side of their bows, steaming parallel and uncomfortably close to the *Blackfin*'s northerly track, bore watching.

Easing west, Hunter had a quick meal while mulling time and distance to the nearest exit. At ten knots—

A whooping alarm went off in the maneuvering room. "Reactor scram!" announced the engineering officer of the watch. At the same time a warning light on the reactor control panel flashed GROUP SCRAM. A single control rod group had dropped into the reactor core, shutting it down. But how?

Up forward the OOD acknowledged the report, then ordered, "All stop. Make your depth one-two-zero feet." Next he grabbed a 1MC mike and announced through the ship, "Rig ship for reduced power."

Air-conditioning cycled off; ventilation shifted to slow speed; atmosphere controls cycled off, too. Other nonessential equipment stopped operating.

Men jumped to essential controls; the throttleman spun the throttles shut; the annunciators rang up ALL STOP. The *Blackfin*'s prop started winding down, the sudden loss of power scrubbing off her speed as she came to the depth ordered by the OOD.

The engineers worked fast to find the problem. Something in the system, perhaps a mechanical problem, perhaps human error, had triggered the reactor shutdown.

Hunter felt like he was in a movie with a last-minute complication that put the hero in peril. He stubbed out a cigarette and mopped his brow, shifted his weight from foot to foot. "OOD, answer bells on emergency propulsion motor," he ordered.

The emergency propulsion motor, or EPM, drew its power

from the ship's storage batteries. The EPM could move the ship at three knots—but not for long without draining the batteries. It was only a temporary fix to keep some way on the ship until the emergency diesel could be put online. For that the *Blackfin* would have to come to PD and snorkel to pipe air into the diesel and discharge its exhaust. A snorkel tube sticking out of the water made an excellent target for Soviet small-object radar.

"Stand by to snorkel," Hunter ordered.

The OOD acknowledged the order, then cleared baffles, after which he brought the ship to periscope depth. The chief of the watch stood by to raise the snorkel. The OOD had his hands full: He had limited power with which to maneuver to clear baffles, and sonar had to report all contacts. They couldn't just pop to the surface like a cork. There were too many Soviet ships and helos up there hunting for the *Blackfin*.

Hunter calmly monitored unfolding events in the engineering spaces. He had complete confidence in his crew and was sure that they'd soon find and fix the problem. He had trained them to deal with any emergency, especially one as serious as a reactor casualty. No one panicked. The engineering watch calmly followed the rigid procedures established to ensure a safe recovery and reactor start-up from a scram. He was more concerned about counterdetection than he was about the *Blackfin*'s nuclear reactor.

In typical fashion, the Soviets had set up an area search employing surface ships and aircraft. Earlier, Hunter had seen helos using a hop-and-skip technique like dragonflies zipping from flower to flower as they searched areas where they thought the *Blackfin* had to be. When they didn't find her, they skipped to the next area. The helos, each equipped with dipping sonar, hovered for three or four minutes fifty to sixty feet above the sea, listening. Other helos dropped patterns of passive and active sonobuoys.

Under ideal conditions the active sonobouys had a range of four thousand to eight thousand yards. Conditions in the Barents op area weren't ideal, and Hunter counted on that to foil their search. Still, some of the helos had come too damn close for comfort.

The engineering officer of the watch—the EOOW—roused Hunter from his ruminations. "Conn, maneuvering. The cause of the scram was operator error. Commencing a fast scram recovery."

Operator error? Hunter cursed silently. After all the training and instruction, how could it happen? Especially now. Hunter blew through his teeth. What the operator error was and who was responsible for it would be determined and dealt with later. There'd also be a report to submit, but right now they had to get full power to the screw. He caught the OOD's eye. "This is a hell of a way to end a patrol."

The OOD nodded his agreement, then uncrossed his fingers. "We'll be out of here in a few minutes, Captain."

He was right. Ten minutes later the EOOW reported, "Reactor's critical."

Hunter gave a thumbs-up as the OOD, on the 1MC, ordered, "Secure snorkeling; secure from reduced electrical power." Switching to the 21MC, he ordered, "Maneuvering, conn. Answer bells on the main engines." To the diving officer he said, "Make your depth four-five-zero feet; all ahead two-thirds." After the repeat-backs, the OOD returned Hunter's thumbs-up.

Emboldened by the weak performance of Soviet sonar—its lack of range detection and definition—Hunter worked the *Blackfin* around the buzzing surface patrols and skipping-and-hopping helos. The trick was to avoid being trapped in the funnel-like area around the Kola Inlet and the Rybachiy Peninsula.

It took several hours to carefully maneuver outside the busy north-south transit lanes connected to the Kola Inlet and to pick around patrol boats. Somewhere east of the Kola Inlet, an underwater explosion, its boom sounding like thunder, reached the *Blackfin*. Then another. Depth charges?

It reminded Hunter of what had happened to the *Gudgeon*, the diesel-boat intel collector that had been discovered snooping by the Soviets so long ago. Hunter vowed it wasn't going to happen to the *Blackfin*. Even so, it was touch-and-go for hours, what with ASW patrols sniffing like the proverbial bloodhounds for a trace of submarine. One of them, active sonar pinging, screws and machinery sounding like the Moscow-Rostov Express, surged in and shot past the *Blackfin* without detecting her. It was dawn when Hunter upped the scope, did a 360-degree search along the cloudy horizon, and saw nothing but open water.

Deep and well clear of the area he ordered, "All ahead full. Let's get the hell out of here."

The *Blackfin* surged forward, for home.

20

INTO THE INTEL ABYSS

THERE WAS A COLLECTIVE SENSE of urgency, even a sigh of relief, aboard the *Blackfin* as she departed her op area for home, leaving behind an empty-handed Soviet ASW force. Once she entered the Norwegian Sea, thoughts turned to reconnection with family and friends. Maybe a little R&R. For sure some cold beer.

Hunter and the ship's officers, relaxed and in a buoyant mood after a successful patrol, got busy writing and assembling the patrol report Hunter would submit to ComSubLant. It included a full narrative of the submarine trails, ASPLs, and underwater hull surveillances, as well as Hunter's observations on how to improve or modify the techniques they had employed in light of current Soviet tactics, as well as which evolutions—under-hull surveillance came to mind—were too risky given that Soviet subs had by now received ample coverage. In the future only the newest classes of Soviet subs would qualify.

The report also included a full narrative along with technical details and the data captured from the Soviet missile tests observed and recorded in the range off Kildin Island. The last part of the report described any new wrinkles observed in Soviet ASW doctrine. Hunter concluded with the observation that the Soviets had not made any changes in their tactical doctrine and that their rigid adherence to outmoded methods thwarted their attempts to block penetration of the Barents Sea area by U.S. submarines.

The most important aspect of the patrol, coverage of the SLBM launch, was given special attention. It would be the first thing analysts would review.

The spooks, meanwhile, set to work tagging and boxing up their data packages of audio- and videotapes, again paying special attention to the SLBM launches. Upon arrival in New London, the intel team would bail out for Fort Meade. Their take had been voluminous: There were dozens and dozens of tape reels and videocassettes for the analysts to work on. How long it would take to review the more routine material was anybody's guess. Maybe years. Like all intelligence agencies, the NSA, after skimming off the cream, moved at a glacial pace when conducting deep analysis. In any event, a series of briefings would likely follow the *Blackfin*'s arrival. Hunter might be called upon to brief the submarine warfare crowd in Washington and Norfolk, CNO Zumwalt, the director of the CIA, even Admiral Rickover. Depending on the significance the CNO and others attached to the mission, Hunter and his crew, even the ship, might be in line to receive awards.

Well clear of the op area, Hunter gave the okay to transmit the encrypted Highlights Message, a summary of significant events and intercepts, especially the SLBM launches. The message also emphasized information that might prove useful to the *Blackfin*'s incoming relief or of wider interest to the intel community, especially those who were planning future Holystone missions. Hunter had written and rewritten the message several times, substituting words and fine-tuning the phrasing to ensure that it conveyed the essence of what was contained in greater detail in the patrol report.

Satisfied that it met his standards for brevity and navalese, Hunter had it encrypted in a virtually unbreakable code, then chose a transmission point east of Greenland, since it was likely that the Soviets would intercept the message and try to use it to pinpoint the *Blackfin*'s position. Of course, all that would do was confirm that yet another U.S. sub had slipped through their porous ASW cordon.

. . .

Two days from home, Hunter radioed his ETA to New London. All hands turned to to give the *Blackfin* a thorough cleaning so that upon arrival she'd look better than when she left, though with Hunter's penchant for cleanliness, that hardly seemed possible. As the deck swabbing, vacuuming, and polishing got under way, the engineers assembled a work package detailing needed postpatrol upkeep. Attached to it was a separate list of preventive and corrective maintenance required to ensure the *Blackfin*'s post-op readiness. The engineers also attached a report on the reactor scram and its cause. Truly, the paperwork was never finished.

Anticipation of homecoming and family reunions made it hard for some of the men to sleep. Standing watches was a way to ease the tension and excitement, which only grew when the Connecticut coastline loomed out of the haze. After a brief stop to disconnect the STASS towed array, the *Blackfin* headed up the Thames. Minutes later she pulled up to the pier crowded with families anxiously awaiting her arrival.

In a quiet moment following the flurry of activity their arrival in New London had unleashed, Hunter pondered the profession he'd chosen. It gave him immense satisfaction to have accomplished something so special that few men in the world had ever done it. If asked what he was going to do next, Hunter, savoring his favorite cocktail and a good cigar, would have answered, "Rewind the clock and get ready for another trip."

EPILOGUE

ADMIRAL ZUMWALT needn't have worried. The SALT talks didn't fail: Nixon and Brezhnev signed the Basic Principles of Relations Between the USA and the USSR in May 1972; then Brezhnev got in his shiny new Cadillac and drove Nixon around Moscow. The *Blackfin* and her crew returned unscathed. If one discounts a few bumps and scrapes from close calls with Soviet subs, all the other Holystone subs returned unscathed, too. Holystone was a great success, its operations extending into the 1980s and 1990s and beyond the collapse of the Soviet Union in 1991. As new and improved U.S. submarines like the *Los Angeles–*, *Seawolf-* and *Virginia*-classes came online to replace the workhorse *Sturgeon*s they, too, were pressed into intel collection service.

After the disintegration of the USSR, the new Russia no longer posed the threat its predecessor once did. Thus, the United States began reducing the size of its military, and as part of that reduction, and in line with treaty obligations, the U.S. Navy began downsizing its nuclear submarine fleet. Even with fewer submarines to deploy around the world, Holystone operations continued, though not at the same tempo as in the heady days when Roy Hunter and the *Blackfin* went north. Today it's a certainty that U.S. submarines spy on China, North Korea, Iran, and other countries.

With the birth of a new, more open, less hostile, and, for a time, less paranoid Russia, the leaders of the former Soviet navy began scrapping many of its older SSNs and SSBNs. Within a few years Russia's nuclear submarine fleet had virtually disappeared, leaving behind a legacy of radioactive contamination that Russia and other countries in the northern region are still struggling to clean up. The numbers of both nuclear and conventional weapons in Russia also declined. In no time at all it seemed that the once invincible Soviet military machine had been reduced to a hollow shell, one that no longer posed a threat to the world.

Of course, the numbers were deceiving. Despite their weapons drawdown, the Russians still have a huge nuclear arsenal, much of it in the form of SLBMs. The Russian Northern and Pacific fleets can still launch these weapons at a moment's notice. Nevertheless, through the mid-1990s and early 2000s, there were signs of increasing cooperation between Russia and the West and with the United States in particular. It appeared then that the new Russia no longer coveted the territory it had lost in Eastern Europe, nor did it seek the return of its former republics that had gained independence. Many observers believed that the Russians were sincere when they said that they wanted to put the nightmare of the cold war to rest. Others weren't so sure, claiming that the Russians, despite all their talk of cooperation, harbored deep resentment over their loss of power and prestige and that sooner or later they would confront the West in a modern iteration of the cold war. In fact, Russia has regained much of its power and prestige, and with it a renewed sense of paranoia manifested in its refusal to be bullied by an America Moscow claims is bent on exporting democracy around the world.

Understandably the United States keeps an eye on developments in Russia, especially its military. As in the past, the United States stays informed of Russia's intentions and capabilities through the use of modern spy technology, including Holystone-type submarine missions. Despite vast improvements in space reconnaissance and other intelligence-gathering technologies, there are things a satellite still can't see and that spies on the ground still can't ascertain. Submarines remain the primary means of gathering intelligence from denied areas beyond the reach of satellites and humans. In that regard not much has changed; the mission and tactics are pretty much the same as they always were.

What, if anything, the Russians are doing to thwart U.S. spy subs is hard to know. The newest Russian submarines, the *Akula*s, for example, are comparable in many respects to modern U.S. subs. The Russians may be using them to hunt our SSNs and SSBNs. Newer, more capable Russian submarines are on the drawing boards and on ship-building ways, but whether or not the Russians have deployed improved sonars and detection technologies in these subs comparable to those the United States has is difficult to gauge, even for experts who have access to officials within the Russian defense establishment. Based on history, it seems fair to assume that Russian capabilities in these fields still lag behind but that the gap is closing fast, propelled by breakthroughs in underwater imaging and space-based ASW technologies that can locate submarines, nuclear or diesel-electric, anywhere under the sea. While these new technologies make seat-of-the-pants submarining a thing of the past, it still takes intelligent, well-trained, and dedicated submariners to man the ships tasked with gathering intelligence. Given that current U.S.-Russian relations are strained and may get worse, Holystone-style intelligence collection will probably always be in demand.

. . .

Under Hunter's command and, later, under the COs who succeeded him, the *Blackfin* returned to the Barents Sea. After a long and successful career she was decommissioned at the end of her service life in the late 1990s. She, like her sister *Sturgeon*s, entered the navy's Nuclear Powered Ship and Submarine Recycling Program in Bremerton, Washington, for dismantling. There, the compartment containing her nuclear reactor was cut out of her hull, sealed, and shipped to the Department of Energy's Hanford Nuclear Reservation in Washington state for burial alongside other submarines' reactor compartments stored in containments specially designed for that purpose.

Roy Hunter went from the *Blackfin* to other commands at sea and ashore. After twenty-five years of distinguished service, he retired from the navy and entered private industry. He's a proud and modest man. People who meet him would never guess he'd commanded a nuclear sub that stalked the red bear. Ask him about it, though, and he'll tell you it was all in a day's work.

. . .

With the breakup of the Soviet Union, many Russian submariners left the navy disillusioned with the shoddy treatment they received during their service and angry that the submarines they and their shipmates took to sea were so badly constructed. Today, many former Soviet and Russian submariners suffer from the effects caused by excessive exposure to radiation; some have died from it. (As an extreme example, a full-body dose of, say, 200 to

300 rem, a measure of radiation, usually results in radiation sickness and 10 to 35 percent mortality in a month.) Their disillusionment didn't begin with the collapse of the Soviet system; rather, it began early in their careers when they learned that serving a rigid and authoritarian regime demanded more than unwavering loyalty: It demanded that they surrender their independence and freedom, if not their lives.

Soviet cold war submariners were dedicated professionals forced to fight two battles, one with the United States, another with their ships. In the end both battles had sapped their spirit. Just as Admiral Dönitz's Type XXI U-boats came too late to save Germany, new and improved Soviet submarines came too late to have an influence on the cold war's outcome. After the cold war, in the new, almost bankrupt Russia, it was hard to justify the continued construction of these new submarines. Those already on the building ways ended up as scrap; new designs were shelved. Until now.

With the end of the cold war, the U.S. sub force faced problems of its own: It had to search for a new mission to justify the enormous cost of building the modern, highly capable submarines the navy said it needed. The navy's penchant for wanting subs capable of doing everything possible had made them almost too costly to procure. Ironically, the mission the sub force seems to have found to justify these expensive submarines is a lot like the old World War II mission: special operations.

In any event, retired U.S. submariners look back on those days of a hot cold war with a twinge of melancholy and nostalgia. And why not? It was a time we won't likely see again: submarines tracking, trailing, and dueling for supremacy of the undersea battleground. Seen from today's perspective, it was a different world and a different navy, not a navy run as it is today, like a business with a marketing plan and a product to sell, but first and foremost a potent fighting force.

．．．

A word about spies and the NSA's black intel hole seems in order.

One of the most infamous cases of Americans spying for the Soviet Union during the cold war concerned John Walker, a navy chief warrant officer and communications specialist on the staff of ComSubLant. Walker, who began spying for the Soviets in late 1967, had a top-secret clearance and access to some of the navy's most sensitive classified materials. He recruited friends and family alike to deliver information to the Soviets that helped them decrypt thousands upon thousands of secret messages sent by U.S. military commands, including ComSubLant and ComSubPac, to their units deployed around the world. He also delivered to the Soviets technical manuals for advanced U.S. spy satellites. Understandably, the KGB considered Walker one of their most important espionage agents. He and his accomplices were arrested in 1985. Convicted of espionage, Walker received a life sentence.

Ronald Pelton, a onetime NSA communications specialist, was another spy who sold his services to the KGB. For almost six years, until his arrest in 1985, Pelton delivered top-secret information to the Soviets about U.S. intelligence operations. One of the most important operations he compromised was known as Ivy Bells (see Appendix One), in which Holystone submarines had placed induction taps and recording devices on Soviet communications cables in the Sea of Okhotsk. Until Pelton compromised the operation, the cable taps had yielded a voluminous haul of intelligence about Soviet military planning. After Pelton revealed their existence, Soviet navy divers found the taps and removed them, though it's still not clear whether Pelton knew the location of all the taps that had been placed or if divers had to inspect every inch of undersea cable the Soviets had looking for them. In any case, Pelton's treachery brought the operation to an abrupt end. Pelton, like Walker, is serving three life terms in prison.

How much damage Walker and Pelton did to the U.S. cold war intelligence collection effort can only be guessed. More to the point, did their actions endanger Holystone submarines and their crews? It's hard to tell. Based on what we know about Soviet ASW capabilities, it's fairly clear that even if the Soviet navy had had information about the timing of Holystone deployments or advance warning of the arrival of Holystone subs in the Barents Sea or the Sea of Okhotsk, there wasn't much they could do about it. In that regard a retired Soviet naval officer, when asked how it was that U.S. submarines penetrated Soviet waters time and again without being detected, replied, in effect, "Oh, we let them do it so we could keep track of them."

Roy Hunter scoffed at that. No way, he said; we were too damn quiet and the Soviets had lousy sonar. It sounded to him like typical Soviet disinformation. Even with help from spies like Walker and Pelton, the Soviets couldn't thwart U.S. submarine intelligence operations. No matter how hard they tried, Holystone intel flowed like a river into the black hole that was the U.S. intelligence vault. So much intel flowed in, not just from Holystone but from other collection platforms and stations around the world, that at times the vault must have overflowed. Holystone, of course, was just one part of the overall effort that helped the United States to gain insight into how the Soviets would fight a war, to assess their strengths and weaknesses, and to pinpoint their vulnerabilities. It also showed the United States how the Soviets viewed U.S. capabilities and intentions. Clearly the Soviet navy posed a formidable seaborne nuclear threat that continued to grow until the end of the cold war. No less threatening was its improving fleet of nuclear attack submarines, which, given time, might have been capable of finding and destroying U.S. SSBNs and SSNs.

Basing its decisions in part on intelligence collected by Holystone subs, the United States altered and adapted its tactical and strategic plans to reflect Soviet objectives and intentions and to ensure that the country could respond to the growing Soviet threat.

Then the cold war ended.

Could the United States have defeated the Soviet Union and won the cold war without Holystone? Did all those recordings of Soviet SSNs and SSBNs, all the videos of submarine hulls and props, of missile and torpedo tests, make a difference? Ask the Russians today. Ask the spooks. Ask the intel community. Above all, ask the Holystone submariners.

APPENDIX ONE

_____

Sand Dollar, Jennifer, and Ivy Bells
Visionaries

During the cold war, it became more and more apparent that submarines, especially nuclear submarines, were incredibly versatile. Not only could they sink ships, they could spy on enemies, transport special operations forces to hostile shores, even launch guided missiles. Their abilities seemed endless, limited only by imagination. Come up with an idea and a sub could do it.

Among the U.S. first-generation nuclear submarines, only the USS *Halibut* was built to carry and launch guided missiles. Operational in 1960, she was a big submarine, 350 feet long and displacing 4,900 tons submerged. Her single reactor driving twin shafts propelled the ship at twenty knots underwater. Her main armament consisted of six torpedo tubes. Built with a massive eighty-foot-long hanger on her bow, she could launch five subsonic Regulus I or four supersonic Regulus II cruise missiles. Unlike ballistic missiles, which assume a ballistic trajectory, cruise missiles have wings and employ continuous propulsion. The Regulus had a turbojet engine and folding wings for stowage aboard a submarine and was capable of carrying a nuclear warhead. Five Regulus-armed nuclear- and diesel-powered submarines made deterrent patrols starting in 1956 through 1964, when the program effectively ended with the appearance of Polaris-launching SSBNs. Suddenly the nuclear-powered *Halibut* and her diesel-powered sisters, *Barbero*, *Growler*, *Grayback*, and *Tunny*, were out of work. Three boats were decommissioned; one became a transport for special operations forces. What to do with the *Halibut*?

The answer came in 1965, when the navy's Special Projects Office realized she'd be ideal for conversion to a spy submarine—not just any spy submarine but one that could conduct underwater surveillance and recovery of Soviet weapons that had been tested at sea, such as torpedoes and missiles and their electronics packages.

The *Halibut* underwent refitting for her new role. It included the installation of thrusters for hovering, a lock-in/lock-out chamber in the old Regulus missile hanger, mushroom anchors fore and aft for fixing her position on the seabed, side-scan sonar, video recording equipment, underwater tethered robotic cameras, and a saturation (mixed gas) diving rig. Thus equipped, the submarine could range over the seabed hunting for Soviet missile debris and other objects of interest.

The *Halibut* proved her worth during a mission to find a sunken Soviet diesel-powered missile submarine, the *K-129*. In early March 1968, the Golf-II-class boat, armed with three nuclear-tipped ICBMs and two nuclear torpedoes, had been ripped open by an explosion while patrolling northwest of Hawaii. She sank in water three miles deep. Shortly afterward the Russians mounted an extensive search for the *K-129* but failed to find her.

With the help of SOSUS, which had heard the explosion and

breakup, the U.S. Navy located the general area in which the Golf had sunk. If she could be found and photographed, or, better yet, if debris such as warheads and coding machines and code books and communications gear could be recovered, ONI would have an intelligence windfall. In an operation code-named Sand Dollar, the navy deployed the *Halibut* to find the *K-129* and photograph the wreckage with her twin robotic cameras. In July 1968, after a three-week search, the *Halibut* found the sub. The photographs she brought back included pictures of the exposed tips of two of the three ICBMs wedged in the sub's conning tower launch tubes. After viewing the photos, officials in the White House and at the CIA realized the navy had stumbled upon a trove of intelligence unlike anything they had ever encountered before. The question was how to get hold of it. Over a five-year period the CIA put together a salvage plan that became the most difficult, complex, and expensive espionage operation of the cold war.

Code-named the Jennifer Project, a special ship with deep-ocean lifting gear was constructed under deep cover and dispatched to the Pacific Ocean in 1974 to retrieve the wreckage of the *K-129*. By then the Soviets had discovered what the CIA was up to but could only stand by and watch it unfold. The ship, the *Glomar Explorer*, raised a portion of the sub—compartments one and two—which contained two nuclear torpedoes and also the remains of six sailors. The wreckage was examined in detail (what was found is still deeply classified), after which the sailors' remains were reburied at sea.

During the long period of preparation for recovery of the *K-129*, the *Halibut* wasn't idle. She continued operations from Pearl Harbor and the West Coast, recovering bits and pieces of Soviet missile hardware and other items of interest to naval intelligence. After review of the materials and the methods used to recover them, an idea began to take form within the brain trust of ONI and the NSA, that when fully developed would call upon the *Halibut* for execution.

The idea was so fantastic that it seemed beyond the realm of possibility even for a submarine. Code-named Ivy Bells, the mission targeted a Soviet undersea communication cable lying on the bottom of the Sea of Okhotsk. There was no proof that such a cable existed, but intel specialists assumed that there was no other way for the Soviets to engage in secure communications between their submarine and missile bases at Petropavlovsk on the Kamchatka Peninsula and Vladivostok on Russia's far eastern coast. It also seemed possible that the cable joined landlines connecting Vladivostok to Moscow. If it could be tapped it would be like opening a door into the mind of the Kremlin itself, exposing its fears, its plans, and its vulnerabilities.

While the intel specialists insisted that such a cable had to exist, they didn't know exactly where it was. If it did exist, who or what would find it and how would they tap it? Answer: the *Halibut* and a special team of navy divers.

As plans and approvals for the mission coalesced in the summer of 1971, attention shifted to the *Halibut*. She underwent an overhaul during which she was outfitted with a fake Deep Submergence Rescue Vessel, or DSRV, on her afterdeck. The DSRV had been designed to rescue submariners from a sunken submarine and was essentially a long, pressure-proof cylindrical tank with lock-in/lock-out chambers from which swimmers could enter and depart. In fact, it was a decompression and airlock chamber designed for use by divers working secretly in deep water. If the *Halibut* could locate the cable on the bottom of the Sea of Okhotsk, divers would have to haul it up from the seabed from four-hundred-foot depths and install specially designed cable taps and recording devices.

The risks were enormous. If the Soviets discovered the *Halibut* in waters considered Soviet territory, they might attack the sub and sink her, causing an international incident that would scuttle Soviet-American relations once and for all.

That was speculation, though. Besides, Holystone subs had been operating in Soviet territorial waters for years and getting away with it. The immediate problem was how to find the cable. The answer lay in an intelligence officer's recollection of cruising down the Mississippi River as a youth and seeing at various points along the shore signs warning boaters not to anchor in areas where telephone cables crossed under the river. Was it possible that the Soviets had posted similar warnings along the shores of the Sea of Okhotsk?

The *Halibut* would soon find out.

She entered the Sea of Okhotsk undetected through the Kuril Island chain near Kamchatka. For days the *Halibut* cruised at PD searching for a posted sign warning of a cable crossing somewhere along the coastline of the southern tip of the Kamchatka Peninsula. Sure enough, the *Halibut*'s periscope watch found what they were looking for stuck on a rocky beach: WARNING. CABLE CROSSING. DO NOT ANCHOR, in Russian of course.

A remote-controlled video camera rig launched from the *Halibut* found the cable on the bottom buried in silt. The *Halibut* took position over the cable in four hundred feet of water and dropped her mushroom anchors to hold her in place. The divers inside the pressure chamber on the *Halibut*'s after deck got ready to lock out and plant the cable taps.

Using saturation diving techniques, the divers had been breathing a mixture of helium and oxygen for days inside the pressurized chamber in preparation for their deep underwater work. Wearing hot water suits to protect them against near-freezing temperatures, the divers relied on diving rigs that utilized an umbilical to supply the breathing mixture, hot water, and two-way communications with the *Halibut*. As a safety precaution, each diver's umbilical contained a steel cord that kept him tethered to the sub.

The divers emerged from the chamber and began the arduous task of exposing the cable, using compressed air delivered through hoses to clear away sand and debris. Once the cable was exposed, the divers connected an induction tap that worked the same way that a suction cup attached to a recorder does on a telephone receiver. The cable itself wasn't pierced or damaged in any way that, if it were inspected, would indicate that it had been tampered with. The battery-powered device contained the induction electronics and a tape recorder that could log hours' worth of recordings of both covered and uncovered telephone conversations between Soviet Pacific Fleet commanders and their superiors in Moscow. The cable contained scores of channels, each of which could be recorded separately and unscrambled later by analysts. The tap was designed to break away in the event the cable was hauled up for servicing.

The *Halibut*'s intel take on that first mission was impressive, but the quality was less than hoped for. To overcome the problems, the *Halibut* embarked a team of SIGINT specialists and returned to the Sea of Okhotsk. This time she came back with recordings that contained material beyond the wildest dreams of those who had dreamed up Ivy Bells. Not only had the tape recordings captured the details of Soviet military operations in all theaters, they also gave analysts a look inside the minds of the top Soviet military commanders themselves and, most important of all, a chance to hear their views on America's military strategy and how to cope with it.

The *Halibut* returned several more times to retrieve taps and plant new and better ones. It soon became obvious that as long as Ivy Bells relied on regular incursions into Soviet territorial waters, chances were good that the Soviets would eventually discover what the *Halibut* was up to. Every time she entered the Sea of Okhotsk, she went equipped with scuttling charges to prevent her capture. To lessen the risk of discovery, the navy developed a more sophisticated tapping device that could be left in place for up to a year.

Bell Laboratories, having extensive experience with undersea cables, designed a self-powered twenty-foot-long podlike tap that could make recordings for up to a year, after which a sub would return to retrieve the tapes and install fresh ones. The Bell Labs taps worked perfectly and provided analysts with an even greater trove of information.

In time, the *Halibut*, showing her age, retired from her tapping missions. She was decommissioned in 1976, her work taken over by the USS *Seawolf* and, later, the highly modified *Sturgeon*-class sub USS *Parche*.

Ivy Bells came to an abrupt end in the 1980s when U.S. spy satellites saw Soviet ships clotted around the area of the cable tap in the Sea of Okhotsk. The question U.S. intelligence officials had was, how had the Soviets discovered it? By sheer chance? A technical failure in the pod that somehow had tipped the Soviets off? Or was it possible that the Soviets had a spy inside U.S. intelligence with information about Ivy Bells? The latter possibility seemed remote, as few people knew about Ivy Bells, and all who did had the highest security clearances.

The spy turned out to be Ronald W. Pelton, a disgruntled

former NSA cryptanalyst. Out of money and facing bankruptcy, Pelton sold out Ivy Bells to the Russians for thirty-five thousand dollars. Ironically, Pelton's treason was discovered via a wiretapped telephone conversation he had with a Soviet KGB defector under surveillance by the FBI. Pelton was arrested in 1985 and convicted of espionage. He is serving three life sentences.

Behind Enemy Lines
U.S. Submarine Special Missions
Against the Japanese Empire

Operation Holystone's roots can be traced to World War II and the Pacific theater of operations. While the British and Germans sporadically employed submarines to carry out secret missions, principally the landing of agents on enemy shores, the U.S. Navy's submarine force, in addition to its primary job of sinking ships, carried out close to three hundred such missions against the Japanese. These missions proved the value of using submarines to conduct clandestine operations that would have otherwise been impossible for conventional forces to mount against a determined enemy.

These missions encompassed everything from evacuating men, women, and children from Japanese-occupied islands to spiriting gold and silver from the Philippines to reconnoitering Japanese-held islands prior to their invasion by U.S. Marines. So while the submarine force was crushing the Japanese navy and merchant marine, it was also executing an extraordinary array of special missions designed to weaken and ultimately defeat that enemy.

The nature of these operations entailed infiltration of Japanese-controlled harbors and groups of islands, a venture often more hazardous than a normal sixty-day war patrol, during which a submarine frequently had to slip inside a screen of escorting destroyers to fire her torpedoes, then endure a vicious depth-charging. Landing a shore party in rubber boats to reconnoiter an invasion beach or sneaking a submarine into a harbor at night to deliver ammo to Philippine guerrillas called for extraordinary reserves of courage and just plain guts. The men who did this faced attack not just by depth charges but also by aircraft and shore batteries.

Not all special missions were as dramatic as landing agents and lugging gold across the Pacific. Mine laying, an important but unheralded task, was simply hard, backbreaking work. Yet every mission successfully carried out was vitally important to the overall war effort.

At war's end, with the accomplishments of the sub force fresh in mind and with the United States facing a growing Soviet threat, a select group of submariners was given a new assignment, one that eventually became known as Operation Holystone. The idea for Holystone sprang from the defeat of the Japanese by the U.S. sub force with its ability to adapt as circumstances dictated. Yet in the days following Pearl Harbor, when no one knew for sure if the United States could retake the Pacific from the Japanese, things looked pretty bleak. By mid-1942 the Japanese had pushed deep into East Asia and the Western Pacific. They controlled the oil-rich Dutch East Indies and were threatening Australia. If Australia fell, the Aussies and Americans, many of whom had fled the Philippines and Malaysia ahead of the Japanese to establish bases in the south, would find themselves at the South Pole. There was literally no place left to run. The Japanese in one bold stroke had conquered over eight million square miles of territory. For the Allies it seemed an impossible task to ever retake it.

Nevertheless, the geography of the region proved a blessing in disguise. While the Japanese controlled most of the Pacific, little of what they had conquered was land. To maintain its far-flung military garrisons—even to maintain the home islands themselves—Japan required a huge web of supply lines and a vast fleet of merchant ships to deliver the food, fuel, and ammunition needed to fight the war in remote areas of the Pacific. After regrouping, the U.S. sub force launched an all-out war of attrition against the Japanese merchant marine. Unlike the Allies, who had begun a mass-production shipbuilding program to replace their losses, especially those inflicted by German U-boats, the Japanese collapsed, strangled by the loss of thousands of ships and the matériel and soldiers they could have transported.

Before the takeover of the Philippines by the Japanese in January 1942, the U.S. Navy had started delivering badly needed supplies by submarine to U.S. and Filipino forces fighting in Bataan and on Corregidor in Manila Bay. As the Japanese tightened their grip, Corregidor, known as the Rock, came under relentless assault. Its American and Filipino defenders would soon face surrender and the infamous Bataan Death March.

The USS *Seawolf* was one of the first submarines to attempt a resupply mission to the Philippines, delivering almost forty tons of ammunition to Corregidor. She was followed by the USS *Trout*, which arrived after running the Japanese blockade off Manila Bay, loaded with thousands of rounds of antiaircraft ammunition and food. Her cargo was unloaded and swapped for two tons of gold bullion in gleaming bars, eighteen tons of silver pesos, and bundles of negotiable securities that would otherwise have fallen into Japanese hands. Weeks later the treasure arrived in Pearl Harbor for shipment to the United States for safekeeping in Fort Knox.

In mid-February 1942, the *Swordfish*, under the command of Lieutenant Commander Chester Smith, received orders to load up and head for the Philippines. While Smith laid out a course for Manila Bay, his submarine was packed with thousands of rounds of .30 caliber and .45 caliber ammo, crates of canned goods and cigarettes, and, for the men on the Rock, bags of mail.

The *Swordfish*, like the *Seawolf* and *Trout* before her, headed north submerged by day, and surfaced by night. Smith had to dodge more Japanese warships and avoid contact with merchantmen, even though such juicy targets were hard to pass up. Approaching Luzon, Smith, after lying offshore submerged during the day, had to then pick his way through minefields outside Manila Bay at night on the surface. The location of the fields marked on Smith's navigation charts came mostly from sketchy information provided by guerrillas and coastwatchers and was therefore open to interpretation. After an exchange of recognition signals with a PT boat escort, and expecting at any moment to be jumped by a Japanese patrol boat or targeted by shore batteries, Smith nosed the *Swordfish* into the bay and tied up at South Dock.

Under the cover of darkness, but with tracers and star shells lighting up Corregidor, the backbreaking job of moving the ammo ashore got under way. Meanwhile, Smith received orders to evacuate Philippine president Manuel Quezon and his wife, son, and two daughters to Panay. In addition, Smith took aboard the Philippine vice president, the chief justice, and three army officers. Quezon was ill and would find the voyage difficult. His wife and daughters would get seasick. His son, however, would have the time of his life climbing all over the submarine and making friends with the crew. With dawn breaking and the passengers aboard, Smith gave the order to head for the safety of deep water.

After disembarking passengers at Panay, the *Swordfish* returned to Corregidor to evacuate the U.S. high commissioner, Francis B. Sayre, and a party of eleven, plus five navy code-breakers to Australia. With the Sayre party aboard, however, there wasn't room for the code-breakers, and they had to be left behind.

On March 11, 1942, General Douglas MacArthur and his family, ordered out of the Philippines, fled via PT boat and B-17 for Australia. A month later U.S. and Filipino defenders surrendered to the Japanese. After arrival in Australia, the pioneering *Swordfish* returned to the business of sinking Japanese ships. In December 1944, under the command of Commander K. E. Montross, she began her thirteenth war patrol. During that patrol, on January 2 she received orders to conduct photographic reconnaissance of Okinawa. The *Swordfish* acknowledged receipt of those orders on January 3, 1945, her last communication. She was never heard from again.

· · ·

While Smith and the *Swordfish* were resupplying Corregidor, Lieutenant Jim "Red" Coe, captain of the old and creaky *S-39*, a prewar-constructed S-boat, or "Sugar boat" as they were known, received orders to undertake a special mission. Coe's *S-39* was attached to the ragtag Asiatic Fleet, which had fought a rearguard action as the Japanese overran the Malay Peninsula. Coe had been patrolling submerged along the equator in waters west of Borneo, looking for targets to attack but not finding any. His earlier attacks on a transport and possibly a submarine had fizzled. Then, on February 28, Coe received a radio message, which he made note of in his patrol report as follows:

> 0136 Set south westerly course for Chebia Island in Toedjoe group in compliance with following orders received from CSAF [Chief of Staff Asiatic Fleet].
>
> Serial 271525 Job for S-39 X CSAF forty-seven X Party about 40 British including Rear Admiral [Ernest J.] Spooner and Air Vice Marshal [Conway Pulford] from Singapore reported on Chebia Island of Toedjoe group Dutch chart six one since Feb twenty X Rescue if possible X On leaving head for Sunda Straits report result X Watch for air and surface patrol X

The British officers, along with a party of British refugees and Australian pilots, had managed to escape from Singapore one step ahead of the Japanese. How they had reached tiny Chebia Island, a lump of sand in the South China Sea, off Sumatra, was anybody's guess. The Aussies had rigged a radio transmitter and sent a message detailing their plight. CSAF assumed that Japanese recon units were in the area and that unless the party was rescued soon, they'd fall into Japanese hands.

> 0200 Patrolling enroute Chebia continuing on surface until 0300 in order to arrive at destination as early as possible.

Finding a lump of coral and sand in an ocean overrun with enemy ships and aircraft demanded extraordinary navigational and submarine skills. Coe and his crew had what it took to find the island and avoid detection, but finding the refugees ashore would be another matter. Shore recon missions were extremely hazardous. They could also be deadly.

1 March 1942

0300   Stopped having arrived ¼ mile off s.w. Chebia Island. Made signals by blinker gun covering entire s.w. side of island at intervals. The signals included the proper challenge for the date, and messages such as, "British Party"; "U.S. Submarine calling British party." No response. It was a bright night with almost full moon, and the submarine was plainly in view of this island and the other small island to s. and w. During the approach on surface from the n.e. we easily [could] have been sighted from Chebia for at least 1 hour and from Kachangang [Island] for at least 2 hours prior to arrival.

0045   Sent Petersen, C.I., E.M. 1c in wherry to beach, Chebia s.w. point. He had full instructions to search island for British, if found to get them started to ship, and if not able to find them to return. He carried a blinker light and a simple code to communicate with ship, and was armed with a service pistol.

0135   Petersen signalled that British were not on island and left beach by wherry.

Petersen reported that he'd made a thorough search of the island and hadn't found the British party, nor any sign of life of any kind. Native shacks had been beaten to the ground, pots and pans scattered everywhere. He found several sets of footprints, military in style, he said, leading to the water, but none returning, indicating that the wearers had left by boat. It appeared that a small

Japanese landing force had been ashore recently, and if the British party was there, they had been taken prisoner and removed from the island. An optimist, Coe held out the possibility that the British might have gotten away earlier by boat.

Coe continued patrolling offshore, signaling, waiting for a response that never came. Twenty-four hours later the *S-39* stood out from Chebia Island empty-handed, the refugees' fate unknown. Coe is reported to have said later, "We were sorry for those people. The Japanese were merciless with prisoners."

Postwar reports claim that the refugees, after surviving an attack on the motor launch they had used to escape from Singapore, were left stranded on Chebia Island. Lacking fresh water and food, and after Spooner and Pulford had died of malaria, the surviving members of the party surrendered to the Japanese.

Red Coe went on to command the USS *Cisco*, which was sunk with all hands by the Japanese during her first war patrol west of Mindanao, Philippines.

While Coe failed to find and evacuate the British party, the mission itself was a great success. It proved once again that submarines could perform tasks other naval units could not, especially when the mission's requirements meant that a sub had to get in close—dangerously close—to enemy territory.

• • •

Prior to the planned invasion of the Palau Islands, code-named Operation Stalemate and scheduled for September 1944, the navy was directed to carry out reconnaissance of the beaches of Peleliu and Yap. The marines needed detailed information about tides, shoals, sandbars, and the like, which would help them decide how to employ Higgins landing boats, LVTs, and amtracs. Aerial photography was unsuitable because it couldn't probe beneath the surf or measure the height of coral reefs. The only way to get this information was to send small landing parties ashore in rubber boats from submarines—in other words, HUMINT. Such recon missions were not new to U.S. subs; several had carried out similar missions early in the war.

Commander Bill Perkins and the USS *Burrfish* were tapped to follow up an earlier photographic reconnaissance of Peleliu by the *Seawolf* and had orders to land a recon party on Peleliu and its neighbor, Yap. Perkins approached Peleliu submerged and completed a photo recon of its beaches from offshore with a special camera rigged to the scope. He noted that Japanese land-based and airborne radar had been detected by the submarine's APR radar detector (an early version of the *Blackfin*'s ESM). Under full darkness, Perkins nosed the *Burrfish* into shallow water off Peleliu and made a careful periscope recon of the island and its approaches, on the lookout for Japanese patrol boats and night fighters. His examination disclosed nothing more than the usual deserted beach and wall of jungle. Fearful of grounding, he eased the *Burrfish* inshore as close as he dared to off-load the recon team.

The landing party, armed only with knives and grenades, consisted of ten men who were members of UDT-10. (Underwater demolition teams were the precursors of today's Navy SEALs.) They were equipped with compasses, face masks, and swim fins and were expert in boat handling and surf riding. After collecting valuable information ashore, the men were recovered without incident; the *Burrfish* then moved on to Yap.

On the night of August 16, following a daylight photo recon, the UDT team landed on Yap's southern tip. They collected good intelligence, but more was needed. Two nights later the *Burrfish* stood off the beach with Perkins on the bridge watching a party of five men paddle ashore.

According to the *Burrfish*'s patrol report, edited here for clarity, between the time they shoved off from the submarine at 2006 and their return at 0315 the next day, something went tragically wrong.

0034 to 0300 Attempting to make contact with rubber boat.

0300 Sighted flashing white light from rubber boat.

0315 Picked up boat [with two men] the only crewmembers in it. [Three] were missing.

0348 Jap radar was picked up on the APR and the ship dived to avoid detection.

0348 to 0640 Patrolled off beach. Changed course [to patrol along rendezvous course line]. At 1829 surfaced but because of extremely black and rainy weather no attempt was made to run to the rendezvous point [ashore]. [Perkins reported that the men were covered with commando black paint and it would have been very difficult to see them in the water.] At 0515 dived and made submerged approach on rendezvous point. Searched all day along beach. None of the men were found.

Perkins's patrol report stated that the remnants of the recon team he'd recovered had found the island's fringing reef and searched for possible boat passages through it. They took soundings, after which they anchored offshore. On the beach they split up into two groups, leaving one man behind as a boat keeper.

Only two men returned to the boat. While one man stayed with it, the other man, after a breather, took a compass reading and swam back ashore. He never returned. The boat keeper and the other man waited well past the midnight rendezvous deadline, then paddled in to the beach in search of their missing mates.

Nothing. With dawn approaching, the two survivors rowed out and rejoined the waiting *Burrfish*.

According to Perkins, after considering all the possibilities, he concluded in his report that the three men had joined up, saw something interesting near the shoreline, decided to investigate, and were captured.

The men in the other recon unit aboard the *Burrfish* pleaded with Perkins to man a boat and search for the missing men. Perkins wouldn't allow it because there was only one hour of darkness left, and they would soon have to dive to avoid detection by Japanese radar, which had been idle all night but would soon be switched on. The next day the weather was squally with near zero visibility. It would have been courting disaster, Perkins wrote, to put a boat over the side and try to fix positions ashore under such conditions. He had no choice but to depart the area and return to base.

The invasion of Yap never materialized. Instead, like other islands in the Pacific, it was bypassed and left to die on the vine as U.S. forces moved on to retake the Philippines. The invasion of Peleliu, which came too late to affect the war's outcome, was a disaster. Thousands of marines died needlessly.

After the war, Japanese documents claimed that the three men missing on Yap had been captured, likely tortured to get information, then sent to a prison camp in the Philippines from which they never returned.

Shore party–style recon ended with the *Burrfish* operation. The loss of those men was a blow to the UDT and submarine force. Theater commanders labeled it too dangerous and a giveaway to the Japanese about future operations. Nevertheless, the value of photo recon and SIGINT collection from Japanese radar installations by submarines wasn't lost on the officers who were involved after the war with planning espionage operations against America's new enemy, the Soviet Union. Clearly submarines could get the goods, and if they could get the goods from territories under Japanese control, why not from territories under Soviet control?

Holystone originated with submarines like the *Swordfish*, *S-39*, *Burrfish*, and others, whose pioneering missions set the stage for what was to come in the cold war.

APPENDIX THREE

Hit and Run

The Galloping Ghosts
Rewrite Submarine History

The German U-boat campaign waged against Allied merchant shipping came close to giving Hitler the one victory he needed most to win World War II—the defeat of Great Britain. In the Pacific, the American submarine campaign waged against the Japanese merchant marine cut off Japan's lifelines and doomed that country to defeat. As Winston Churchill said, "The only thing that ever really frightened me during the war was the U-boat peril." Perhaps Japanese prime minister General Hideki Tojo had similar fears.

Early in the war, both German and U.S. submarine doctrine focused almost exclusively on the destruction of the enemy's battle fleet, but as the war progressed, it become apparent to both sides that submarines were more effective when used against merchant shipping. Grand Admiral Karl Dönitz organized his U-boats into wolfpacks to attack Allied supply convoys; U.S. submarines, under the command of Vice Admiral Charles A. Lockwood, mainly undertook lone-wolf patrols to decimate Japanese merchant shipping. Both Dönitz and Lockwood understood the great advantages submarines had over their adversaries: Their inherent stealth made them hard to find, hard to see, and hard to kill.

Unlike the United States, Germany also had to fight a powerful British fleet in waters close to home—the Baltic, the North Sea, the Mediterranean, the North Atlantic. The Germans believed that in addition to sinking supply convoys, sinking British warships, especially capital ships, would not just weaken the Royal Navy, it would weaken British resolve and morale. With this in mind Dönitz ordered that, whenever possible, U-boat commanders should attack British warships, especially battleships and aircraft carriers.

Dönitz then envisioned a daring hit-and-run attack against the British Home Fleet in its main anchorage in Scapa Flow, which was enclosed by the Orkney Islands at the northern tip of Scotland. The base was protected by patrol boats, block ships, and steel antisubmarine netting. The British, understandably, felt that Scapa Flow was impenetrable. Dönitz, after studying recon photos, tidal data, and other intelligence, thought otherwise. He was convinced that a determined sub skipper could penetrate the British defenses and attack the fleet.

Dönitz selected thirty-year-old Kapitänleutnant Günther Prien for the job. Commanding officer of the *U-47*, Prien possessed the traits Dönitz was looking for: seasoned judgment, experience, great daring. He was also fanatically loyal to Hitler and the *U-Bootwaffe*.

Dönitz presented the plan and asked, "What is your opinion, Prien? Can it be done? Yes or no?"

"Yes, sir."

"Very well, get your boat ready." Dönitz shook Prien's hand.

Prien departed from Kiel, Germany, on October 8. A German photoreconnaissance plane overflew Scapa Flow on October 12. The Germans were excited: A photograph showed that the battle cruiser HMS *Repulse* lay anchored near the *Royal Oak*, a 39,000-ton dreadnought, in the northeast corner of the Flow. With luck Prien could sink them both.

On the moonless night of October 13–14, 1939, Prien surfaced the *U-47*, a snorting red bull painted on her conning tower, just outside Scapa Flow. He had to overcome both the treacherous currents and also find a fifty-foot-wide opening in the antisubmarine defenses posed by the sunken block ships. In addition to these obstacles, Prien, expecting a moonless night, had surfaced to discover a brilliant display of northern lights. Prien noted in his war diary:

> The passage . . . through Holm Sound was accomplished only with the greatest difficulty. I was compelled to pass very close to the block ships, and [overcome] a ten-knot current [running behind us]. No watch was being kept on Holm Sound.

Once again, submarine stealth had paid off. Prien penetrated the defenses, scraping over low-slung antisubmarine cables, and once, temporarily, he ran aground. Inside the Flow, Prien searched for the fleet. Unknown to him, the *Repulse* and major elements of the Home Fleet had earlier departed Scapa Flow; only the *Royal Oak* and seaplane tender HMS *Pegasus* remained. Finally Prien saw the unmistakable shape of a British battleship, the mighty *Royal Oak*, her superstructure and bulging gun turrets illuminated by what he called "the burning sky." He mistook the *Pegasus*, which he saw at anchor beyond the *Royal Oak*, for another battleship. Prien closed in and fired three torpedoes, all of which hit the *Royal Oak*, one of them striking her magazine.

With a tremendous explosion, the burning *Royal Oak* rolled over and sank, taking down with her 833 British sailors. Prien reported:

> Three hits on *Royal Oak*. The ship blew up within a few seconds. After leaving Holm Sound, observed great anti-U-boat activity [with depth charges] in Scapa Flow. Was greatly bothered by brilliance of northern lights.

Two hours after entering Scapa Flow, the *U-47* sped south, out of what Prien called a witches' cauldron. Fighting a strong inflowing current, and easing past block ships with only inches to spare, Prien escaped hunting destroyers and slipped away into the North Sea.

The loss of the *Royal Oak* and her crew was a disaster for the Royal Navy. After the attack, they abandoned Scapa Flow and scattered the British Home Fleet to other anchorages, none of which was safe from attack by German surface warships. In Germany, Prien, now known as the Ghost of Scapa Flow, and his crew were welcomed as heroes. Having proven the value of a lone submarine set loose in an enemy harbor, Prien carried on with his war against merchantmen in the North Atlantic. In March 1941, the destroyer HMS *Wolverine* caught Prien and the marauding *U-47* on the surface off Ireland. Prien dived. Crippled by depth charges, the *U-47* tried to evade but was sunk with all hands. Prien was credited with sinking thirty ships and damaging another eight.

• • •

The value of stealthy lone-wolf submarining wasn't lost on Commander Eugene B. Fluckey, USN. Fluckey, a daring innovator of submarine tactics, would surely have credited Günther Prien with setting the standard for penetration of a harbor undetected, something Fluckey would refine and make his own. Fluckey proved that submarines could carry out a multitude of missions, even coastal bombardment with rockets, a tactic he pioneered and one that would one day influence cold war submarine doctrine and operations, including Holystone. He also refined the art of blowing up trains, when he sent a demolition team ashore on Karafuto, Japan, to set charges that wrecked a highballing steam locomotive and its passenger cars. It isn't a stretch to say that Fluckey's forays into demolition and rocketry were a practical lesson that hastened the development of the submarine-launched Polaris missile.

The idea of firing rockets from a submarine to bombard enemy positions ashore had been examined and discarded by the submarine force as impractical and, well, too new and therefore potentially unsettling to the guardians of the status quo. Nevertheless, Fluckey prevailed. He departed for his twelfth war patrol after equipping his submarine, the USS *Barb*, with a Mk 51 pipe-rack-style rocket launcher, a type used mainly for saturation shore bombardment, installed on the sub's main deck forward of the conning tower. It could fire twelve five-inch rockets in less than half a minute. Fluckey shoved off bound for Japan and a date with destiny.

Man battle stations rockets!

The *Barb* hit Japanese coastal cities from Hokkaido to Shiritori with rockets. Gasoline storage facilities and godowns filled with supplies went up in flames. Then and there Fluckey realized that anything was possible, especially bigger, more powerful rockets. Maybe they could even be launched from a submerged submarine. Time would tell.

Before his foray into rocketry, Fluckey had amassed an enviable record of sinking Japanese ships. By January 1945 his tonnage sunk to date totaled eleven ships, including an escort aircraft carrier and a converted light cruiser. Nicknamed "Lucky," Fluckey believed a man made his own luck. Therefore, patrolling off the coast of China, where Japanese targets had seemingly gone to ground, Fluckey analyzed traffic patterns based on information provided by coast watchers and spies in China. He realized that Japanese ships were travelling by day, when they had a better chance of surviving and when it was almost impossible for a sub to attack so close to the coast. At night they holed up in harbors their captains believed were impervious to attack.

Accordingly, Fluckey tracked two targets by day but lost them at night. It didn't take long to figure out that they'd anchored in-shore. But Fluckey faced a host of obstacles getting to them, mainly minefields, shallow water, and clots of Chinese junks that would impede the *Barb*'s maneuvers.

Fluckey reported:

> 0030 Started an inshore surface search for convoy anchorage. Maneuvering constantly to avoid collision with junks. Entourage consists of several hundred darkened junks.

Undeterred, and realizing that the junks could provide cover as well as early warning of mines, Fluckey pressed his attack on the ships he believed were anchored in Namkwan harbor (now Shacheng Gang), located about 120 miles south of Wenchow (now Wenzhou), China. Fluckey knew that his advantage consisted of surprise. He also knew that the Japanese wouldn't know what had hit them, and that when they finally figured it out the *Barb* would be long gone. Fluckey believed that "stealth, stupefying surprise, and a sprinkle of serendipity [were] *Barb*'s hallmarks." He proceeded up the narrow, poorly charted, and mined channel into the harbor, sometimes maneuvering in less than forty feet of water.

0300 Rounded Incog Island and contacted a very large group of anchored ships in the lower reaches of Namkwan Harbor! Slowed to take stock of the situation.

Fluckey had hit the *Barb* jackpot. Instead of two ships, he'd found a convoy of thirty ships! They, along with three escorts, lay anchored in three lines parallel to the coast, five hundred yards apart, making a solid wall of overlapping targets for the *Barb*'s torpedoes.

Man battle stations torpedo!

Fluckey's patrol report stated:

Atmosphere throughout the boat is electric. The men are more tense than I've ever seen them. Range 6,000 yards. Made ready all tubes. Our biggest job will be to prevent too many torpedoes from hitting one ship!

[I] chose one of the large ships to the left of center of the near column as target.

Fired one. Fired two. Fired three. Fired four. Shifted target to right for ships ahead in near column. Fired seven. Fired eight. Fired nine. Fired ten. All ahead flank! Commanding officer manned bridge. Timed and observed eight hits.

Explosions erupted in the convoy. Smoke and fire boiled from damaged and sinking ships. Tracers and searchlights laced the sky, the Japanese certain they were under attack by planes.

Fluckey spun the *Barb* on her heel and, employing broken-field running through the junk fleet, highballed it for deep water, where, as Fluckey observed, life began at forty fathoms. With gunfire well astern, the *Barb* made tracks for Midway.

Eugene Fluckey had just completed one of the most daring and successful submarine raids in history, for which he was awarded the Medal of Honor. The lessons taught by Lucky Fluckey—innovation and persistence—rang through the sub force for decades. His doctrine of stealth, stupefying surprise, and a sprinkle of serendipity became the hallmark of the sub force, too, as it moved into its cold war phase. Fluckey proved that with submarines, anything was possible.

Fluckey carried on his tradition of innovation as postwar ComSubPac and later in various assignments including director of ONI. In that position, his vision helped shape the role Holystone played in America's defeat of the Soviet Union. Fluckey, the Galloping Ghost of the China Coast, died in 2007.

• • •

While Fluckey and the *Barb* were busy torpedoing ships in Namkwan harbor, Lieutenant Commander George L. Street, a veteran of nine war patrols in the USS *Gar*, took command of the USS *Tirante*, a new submarine. Though she arrived late in the Pacific when targets were scarce, Street knew what it took to succeed in submarine warfare and was determined to prove it as CO of the *Tirante*. Submarines were scouring the waters off Japan and China for ships, haunting harbors as *Barb* had, for anything worthy of a torpedo. In 1944 alone, almost half of the ships sailing from imperial waters ended up on the bottom. Now it was March 1945, and the Japanese merchant marine had all but evaporated.

Street conducted *Tirante*'s first war patrol in the East China and Yellow seas. Hoping to blood his ship early, he attacked and sank a small ship off Kyushu. He torpedoed another a few days later, followed by the *Nikko Maru*, a 5,500-ton transport loaded with troops and their equipment. For her efforts, the *Tirante* suffered a stout depth-charging by escorts, one of which Street targeted and apparently sank with one of the new homing torpedoes he carried, which had recently been introduced into the fleet.

On the night of April 12–13, Street received a radio message of the type known as Ultra, with information about a convoy holed up in a harbor in Quelpart Island, also known as Cheju Do, south of Korea. Ultra had played a vital role in the submarine war, giving skippers on patrol an immeasurable advantage over the Japanese.

By the spring of 1943, the United States had cracked both the Japanese naval and merchant marine codes. This code-breaking enterprise, known as Ultra, for ultrasecret, enabled American submarines to be routinely deployed with accurate information about Japanese convoys, including detailed descriptions of their movements and even their cargoes, extracted from decoded radio traffic. Often the information was sent to patrolling submarines within minutes of its receipt. It allowed ComSubPac to direct subs to individual ships with great precision. After that it was up to the individual CO to find and attack the target. Without Ultra, the submarine war would have been a long, tedious process of hunting for *maru*s over an immense expanse of water, guided by planning, luck, and the hope that if you crisscrossed enough square miles of ocean *something* would show up sooner or later. George Street knew what he had in Ultra and how to use it.

The *Tirante* approached the anchorage at Quelpart at night on the surface via a long, narrow channel. Ultra had also provided information on the location of a large minefield sewn between the coasts of Quelpart and Korea, which Street had carefully avoided. From Street's patrol report:

> 14 April 0000 Approaching Quelpart Island northwestern side. 0029 Radar contact. Patrol boat. Went to tracking stations and worked around him. Patrol was suspicious for a short time; then went back to sleep. Continued working up the anchorage.

The *Tirante* sped up the thirty-mile-long channel at flank speed, the roar of her diesels echoing off the surrounding hills. The bridge watch smelled cattle and vegetation. There was no moonlight to help identify landmarks. All Street had to go on was the ragged outlines of the narrow channel displayed on the radar scope. Then:

> 0223 Radar contact. Another patrol boat. Avoided by going close inshore. He was patrolling back and forth in front of the anchorage, had radar and was echo-ranging in the bargain. He also became suspicious, but our tactics of running inshore confused him, and he continued routine patrolling. The only chart of any use was the Jap [aircraft pilot] chart labeled "Japan Aviation Chart, SouthernMost Portion of [Korea] No. V3-36." No soundings were shown. Hoped the place wasn't mined and that none of the five shore-based radars reported on Quelpart were guarding the harbor.

Approaching the anchorage—it was, someone said, like sticking your head into a cave on a dark night—Street called away battle stations. The *Tirante* was maneuvering in water only seven fathoms—forty-two feet—deep, not enough to cover the ship. If there were any Japanese ships in there, they were invisible or had upped anchor and sailed. Street started around the small island off the anchorage.

> 0340 Bridge made out the shapes of the ships in the anchorage. Radar officer confirmed sharp pips of ships. . . .

The *Tirante* paused. A thump from the outer doors opening on the six forward torpedo tubes. Then, *Fire!* A line of bubbles streaked for the target. Minutes later:

> A tremendous beautiful explosion. A great mushroom of white blinding flame shot 2,000 feet into the air. . . . Then a tremendous roar flattened our ears against our heads. The jackpot, and no mistake! In her light camouflage *Tirante* stood out like a snowman in a coal pit.

Street fired more torpedoes, then got out of there. More ships erupted in flame as the *Tirante* sped for the open sea, frigates chasing. With dawn breaking, Street dived and evaded them submerged. The frigates unleashed a terrific depth-charging where they thought the *Tirante* was but found nothing. As Street noted, they heard depth-charging and saw planes all day. The area would be hot for days.

The *Tirante* arrived in Midway to a heroes' welcome complete with brass band and movie cameramen. ComSubPac confirmed the sinking of the 4,000-ton *Juzan Maru* and two frigates at Quelpart. Street, like Fluckey before him, had proven what a well-skippered and -crewed submarine could accomplish even under the most dangerous circumstances. For his exploits Street, the Ghost of Quelpart, received the Medal of Honor.

Street wasn't finished. On another patrol he again entered a harbor and sank another ship as well as a host of picket boats and small craft essential to Japan's war efforts. Street retired from the navy after serving in a number of capacities related to submarine warfare and its increasing importance to the cold war and Holystone. He died in 2000.

Prien, Fluckey, Street, and others proved the value of submarine stealth in the pursuit of difficult objectives. Never was this made clearer than during the cold war, when the objectives entailed not the sinking of ships but the gathering of intelligence to defeat an enemy. Building on their pioneering exploits, no matter that Prien was an enemy, the sub force adapted to a cold war that was no less deadly for the fact that submarines didn't fire torpedoes but instead waged a battle that relied on stealth, stupefying surprise, and yes, a sprinkle of serendipity.

ACKNOWLEDGMENTS AND SOURCES

A book like *Stalking the Red Bear* isn't written in a vacuum. Aside from the operational scenarios unique to the *Blackfin*, it builds from and relies on the work of others for insights, conclusions, history, and technical matters that can be difficult if not impossible to develop from scratch. Therefore I thank the many writers who tackled Holystone and the cold war before I ever got there. They paved the way, and I followed. My contribution will, I hope, add something of value to a part of the Holystone story that until now has not been told.

I also want to express my sincere gratitude to "Roy Hunter" for his help and patience and, above all, his willingness to sit down and tell me what I needed to know to write his and his shipmates' stories. I thank him for letting me pester him as often as I did about details and just one more explanation of how complicated things aboard submarines work.

For the portrayal of Soviet submarine operations in the Barents Sea, I turned to a variety of sources. Among them were articles in

Russian and American periodicals, postings on Web sites devoted to Russian-Soviet submarine history, studies produced for international organizations and defense institutes, and books about cold war–era Soviet submarine operations. I also spoke with experts in the field who offered advice and directed me to sources.

In particular, I want to acknowledge two important sources that I used for the description of the Soviet submarine patrol from Polyarnyy: "An Ordinary Deployment," an article by Captain Second Rank A. Stakhayev, originally published in the January 1994 issue of *Morskoi Sbornik* and reprinted in English in the *U.S. Naval Institute Proceedings*, July 1994; and "Life Aboard a Soviet Destroyer and a Soviet Submarine," a RAND paper written by Sally W. Stoecker in September 1983 and published by the Defense Technical Information Center, accession no. AD-A158 864, in 1995. My sincere thanks to both authors. I also want to thank Michael DiMercurio, a cold war submariner and author, who in his book *Barracuda Final Bearing* provided the inspiration for the attack teacher scenario and depictions of operations aboard a 637-class submarine.

Authoritarian trends in Russia have resulted in a return to Soviet-style secrecy and censorship. The Kremlin has exercised increasing control over the news media and journalists, as well as publishing and scholarship. It has also restricted access to archives that had earlier been opened to scholars conducting legitimate research into the history of the cold war. Today, much as it did in the past, the Kremlin threatens writers and scholars it doesn't approve of with arrest—or worse—and confiscates any publications and reports it deems critical of the current regime. In such an atmosphere it's not surprising that material formerly available on Soviet-era submarine operations is now virtually impossible to acquire. In addition, the FSB, successor to the KGB, has had a chilling effect on the free exchange of information. Understandably, the former submariners whom I contacted in Russia declined to divulge any details of their cold war service. Perhaps in time this will change.

Nevertheless, I discovered that except for vocabulary and phraseology, U.S. and Soviet submarine operating procedures were amazingly similar. What was not similar was the complete trust U.S. commanders placed in their submarine crews. There were no *zampoliti*—political officers—aboard U.S. subs to watch and approve every move the captain and crew made. Soviet-era submariners have expressed amazement that U.S. subs operate unfettered by shore controllers. Independence—trust, if you like—is one of the hallmarks of the U.S. sub force.

. . .

As in everything, my wife, Karen, played a big part in *Stalking the Red Bear*. She's a tough critic, and her insights and objectivity kept me on track and made this a better book. She also suggested ways to take some of the rough edges off a narrative that sometimes got too complicated or too dense. Thanks, babe.

As for research, I was surprised, if not dismayed, to discover that many of the standard texts about nuclear submarines and their operations, especially their tactics, weapons, and sonar, were, if not flat-out wrong, often wildly at variance with the hands-on experience of Roy Hunter and others like him. This was true for strategic and tactical issues as well, especially in the fields of intelligence gathering, nuclear weapons, SSBNs, and Soviet ASW doctrine. I would also urge caution when using material about submarines found on the Internet, as much of it is misleading and inaccurate.

I want to acknowledge the help and advice I received from

individuals who are experts in their fields. Alena Aissing, university associate librarian, Germanic and Slavic Studies and European History at the University of Florida George A. Smathers Libraries; Steve Ernst; Heather Florence; Paul Lapinski, formerly of Kollmorgen Electro-optical; Wendy Gully, Archivist, Submarine Force Library and Museum, Groton, Connecticut; Armando Rodriguez; and Nina Kudryashova. A special thanks to Mary Lee Fowler, daughter of James "Red" Coe, for providing the patrol report and other information concerning the *S-39*'s mission to Chebia Island. For a description of submarine family separation, I'm indebted to Roy Hunter's daughter.

A special thanks to the late Captain Edward L. Beach, USN (ret.), a submariner's submariner if ever there was one. Beach loved the navy and submarines. His stories grabbed hold of me and never let go. I had the good fortune to meet Captain Beach at a book signing and to chat with him at length about his career. For the kid who grew up reading his books, it was a dream come true.

It follows, then, that among all the books I read and studied while writing *Stalking the Red Bear*, the one that offered inspiration when I needed it most and provided insights and guidance into the world of nuclear submarines turned out to be a novel written by Ned Beach entitled *Cold Is the Sea*. Written in 1978, long after Beach had retired from the navy, it's the story of three former shipmates who had served together in submarines during World War II and find themselves back in action during the cold war. In typical Beach fashion, the story involves heroism, duty, and camaraderie, which he rendered in fine style. Beach had an eye for the telling detail, and his descriptions of shipboard routine and how things on submarines work and look are unmatched. Especially valuable to me were his descriptions of the nuclear navy of the early 1960s, the period Beach wrote about in *Cold Is the Sea*.

The story helped me understand not only what I was writing about but also how it looked back then, which, luckily, wasn't so different from the 1970s of Roy Hunter.

Finally, a special thanks to my dad, who served in submarines during World War II, in the USS *Rasher*.

GLOSSARY

AGI: A type of intelligence-gathering ship used by both the Soviets and NATO.

ASPL: Absolute sound pressure level. Intensity of sound measured underwater.

ASW: Antisubmarine warfare.

Arctic circle: Imaginary line separating the earth's arctic zone from the northern temperate zone.

Baffles: The conical area behind a submarine where the noise from hydrodynamic flow and propeller turbulence greatly reduces sonar's detection ability. When a submarine clears baffles, it maneuvers left or right to search the area behind it for an intruder.

Ballast tanks: Tanks used to submerge and surface a submarine by filling them with seawater (flooding) or blowing them dry with compressed air (deballasting or dewatering.)

Bearing: Direction to a target expressed in degrees: 000 north, 090 east, 180 south, etc.

Bearing rate: The rate of change of a target's bearing. Expressed in degrees left or right per minute.

Biologicals: Sea life; the noise it creates, which can be heard on sonar.

Blue Nose: A sailor who has crossed the arctic circle and been inducted into the Order of the Blue Nose.

Boomer: An SSBN.

Boundary layers: Layers of varying temperatures in the ocean, which affect sound propagation and reception by bending sound waves.

BOQ: Bachelor officers' quarters.

BQQ-5 sonar: A low-frequency active and passive submarine sonar system.

BQR-7 sonar: Submarine sonar system whose hydrophones are installed around a sub's bow and conform to its shape.

BQS-14 sonar: Short-range under-ice and mine avoidance submarine sonar installed in the front of the sail.

Bridge: Small cockpitlike space atop a submarine's sail from which the ship is conned while on the surface.

Broadband: Sound encompassing all frequencies. Background noise heard by sonar.

Bubble: A submarine's angle in the sea expressed in degrees, as in "Five degree down bubble."

Bubble head: Submariner.

CCP: Central command post. Control room of a Russian submarine.

Christmas tree: A submarine's hull opening indicator. Green for closed; red for open.

CIA: Central Intelligence Agency.

CinCLantFleet: Commander in Chief Atlantic Fleet. The four-star admiral in command of the U.S. Navy's Atlantic Fleet, including ComSubLant, who is a reporting subordinate. Also refers to the organizational structure.

CO: Commanding officer.

COB: Chief of the boat, pronounced "cob." Senior enlisted man in a submarine; the XO's (see page 282) top assistant.

COMINT: Communications intelligence. Collection of foreign communications including messages sent by radio and other means.

Compartment: A space aboard a submarine bounded fore and aft by bulkheads and port and starboard by the ship's pressure hull.

COMSEC: Communications Security. Protection of U.S. communications systems.

ComSubLant: Commander Submarines Atlantic. Refers to both the flag officer in charge of the fleet and its organizational structure.

ComSubPac: Commander Submarines Pacific.

CNO: Chief of naval operations.

Conn: To maneuver a ship. The OOD (see page 280) has the conn and is addressed in tactical situations as, "Conn, [this is] sonar." The OOD responds, "Conn, aye [yes]." The modern term is "driving," as in "submarine driver."

Contact: A target; a ship.

Control room: Operations center of a U.S. submarine.

Counterdetection: Detection of a friendly submarine by a hostile one, or vice versa.

Cryptanalyst: A specialist in coded communications.

DIA: Defense Intelligence Agency.

Double hull: A submarine designed with an inner pressure hull surrounded by an outer superstructure hull. The space between the hulls is used for ballast tanks and other equipment.

Diving planes: Movable horizontal appendages attached to the sail (on *Sturgeon*-class submarines) and at the stern, that control diving depth and angle.

Duty officer: Officer in charge of the ship when it's moored or in dry dock.

EPM: Emergency propulsion motor. A DC motor that takes its power from a submarine's storage battery.

ESM: Electronic signals measures. A mast with receptors for passive detection of radar and other electronic emissions. Supplements ESM receptors in the Type 15D periscope.

Familygram: Short, personal radio messages sent to deployed submariners from home.

Fire-control party: Personnel who operate a submarine's target tracking computers and related equipment for the purpose of firing torpedoes or launching weapons at hostile ships.

GIUK Gap: Greenland–Iceland–United Kingdom gap. A narrow part of the Atlantic ocean between Greenland and the UK. Soviet subs had to transit the gap to reach the Atlantic Ocean from the Barents Sea. SOSUS (see page 281) and patrolling U.S. subs monitored Soviet subs operating in the area.

Goat locker: Chief petty officers' quarters aboard a submarine.

Group scram: A scram (see page 280) that releases some but not all of a reactor's control rods to shut down the reactor.

Helm: Refers to both a ship's rudder and the equipment that controls it. Also the individual steering the ship, called a "helmsman."

HY-80 steel: High-yield alloy steel capable of withstanding 80,000 psi used to construct submarine hulls.

HUMINT: Human intelligence; secret agents or spies.

ICBM: Intercontinental ballistic missile.

KGB: *Komitet Gosudarstvennoy Bezopasnosti.* Soviet Committee of State Security; Soviet state security service.

KH-8: One of the early Keyhole series of U.S. area reconnaissance and close-look imaging satellites.

MAD: Magnetic anomaly detector. Airborne magnetometer used to detect disturbances in the earth's magnetic field caused by a submarine's steel hull.

Michman: Warrant officer in the Soviet navy.

MI6: British Secret Service; equivalent of CIA.

Mk 37 torpedo: Wire-guided, homing submarine torpedo armed with a warhead packed with 300 pounds of HBX high explosive.

Mk 113 fire-control system: Computerized submarine fire-control system used in *Sturgeon*-class submarines.

NATO: North Atlantic Treaty Organization. A military alliance established for collective defense in response to an attack on any member country.

NSA: National Security Agency.

Nuclear fission: The splitting of an atomic nucleus and consequent release of energy. Controlled fission occurs in nuclear reactors; uncontrolled fission occurs in nuclear weapons.

OBA: Oxygen breathing apparatus. Emergency breathing mask and associated gear.

OCS: Officer Candidate School.

OOD: Officer of the deck. Officer in tactical command of a ship. Represents the commanding officer and requires CO's permission to carry out certain evolutions.

1MC: Submarine general announcing system.

ONI: Office of Naval Intelligence.

Op orders: Operation orders; a document setting out parameters of a military deployment.

PD: Periscope depth.

Periviz: A video system built into submarine periscopes capable of relaying images to a slaved video monitor in the control room.

Poopie suit: Blue coveralls worn by submariners.

Sail: Finlike projection atop a submarine containing the bridge and housing periscopes and masts.

SALT: Strategic Arms Limitation Treaty. Signed by President Nixon and General Secretary Brezhnev in May 1972.

Scram: Emergency shutdown of a nuclear reactor. The word may have come from "safety control rod axe man." When the first nuclear reactor, built in Chicago by Enrico Fermi, went critical, a man stood ready with an axe to cut the rope holding up the control rod. The rod would then drop into the reactor and quench the chain reaction.

Shakedown: Period when a ship undergoes adjustment and fine-tuning after commissioning or overhaul.

SIGINT: Signals intelligence. Electronic communications collection, including telemetry, instrumentation, infrared, etc.

SINS: Ship's inertial navigation system. A navigation system that works by tracing a ship's movement from its known starting position. Requires periodic updates from external sources such as global positioning satellites.

Sonar: Sound Navigation and Ranging. System comprised of sound receptors and computers for detecting the presence and location of a ship. A sound wave fired into the sea and reflected back from a target (active sonar) gives an accurate reading of the target's range and bearing. Submarines rarely use active sonar because it gives away their position. Listening to the noise produced by a target (passive sonar) can reveal its bearing and often its classification, i.e., surface ship or submarine.

SOSUS: Sound Surveillance System. An underwater hydrophone network extending from the East Coast of the United States to the western edge of the Barents Sea. Also installed in the Pacific off the West Coast of the U.S.

SLBM: Submarine-launched ballistic missile.

Spec ops: Special operations.

Spherical array: Sonar hydrophones arranged in a spherical shape inside the bow, or nose cone, of a submarine. Also known as a "conformal" array.

SSBN: Ballistic missile submarine, nuclear.

SSN: Attack submarine, nuclear.

STASS: Submarine towed array sonar system. A towed cable equipped with sonar receptors.

Starpom: Executive officer (XO) in the Soviet navy.

SUBROC: Submarine rocket. A tactical ASW nuclear ballistic missile launched from submarines.

Sound signature: Broadband noises and narrowband tonals that identify a ship by class or type.

Thermal layer: Layers of warm or cold water near the ocean's surface, which bend sound waves above or below them. Thermal layers complicate sonar's ability to detect ships.

TMA: Target motion analysis. The method of maneuver to establish a target's course, speed, and range based on sonar or visual inputs. The fire-control party uses the acquired data to aim and fire torpedoes or missiles at the target.

Transient: Short-duration noise emanating from a submarine. Can be caused by the opening and closing of torpedo tube shutters and hatches, even dropped tools.

UQC: Underwater telephone; also called a "Gertrude" in the U.S. Navy.

Uranium-235: An isotope of uranium. When bombarded with slow neutrons it undergoes rapid fission, releasing energy. In a submarine reactor, the energy heats water to make steam to drive the submarine.

VHF: Very high frequency. Radio transmissions broadcast at 30 MHz (megahertz) to 300 MHz.

VLF: Very low frequency. Radio transmissions broadcast at 3 kHz (kilohertz) to 30 kHz.

Wardroom: Officers' messroom and conference room aboard a ship. A place where officers can eat, relax, and also plan operations at sea.

XO: Executive officer, second in command.

***Zampolit*:** Political indoctrination officer assigned to Soviet navy ships.

BIBLIOGRAPHY

Allbeury, Joseph. *Russian Cobra, Foxtrot-Class Submarine*. Sydney, Australia: Jasper Communications, 2002.

Andrew, Christopher, and Oleg Gordievsky. *KGB: The Inside Story of Its Foreign Operations from Lenin to Gorbachev*. New York: HarperCollins, 1990.

Bamford, James. *Body of Secrets: Anatomy of the Ultra-Secret National Security Agency*. New York: Doubleday, 2001.

———. *The Puzzle Palace*. New York: Houghton Mifflin, 1982. (The two best books there are on the NSA; an invaluable resource.)

Beach, Edward L. *Cold Is the Sea*. New York: Dell, 1978.

———. *Submarine*. New York: Henry Holt, 1946. (One of the best books ever written about World War II U.S. submarine operations; the primary source for the *Tirante* episode and patrol reports.)

Bellona Foundation. "The Russian Northern Fleet Nuclear Submarine Accidents." Report no. 2:96. Available at http://spb.org.ru/bellona/ehome/russia/nfl/nfl8.htm.

Burrows, William E. *Deep Black: Space Espionage and National Security*. New York: Random House, 1986.

Busuttil, W., and A. M. C. Busuttil. "Psychological Effects on Families Subjected to Enforced and Prolonged Separations. . . ." *Sexual and Relationship Therapy* 16, no. 3 (August 2001): 207–28.

Chipman, Donald. "Admiral Gorshkov and the Soviet Navy." *Air University Review*, July–August 1982.

Cote, Owen R., Jr. "The Third Battle: Innovation in the U.S. Navy's Silent Cold War Struggle with Soviet Submarines," Naval War College *Newport Papers* no. 16, 2003.

Crankshaw, Edward (commentary and notes). *Khrushchev Remembers*. New York: Little, Brown, 1970.

DiMercurio, Michael, and Michael Benson. *The Complete Idiot's Guide to Submarines*. New York: Alpha Books, 2003. (An insider's view of a U.S. nuclear submarine, comprehensive and humorous to boot.)

Dönitz, Karl. *Memoirs: Ten Years and Twenty Days*. Annapolis, MD: Naval Institute, 1990.

Dorril, Stephen. *MI6*. New York: Free Press, 2000.

Drew, Christopher, Michael L. Millenson, and Robert Becker. "Enemies Below," *Chicago Tribune*, January 6–11, 1991.

Fluckey, Eugene B. *Thunder Below*. Chicago and Urbana: University of Illinois Press, 1992. (A well-written tale by a master submariner; the source material for the description of the *Barb*'s operations off the coast of China.)

Friedman, Norman. *Submarine Design and Development*. Annapolis, MD: Naval Institute, 1984.

———. *U.S. Submarines Since 1945*. Annapolis, MD: Naval Institute, 1994.

Gaddis, John Lewis. *The Cold War: A New History*. New York: Penguin Press, 2005.

Goldstein, Lyle J., and Zhukov, Yuri M. "A Tale of Two Fleets: A Russian Perspective on the 1973 Naval Standoff in the Mediterranean." *Naval War College Review*, Spring 2004.

Herrick, Robert Waring. *Soviet Naval Strategy*. Annapolis, MD: Naval Institute, 1968.

"How Submarine Intelligence Collection Made a Difference—Lessons from the Past." Published proceedings of the Naval Submarine League History Seminar, April 11, 2007.

Huchthausen, Peter. *K-19: The Widowmaker*. Washington, DC: National Geographic, 2002.

Huchthausen, Peter, Igor Kurdin, and R. Alan White. *Hostile Waters*. New York: St. Martin's Press, 1997. (Both Huchthausen books provided invaluable source material and detailed insights into Soviet submarine operations.)

Jones, Roger S. *Physics for the Rest of Us*. New York: McGraw-Hill, 1993.

Köhl, Fritz, and Eberhard Rössler. *The Type XII U-boat*. Rev. ed. Annapolis, MD: Naval Institute, 2002.

Lockwood, Charles A., and Hans Christian Adamson. *Hell at Fifty Fathoms*. Philadelphia and New York: Chilton, 1962. (A history of submarine disasters including the loss of the USS *Cochino*.)

Military Analysis Network. Online at http://www.fas.org/man.

Missing Air Crew. Online at http://www.missingaircrew.com. Excerpts from *The Naked Warriors: The Elite Fighting Force That Became the Navy SEALs*, by Francis D. Fane. (An important source for the depiction of the *Burrfish* operation; also for the patrol report narrative.)

National Museum of American History. "Family Support/Supporting Families." Online at http://americanhistory.si.edu/subs/ashore/familysupport. (Basic source material for the depiction of submarine wives and families during long deployments.)

Pavlov, A. S. *Warships of the USSR and Russia, 1945–1995*. Annapolis, MD: Naval Institute, 1997.

Penkovskiy, Oleg. *The Penkovskiy Papers*. Garden City, NY: Doubleday, 1965.

Polmar, Norman, and K. J. Moore. *Cold War Submarines*. Dulles, VA: Brassey's, 2004.

Polmar, Norman, and Jurrien Noot. *Submarines of the Russian Navies, 1718–1990*. Annapolis, MD: Naval Institute, 1991. (Polmar's books are the gold standard for detailed specifications and histories of submarine development. Good source material for anyone delving into submarine operations.)

Prien, Günther. *I Sank the Royal Oak*. London: John Spencer, 1957.

Richelson, Jeffrey. *American Espionage and the Soviet Target*. New York: William Morrow, 1987.

Rhodes, Richard. *Dark Sun: The Making of the Hydrogen Bomb*. New York: Simon & Schuster, 1995.

———. *The Making of the Atomic Bomb*. New York: Simon & Schuster, 1986.

Roscoe, Theodore. *United States Submarine Operations in World War II*. Annapolis, MD: Naval Institute, 1949. (A dated but still valuable source for information about U.S. submarine operations, especially for the special missions against the Japanese outlined in Appendix Two of *Stalking the Red Bear*; also for related submarine patrol report narratives.)

Sasgen, Peter. *Red Scorpion: The War Patrols of the USS Rasher*. Annapolis, MD: Naval Institute, 1995.

Sontag, Sherry, and Christopher Drew. *Blind Man's Bluff*. New York: Public Affairs, 1998. (An excellent and groundbreaking overview of Operation Holystone.)

Stakhayev, A. "An Ordinary Deployment." *Proceedings of the United States Naval Institute* 120, no. 7, issue 1097 (July 1994): 79–82. Reprinted from *Morskoi Sbornik*, January 1994. (One of the few published articles about Soviet cold war submarine operations.)

Stoecker, Sally W. "Life Aboard A Soviet Destroyer and A Soviet Submarine." RAND Paper no. P-6910, September 1983. Defense Technical Institute Information Center accession no. AD-A158 864, 1995.

Soviet Submarine Recce Guide. Technical Training Naval Intelligence Officer Intelligence Specialist (IS). Armed Forces Air Intelligence Training Center, Naval Intelligence Branch, Lowry Air Force Base, Colorado. (A book of Soviet submarine silhouettes for identification at sea.)

U.S. Naval Institute Proceedings. Various issues.

USS *Burrfish* patrol report (declassified), August 24, 1944. PDF courtesy of Mark Swank.

Submarine Review. Various issues. Published by the Naval Submarine League.

Submarine Wives Club. Online at http://www.submarinewivesclub.org. (A survival guide for submarine wives; rare source of information on the topic.)

To Use the Sea: Readings in Seapower and Maritime Affairs. 2nd ed. Annapolis, MD: Naval Institute, 1977.

Vego, Milan. *Soviet Naval Tactics*. Annapolis, MD: Naval Institute, 1992. (An easy-to-understand explanation of a difficult subject.)

Wolfpack. Alexandria, VA: Time-Life Books, 1989.

Zumwalt, Elmo R., Jr. *On Watch*. New York: Quadrangle, 1976.

INDEX

Note: For further definitions, see Glossary.

A-1 SLBM, 42
A-3 SLBM, 42
absolute sound pressure level. *See*
    ASPL
AGI ships, Soviet, 92–93, 136, 170
aircraft carriers
    Soviet exercise vs., 191–94
    Soviet missiles vs., 158
Akula Russian submarines, 231
Amethyst SS-N-7 Soviet missiles, 158
antisubmarine warfare (ASW), *ix*
    NATO, 201–2
    post-USSR improvement in
        technologies of, 231–32
    SOSUS in, 64–65
    Soviet, 5, 16, 42, 66–68, 74–76, 100,
        204–5
        aircraft, 115
        radar, 63, 113–14
        satellites, 113
        by surface ships, 114
APR radar detector, 253, 254
Archerfish (USS submarine), 47
arctic circle, induction ceremony at,
    108–9
arctic pack ice, 119–20
    sonar system for, 47

ASPL (absolute sound pressure level),
    17, 146, 149, 155, 160–61, 164,
    211
    accuracy of, 157, 159
ASW. *See* antisubmarine warfare
Atlantic Drift, 63, 119, 170

baffles, clearing of, 116–17, 154, 164,
    203
ballast-control panel, 94
ballast tank vent switches, 96–97
Barb (World War II submarine), 210,
    261–64
Barbero (submarine), 238
Barents Sea
    Blackfin's entrance to, 115, 118–20
    description of, 62–63
    reports of intel missions in. See
        patrol reports
    shallow underwater visibility in, 178
    Soviet radar sites on, 63
    temperature boundary layers in, 63,
        170
    U.S. gathering of intelligence in,
        6–7, 116–18
        slide presentation watched by
            Zumwalt, 12–14

Bataan, 247
Beach, Edward L. (Ned), *Cold Is the Sea*, 273–74
Bear Island, 64, 201
Bear Island Trench, 62
Bell Laboratories, 243
Beriev Be-12 Chaika (NATO designation: Mail), 66, 115, 190
Bismarck (German battleship), 107–8
Blackfin (submarine)
  in attack teacher, 15–19
  crew of, 47, 50–51, 103
  enhancements to, 44–45
  food on, 105–7, 189, 191
  in Holystone operation
    briefing, 59–65, 70, 76
    coming on station, 115, 118–22
    counterdetection by Soviets, 220–25
    departure, 89–93, 96–98
    ICBM test, 207, 211–20
    op order, 60, 65, 76, 104, 106, 107, 118, 120, 209
    as pseudonym, *xii, xix*
    return home, 211, 224–28
    route to Barents Sea, 99–109
    rules of engagement, 65, 209
    Soviet anticarrier exercises observed, 191–97
    stalking intelligence in Barents Sea, 135–38, 141, 143–48, 155–61
    Type II submarine interception, 148–49, 152–65, 177–84, 186–88
  later career of, 232
  movies on, 107
  nuclear reactor in, 54–56
    scramming, 221–23, 227
  as perfect antiship weapon, 37
  predeployment maintenance of, 31–33
  as pseudonym, xii, xix
  shakedown cruise of, 35–38, 53, 56
  statistics on displacement of, 47
  as *Sturgeon*-class submarine, 21
  test depth of, 48, 98
Block Island, 91, 92

Block Island Sound, 35
Blue Nose Induction Ceremony, 108–9
BQQ-5 sonar system, 47
BQR-7 sonar system, 47, 215
BQS-6 under-ice sonar, 120
BQS-14 sonar system, 47
Bremerton (Washington), 232
Brezhnev, Leonid, Nixon's meeting with, 13, 61, 208, 229
Brisbane (Australia), 78
Bulganin, Nikolai, 181
Burrfish (World War II submarine), 253–56
Butch Cassidy and the Sundance Kid (movie), 107

carbon monoxide, 101
CCP. *See* central command post
central command post (CCP; Soviet), 168–69
Central Intelligence Agency (CIA), 91, 92, 140, 213, 214, 226
  K–129 disaster and, 239
Charlie-class Soviet SSGNs, 113, 116, 157, 211
  mission and statistics of, 158
Chebia Island, 250–52
"chicken switches," 94
chief of the boat. *See* COB
chief of the watch, 94, 96
  Soviet *(michman)*, 167–68, 172
China
  Fluckey's raids on, 210, 260–64
  U.S. nuclear submarine spying on, 230
Churchill, Winston, on U-boat attacks, *xv*, 257
CIA. *See* Central Intelligence Agency
CinCLantFleet (Commander in Chief Atlantic Fleet), 59
COB (chief of the boat), 31, 50, 77, 79, 87, 103
  wife of, 84
Cochino, USS (diesel-electric submarine), loss of, 71–73, 149
Coe, Jim "Red," 249–52
Cold Is the Sea (novel), 272–73
cold war, 1–2, 230, 236

commissaryman, 105
ComSubLant (Commander
    Submarines Atlantic), 28, 59,
    92, 104, 182, 184, 225
  radio messages from, 102, 147–48,
    207–8, 211
  Soviet spy in, 234
ComSubPac, 264, 265, 267
  Soviet spy in, 234
Corregidor, 247–49
counterdetection, 30, 115–18, 159,
    160, 164, 170, 187, 195–97, 209
  of Blackfin by Soviets, 220–25
covered systems, Soviet, 137–39
Crabb, Lionel "Buster," 181–82
Crypto City, 139, 140
Cuban missile crisis, 204

damage-control drill, Soviet, 171–72
damage-control trainer, 30
dead-reckoning tracer. See DRT
decompression and airlock chamber,
    240–42
Deep Submergence Rescue Vehicle
    (DSRV), 240
Defense Intelligence Agency (DIA),
    91, 92, 140
degaussing of Soviet submarines,
    131–32
Denmark Strait, 99, 100, 103, 107–9
depth charges
  Japanese, 265, 267
  Soviet, 114, 224, 246
DIA. See Defense Intelligence Agency
diving alarm, 96, 168
diving officer, 94, 98
diving planes, fairwater, 94
diving trainer, 30
Dönitz, Karl, 38, 39, 233
  Scapa Flow raid envisioned by,
    258–59
  submarine strategy of, 257–58
DRT (dead-reckoning tracer), 160
DSRV. See Deep Submergence Rescue
    Vehicle

Echo-class Soviet submarine,
    ramming by, 73
Echo II Soviet SSGNs, 194–96

Eden, Anthony, 181
Electric Boat Division, 23, 41, 44, 91
Electronic Signals Measures (ESM),
    15, 45, 195, 215, 253
electro-optical sensor, Soviet, 115
ELINT (electronic intelligence), 215
  Soviet AGI ships with, 92–93
emergency blow activators, 94
engineering officer, 28, 32
  qualification for, 25
engineering officer of the watch
    (EOOW), 53, 221, 223
  qualification for, 24–25, 99
engine-order telegraph, 94
enlisted men (crew)
  Soviet, 70, 169, 172
  U.S., 47, 50–51, 103
    nuclear submarine qualification,
    28, 99–100
  See also submariners
EPM (emergency propulsion motor),
    221–22
ESM. See Electronic Signals Measures
executive officer (XO), 28, 32, 99,
    103, 104, 147–48, 189
  wife of, 84

fairwater diving planes, 94
families of submariners, 7–8, 30–31,
    80–87
  Soviet, 129, 132, 206
familygrams, 80–81, 101, 155
15D periscope, 45, 137, 141
fire, simulated, 30, 171–72
fire control, 95, 160, 215
fishing fleets, 174–75
Fluckey, Gene, 209, 210, 260–64, 267,
    284
food
  on Soviet submarines, 130–31, 200,
    204
  on U.S. submarines, 105–7, 189,
    191
Fort Meade (Maryland), 139, 226
Foxtrot (Soviet submarine), 74
Franz Josef Land, 62
French Connection, The (movie), 107
frequency hopping, 139
Frunze Higher Naval School, 126

FSB, 270
Fulton, USS (submarine tender), 31–32, 90, 106, 107

Gadzhiyevo (Soviet Union), 60
Galloping Ghost of the China Coast. *See* Fluckey, Eugene B.
Gambit reconnaissance satellite, 111
Gar (World War II submarine), 264
Gayler, Noel, 92
General Dynamics, 23, 91
General Electric, 48
George Washington, USS (submarine), 161
German rocket scientists, 2
Glomar Explorer (lifting-gear ship), 239
"goat locker," 50
Golf-class Soviet submarines, 150, 238
Gorshkov, Sergei G., 112–13, 127, 129
GPS (global positioning satellites), 95, 102
Grayback (submarine), 238
Great Patriotic War. *See* World War II
Grechko Naval Academy, 69, 126
Greenland–Iceland–United Kingdom Gap (GIUK Gap), 64, 99
Greenwich Mean Time (Zulu), 100
Gremikha (Soviet Union), 190
Groton (Connecticut), 23, 44
Growler (submarine), 238
GRU (Soviet military intelligence), 213
Gudgeon, USS (submarine), Soviet ASW attack on, 75–76, 224
guided missile submarines (SSGNs)
    first U.S., 237–43
    Soviet, 113, 116, 157, 158, 194–96
GUPPY (greater underwater propulsive power), 71
gyrocompass, 95

H-6 Soviet warhead, 186
hafnium, 55
Halibut, USS (submarine), 237–43
Hanford Nuclear Reservation, 232
Hawaii, *K-129* sinking north of, 238–39

helicopters, Soviet, 115, 195, 215, 217, 219–20
    hop-and-skip technique, 222–23
Highlights Message, 226–27
Hitler, Adolf, 38
Holland, John P., 42
Holm Sound, 258
Holy Loch (Scotland), 64, 169
Holystone operation, *ix–xi*, 6, 8, 21–23, 236
    basic rules for, 30
    excellent results from, 28–29, 229
    Hunter assigned to, 22, 23, 28–29
    NSA analysis of, 138–41
    pioneering mission of, 71–73
    post-USSR, 230–32
    reports from, 74–76
    rules of engagement of, 65
    spying and, 235
    World War II origins of, 246, 256
    See also Blackfin
Hood, HMS, 107–8
Hormone helicopter (Soviet), 115
Hotel-class Soviet submarines, 150
hot water suits, 242
HUMINT (spies), 4, 170, 212–13, 253
    Soviet, in U.S., 234–35, 243–44
Hunter, Roy, *xix*, 7, 44, 269
    addressing the crew by, 51
    assigned to Holystone, 22, 23, 28–29
    in at-sea trial of *Blackfin*, 36–37, 53, 57
    in attack teacher, 15–19
    background of, 22–23
    daughter of, 272
    family of, 82–84, 89, 106
    later career of, 232
    as OOD previously in Barents Sea, 116–18
    as pseudonym, *xii*, *xix*
    See also Blackfin
hydrophones. *See* SOSUS

ICBMs
    Soviet, 2, 7
        Blackfin surveillance, 207–8, 211–20

HUMINT intelligence on, 4, 213
  misfires, 217, 219
ice, submarines and, 119–20
Iceland, 99, 107
IMC (communications system), 51,
  89, 96, 97, 221
intelligence
  divergent opinions on meaning of,
    3–4
  on Soviet Union, U.S. need for, 3–4
  submarines' gathering of, 4–6
  See also HUMINT
interior communications (IC), 51
Iran, U.S. nuclear submarine spying
  on, 230
Ivy Bells operation, 234, 240–44

Japan
  scythe propeller construction from,
    163
  Ultra breaking of codes of, 265
  U.S. World War II submarine
    offensive vs., 78–79, 245–56
Jennifer Project, 239
Jimmy Carter, USS (submarine), 44
Joe One (Soviet A-bomb), 5
Juliet (SSG Soviet submarine), 194
Juzan Maru (Japanese ship), 267

K–3, Leninskiy Komsomol (submarine),
  68, 149, 151
K–8 (Soviet submarine), 150
K–19 (Soviet submarine), 150–51
K–129 Soviet submarine, sinking of,
  238–39
Ka-25 Hormone helicopter (Soviet),
  115
Karafuto (Japan), 261
Kashin-class destroyers, 113, 114
kashtan microphone, 169
KGB (Soviet State Security
  Committee), 213, 234, 244,
  270
Khrushchev, Nikita, 1, 13, 181
  submarine buildup by, 68
Kiel (Germany), 258
Kildin Island, 118, 193–94, 202, 207,
  209, 214, 226
King Neptune ceremony, 108–9

Kola Inlet, 12, 60, 118–19, 131, 135,
  141, 143, 190, 194, 211, 220,
  223–24
Kola Peninsula, 6, 12, 59, 60, 63, 67,
  111, 119
  Soviet bases on, 190
Kotlin-class destroyers, 113, 114
Kresta-class cruisers, 216
  anticarrier operations by, 191–94
  in counterdetection of *Blackfin*,
    220
Kretschmer, Otto, 185
Kuril island chain, 6, 241

Labrador Basin, 100
Laird, Melvin, 73
Lapon, USS (submarine), 183
LCM landing craft, 91
Leningrad (Soviet Union), 69, 126,
  158
Lockwood, Charles A., 185, 257–58,
  284
Los Angeles–class submarines, 43, 44,
  47, 229

M16's underwater surveillance of
  Ordzhonikidze (cruiser), 181–82
MacArthur, Douglas, 249
MAD (magnetic anomaly detector),
  201
  Soviet, 115
Mail (Beriev Be-12 Chaika), 66, 115,
  190
map, *xvi–xvii*
May, H. J., 184
mine laying, in World War II, 246
mines from World War II, 131–32
missiles
  Soviet
    for anticarrier warfare, 193–97
    ICBM misfires, 217, 219
  See also nuclear-tipped ballistic
    missiles
Mk 14 torpedoes, 184–86
Mk 113 fire-control system, 160, 215
Montross, K. E., 249
Moscow
  Gorshkov headquartered in, 112
  Nixon-Brezhnev summit in, 61

movies, 107, 199
MR-600 Topsail radar (Soviet),
113–14
Murmansk (Soviet Union), 60

Namkwam harbor (China), 210,
262–63
National Security Agency (NSA), 5,
192, 214, 226, 240
SIGINT information collected by,
138–40
sound signatures analyzed by, 157
Soviet spy in, 234–35
National Security Council, 91
NATO (North Atlantic Treaty
Organization), 201–2, 204
Nautilus, USS (nuclear-powered
submarine), 41–42, 146, 149,
161
navigation, Soviet, 127
navigator, 102, 118
New London (Connecticut), 57, 59,
62, 227
Soviet AGI ships outside of,
92–93
submarine school at, 19, 21, 27,
29–30
Nikko Maru (Japanese transport),
265
Nixon, Richard M.
Brezhnev meeting of, 13, 61, 208,
229
territorial limit approved by, 61
noise
components of, 46
hydrodynamic flow, 163–64
problem of, 161–64
Soviet attitude to, 164
transient, 163
Norfolk (Virginia), 8, 28, 59, 76, 171
North Cape (Norway), 71, 119, 148
North Korea, U.S. nuclear submarine
spying on, 230
North Pole, 119
Norwegian Sea, 62
Novaya Zemlya, 62, 139, 150, 190
November-class Soviet submarines,
68, 74, 127, 132, 146, 149,
157

NROTC (Naval Reserve Officer
Training Corps), 23–24, 26
NSA. *See* National Security Agency
Nuclear Powered Ship and Submarine
Recycling Program, 232
nuclear-powered submarines, 2, 4–5
atmosphere inside, 101
clothing on, 188
control room of, 93–96, 168
faster submerged then surfaced, 48,
97
garbage from, 102
long-range navigation by, 95
patrol reports by, 74–76, 104–5,
197, 225–26
Soviet, 2, 113
American collisions with, 73
construction problems, 68–69
crew, 70, 169, 172
diving depth of over 3,000 feet,
69
first, 68
food, 130–31, 200
officer personnel, 69–70
overage commanders, 124–25
political officer (*zampolit*), 70,
128, 130, 131, 133, 169, 202,
204–6, 271
spare-parts problem, 129
total number, 69
U.S.
downsizing of fleet after end of
USSR, 229–30, 233
history of, 41–44, 237–56
See also reactors
nuclear power school, 24
nuclear-tipped ballistic missiles, 2–3
Regulus, 237–38
SUBROC, 48, 109

oceanographic research ship, Soviet,
190
Office of Naval Intelligence (ONI), 5,
140, 156–57, 192, 214, 239,
240, 264
Okhotsk, Sea of, 6, 234
Soviet cable under, 240–43
Okinawa, 249
ONI. *See* Office of Naval Intelligence

OOD (officer of the deck), 15–17, 36, 50, 56–57, 102, 103, 120
  in Barents Sea intelligence gathering, 141, 143, 147, 152, 156, 177, 190, 191
  in *Blackfin*'s departure, 90–91, 93, 94, 96–98
  counterdetection mistakes by, 116–18
  qualification for, 24, 99
  and reactor scramming, 221–23
  Soviet, 167
  spooks and, 137
Ordzhonikidze (cruiser), British underwater surveillence of, 181–82
oxygen breathing apparatus (OBA), 30
oxygen candles, 101
oxygen generator, 101
  Soviet, 173–74

P-3 Orion sub hunter, 201
P-5 antiship missiles, 195, 196
P-6 antiship missiles, 195, 196
Pala Bay, 131
Palau Islands, 252
Parche, USS (submarine), 44, 243
patrol reports, 74–76, 104–5, 197, 225–26
  of *Burrfish*, 254
PCO (prospective commanding officer), 25–26
PCO school, 27
Pearl Harbor (Hawaii), 78, 239, 248
  PCO school at, 27
Peenemunde (Germany), 2
Pegasus, HMS, 259
Peleliu Island, 252, 253
Pelton, Ronald, 234–35, 243–44
periscope depth (PD), 57, 102, 135–36, 147, 154–55, 194, 215, 216, 241
  by Soviet submarines, 172–73
periscopes
  cleaning of, 120
  Soviet, 168
  stand for, 95
  Type 2F, 45
  Type 15D, 45, 137, 141

periviz, 45, 93, 136, 141
Perkins, Bill, 253–55
Perth (Australia), 78
Petropavlovsk (Soviet Union), 240
Petya-class frigates, 113, 114, 142–43, 205, 214–15, 219
  in counterdetection of *Blackfin*, 220
Philippines
  gold and silver from, in World War II, 245, 247–48
  World War II resupply by submarines to, 247–49
plotting table, 95
Polaris submarines, 42–44, 64, 150, 161, 208, 238
  Soviet espionage vs., 114, 169
Poluchat-I class Soviet submarines, 184
Polyarnyy submarine base (Soviet Union), 60, 62, 206
  Soviet submarine departures from, 123–24, 132, 167, 270
poopie suits, 188, 214
Powers, Francis Gary, 13, 211
Prien, Günther, 209–10, 258–60, 268, 285
Project 671, 201
propeller blade rate, 162–63
propellers, scythe, 162–63
propulsion control console, 53–54
prospective commanding officer. *See* PCO
PT boat, MacArthur on, 249
Pulford, Conway, 250, 252

quartermaster, 118, 120, 189, 194
Quelpart Island, 265–67
Quezon, Manuel, 248

R-13 Sark SLBM, 150
radar, Soviet, 63, 113–15, 137
radiation control techniques, 30
radiation exposure, Soviet, 125, 128, 151, 232–33
rafts, sound-insulated, 162
razvedka (reconnaissance), 169–70
reactors, 54–56
  of dismantled submarines sent to Hanford, 232
  scramming of, 55, 221–23, 227

reactors (*continued*)
Soviet, 200–201
VM-4P, 158
Regulus cruise missiles, 237–38
Repulse, HMS, 258, 259
Rickover, Hyman G., 2, 41, 55, 68,
161, 226
officers chosen by, 23–27
rockets
Soviet ASW, 114
U.S. coastal bombardment with,
261
Royal Oak, HMS, 210, 259–60
Russia (post-Soviet)
Holystone operations continued
against, 229–30
increasing secrecy and censorship
in, 270
nuclear submarine decline in, 230,
233
Rybachiy Peninsula, 202, 223

S-39 (submarine), 249–52, 256
SALT. *See* Strategic Arms Limitation
Treaty
Sand Dollar operation, 239
satellites
global positioning (GPS), 95, 102
KH-8 Gambit reconnaissance, 111
Soviet ASW, 113
spy, 59, 234
saturation diving technique, 241–42
Sayre, Francis B., 249
Scapa Flow, German penetration of,
209–10, 258–60
Scorpion, USS, sinking of, 8, 69
scrambler phones, 140
SEALs, 253
Seawolf, USS (World War II
submarine), 247
Seawolf-class nuclear submarines, 43,
44, 229, 243
Semipalatinsk (Soviet Union), 1,
207
Severomorsk naval base, 12, 60, 62
ASW ships at, 113–15
civilians at, 112
description of, 111–12
ship-control station, 94

SIGINT (signals intelligence)
on Holystone mission, 60, 135, 190
NSA collection of, 138–40
on Soviet AGI ships, 92–93
Soviet collection of, 170
of Soviet Okhotsk cable, 242
in World War II, 255
signal-to-noise meter, 160
signal-to-noise ratio, 157
SINS (ship's internal navigation
system), 95, 102
637 class. *See Sturgeon*-class
submarines
Skate-class submarines, 42
Skipjack-class submarines, 42
Skylark, USS (submarine rescue
vessel), 36
SLBM (submarine-launched ballistic
missile), 42, 91, 92, 150, 195,
207–8, 216, 226, 230
Smith, Chester, 248–49
snorkel, 222
sonar
in automatic target following, 160
on *Blackfin*, 35–36, 47, 62, 97–98,
136, 142–43, 146, 153–54, 177,
214, 215
in point-blank survey of Victor,
181
in Soviet firing exercise, 187–89
BQS-6 under-ice, 120
description of, 45–47
in simulated Soviet ASW attack,
15–18
Soviet, 67–68, 115, 117–18, 170,
175–76, 201–2
in counterdetection of *Blackfin*,
220, 222–23
weak performance, 223–24
STASS, 35–36, 47, 91, 227
sonobuoys, 201
Soviet, 115, 222–23
Sosnovy Bor (Soviet Union), 126
SOSUS (Sound Surveillance System),
63–65, 148, 161–62, 201
in locating *K-129*, 238–39
Soviet espionage on, 114
sound signature of submarines, 46,
156–57

Sound Surveilance System. *See*
  SOSUS
Soviet Pacific Fleet, 3
Soviet Red Banner Northern Fleet, 3,
  6–7
  ASW operations of, 5, 16, 42,
    66–68
  See also Severomorsk
Soviet Union
  atomic and hydrogen bomb tests of,
    1, 5, 7, 139
  cold war expenditures of, 1
  simulated surprise nuclear attack by,
    6
  twelve-mile territorial limit of, 61,
    209, 214
  U.S. need for intelligence on, 3–4
spectrum spreading, 139
spies. *See* HUMINT
Spitsbergen, 62, 119
spooks (intelligence operatives), 5,
    103, 136–38, 155, 187, 193,
    197, 217, 226
Spooner, Ernest J., 250, 252
SS-1 submarine, 42
SSBNs (strategic ballistic missile
    submarines), 22–23, 42, 158,
    230
  lack of Soviet contact with,
    169–70
  Soviet, 61, 63–64, 113, 207
SSGNs (guided missile submarines),
    Soviet, 113, 116, 157, 158,
    194–96
SS-N-6 Soviet missiles, 208
SS-N-7 Soviet missiles, 158
SSNs (attack submarines), 23, 64, 158,
    230
  Soviet, 113
  Soviet detection and tracking of,
    170
Stakhayev, A., 270, 285
Stalemate operation, 252
starpom (Soviet executive officer), 132,
    167, 168, 173
STASS (submarine towed array sonar
    system), 35–36, 47, 91, 227
STEST-68 Soviet torpedoes, 186
steward, 106

Stoecker, Sally W., 270, 285
Strategic Arms Limitation Treaty
    (SALT), 13, 61, 62, 91, 141,
    208, 229
Street, George L., 209–11, 264–68
Sturgeon-class submarines, *ix*, 21, 43,
    44, 47
  dismantling of, 232
  Soviet Victors and Charlies
    comparable to, 157, 158, 201
submariners
  brotherhood of, 151, 185
  family and other problems of, 7–8,
    30–31, 80–87
    Soviet, 129, 132, 206
  mystique of, 77–78
  pronunciation of word, 37
  Soviet, 125–29
    qualification by, 172
    radiation poisoning, 125, 128,
      151, 232–33
submarines
  attack teacher for, 15–19
  coastal bombardment with rockets
    by, 261
  disasters to, 8, 43–44, 68–69,
    149–51, 238, 284
  German, Scapa Flow raid, 209–10,
    258–60
  lurking in coastal waters, 2–3
  noisiness of, 46–47
  with nuclear missiles, 2–3
  nuclear-powered. *See* nuclear-
    powered submarines
  railroad demolition teams from,
    261
  Soviet ASW, 67
  stealth of, 5, 100, 209–10, 259, 262,
    268
  before World War II, 78
SUBROC ballistic missiles, 48, 109
"Sugar boats," 249
supply officer, 32, 59, 106
surface-to-air missiles, Soviet, 114
surface-to-surface missiles, Soviet,
    194–97
Swordfish (World War II submarine),
    248–49, 256
Szilard, Leo, 41

Tang-class submarines, 40–41, 75
target motion analysis. *See* TMA
Tautog (USS submarine), collision of, 73–74
Thames River, 90–91
thermoclines, 170
Thrasher-class attack submarines, 43–44, 69
Tirante (World War II submarine), 210–11, 264–67
TMA (target motion analysis), 36, 159–60, 193
Tojo, Hideki, 257
Topsail radar (Soviet), 113–14
torpedoes
    acoustic homing, 185, 188
    of *Blackfin*, 48–50
        mock attacks, 103
        ready for firing, 109
    invention of, 184
    Soviet, 185–86
        firing exercise, 183–84, 187–88
        on Hormone helicopters, 115
        on surface ships, 114
        test range north of Kildin Island, 202–4
        on Victor submarines, 158
        wake-homing, 192
    U.S., in World War II, 263
Torpex, 186
Trout (World War II submarine), 247
Tuloma River, 60, 133, 167
Tunny (submarine), 238
turns-per-knot ratio, 157
Tusk (USS GUPPY submarine), 71–73
Twin Dolphins, 25, 78
Type I submarine (Soviet), *Blackfin*'s tracking of, 143, 145–47
Type II submarine (Soviet), 116
    Blackfin's interception of, 148–49, 152–65, 177–84, 186–88
Type XXI U-boats, 38–40, 233

U-2 spy plane, 13
U-47 (submarine), 258–60
U-2511 (submarine), 39, 40
U-3008 (submarine), 40
U.S. Naval Academy, 23, 105

U.S. Navy
    Soviet spies in, 114
    Special Projects Office, 238
    See also ComSubLant; ComSubPac; Office of Naval Intelligence (ONI)
UDT-10 demolition teams, 253, 255
Ultra (U.S. code-breaking), 265
United States, cold war expenditures of, 1
UQC underwater telephone, 117, 120, 183, 216–17, 219, 220
uranium, enrichment of, 200

Varlamova Bay, 60
Varzino (Soviet Union), 190
Victor-class Soviet SSNs, 68, 113, 116, 155–65, 199–206
    anechoic tiles of, 178
    Blackfin's underwater surveillance of, 176–81, 211
    disaster averted on, 199
    mission and characteristics of, 158
    mission in Barents Sea by, 167–76
    possible contact with U.S. submarine, 203, 205
    "spinners" of, 178
    videotaping Soviet exercise, 195–97
Vietnam War, 13
Virginia-class submarines, 43, 44, 229
Vladivostok (Soviet Union), 240
VLF (very low frequency) communications, 80–81, 102, 141, 155, 173

Walker, John, 234
Walter hydrogen peroxide closed-cycle system, 40
weapons officer, 32
Weinberger, Caspar, on spying, *xv*
Whitehead, Robert, 184, 185
White Sea, 158, 190, 211
Wolverine, HMS, 260
World War II
    Bismarck-Hood battle in, 107–8
    German submarines in, 38
        losses, 78
        nearness to victory, 257

Type VIIC, 39
Type XXI, 38–40, 233
mines from, 131–32
submarine stealth in, 209–11, 259, 262, 268
torpedo failures in, 184
U.S. submarines in, 37, 38, 41, 79
"Christmas tree" lights, 96
size of fleet, 78
special missions vs. Japan, 245–56
Ultra code-breaking in, 265

Yankee-class Soviet submarines, 113, 183, 208, 211, 215–17, 219

Yap Island, 252, 253, 255
yeoman, 104

zampolit (Soviet political officer), 70, 128, 130, 131, 133, 169, 202, 204–6, 271
zigzagging, 159–60
Zulu (Greenwich Mean Time), 100
Zumwalt, Elmo R., 226, 229
submarine intelligence-gathering viewed by, 12–14, 76
surface warfare stressed by, 11–12, 21–22